A POUND OF FLESH

A POUND OF FLESH

MONETARY SANCTIONS AS PUNISHMENT FOR THE POOR

ALEXES HARRIS

A Volume in the American Sociological Association's
Rose Series in Sociology

Russell Sage Foundation • New York

Library of Congress Cataloging-in-Publication Data
Names: Harris, Alexes, author.
Title: A pound of flesh : monetary sanctions as punishment for the poor /
  Alexes Harris.
Description: New York : Russell Sage Foundation, [2016] | Series: American
  Sociological Association's Rose series in sociology | Includes
  bibliographical references and index.
Identifiers: LCCN 2015047289 (print) | LCCN 2016006344 (ebook) | ISBN
  9780871544612 (paperback) | ISBN 9781610448550 (ebook)
Subjects: LCSH: Fines (Penalties)—Social aspects—United States. | Sentences (Criminal
  procedure)—Economic aspects—United States. | Public welfare—Law and legisla-
  tion—United States. | BISAC: SOCIAL SCIENCE / Sociology / General. | SOCIAL
  SCIENCE / Criminology. | LAW / Criminal Law / Sentencing.
Classification: LCC KF9745 .H37 2016 (print) | LCC KF9745 (ebook) | DDC 364.6/8—
  dc23
LC record available at http://cp.mcafee.com/d/2DRPoAcygQ96Qm7S3hO
  -e7nsdTdFTd7bVEVjuujd79JeVEVvd7arNEVhodFTd7bVEVjuuphdEETsd
  7bzb3O9JnoSY-Eazjif Y01dNFF7-00CPhOYNXN1N_HYMZtVxBPHTbFFzDe
  d78VZMQsIcsJteOaaJXEYG7DR8OJMddECQjt-hojuv78I9CzATsS03fJq
  77RJN6FD4XELTo79L6zATqBmMkvmT4qCjr8VxUS91Emd426PQQge
  Ryq83hOeuKYehvooshjdFK6SNV_9oUNm-Ws

The paper used in this publication meets the minimum requirements of
American National Standard for Information Sciences--Permanence of Paper
for Printed Library Materials. ANSI Z39.48-1992.

Text design by Suzanne Nichols.

RUSSELL SAGE FOUNDATION
112 East 64th Street, New York, New York 10065
10 9 8 7 6 5 4 3 2 1

The Russell Sage Foundation

The Russell Sage Foundation, one of the oldest of America's general purpose foundations, was established in 1907 by Mrs. Margaret Olivia Sage for "the improvement of social and living conditions in the United States." The foundation seeks to fulfill this mandate by fostering the development and dissemination of knowledge about the country's political, social, and economic problems. While the foundation endeavors to assure the accuracy and objectivity of each book it publishes, the conclusions and interpretations in Russell Sage Foundation publications are those of the authors and not of the foundation, its trustees, or its staff. Publication by Russell Sage, therefore, does not imply foundation endorsement.

Previous Volumes
in the Series

Karl Alexander, Doris Entwisle, and Linda Olson

Making Hate a Crime: From Social Movement to Law Enforcement
Valerie Jenness and Ryken Grattet

Market Friendly or Family Friendly? The State and Gender Inequality in Old Age
Madonna Harrington Meyer and Pamela Herd

Nurturing Dads: Social Initiatives for Contemporary Fatherhood
William Marsiglio and Kevin Roy

Passing the Torch: Does Higher Education for the Disadvantaged Pay Off Across the Generations?
Paul Attewell and David Lavin

Pension Puzzles: Social Security and the Great Debate
Melissa Hardy and Lawrence Hazelrigg

Social Movements in the World-System: The Politics of Crisis and Transformation
Dawn Wiest and Jackie Smith

They Say Cut Back, We Say Fight Back! Welfare Activism in an Era of Retrenchment
Ellen Reese

Trust in Schools: A Core Resource for Improvement
Anthony S. Bryk and Barbara Schneider

Forthcoming Titles

Family Relationships Across the Generations
Judith A. Seltzer, Emily Wiemers, and Suzanne M. Bianchi

Golden Years? Social Inequalities in Later Life
Deborah Carr

Interracial Romance and Friendship in Adolescence and Adulthood
Grace Kao, Kara Joyner, and Kelly Stamper Balistreri

Urbanization's Changing Nature: Industrial Hazards, Systemic Risk, and the Remaking of American Cities
Scott Frickel and James R. Elliott

The Rose Series in Sociology

The American Sociological Association's Rose Series in Sociology publishes books that integrate knowledge and address controversies from a sociological perspective. Books in the Rose Series are at the forefront of sociological knowledge. They are lively and often involve timely and fundamental issues on significant social concerns. The series is intended for broad dissemination throughout sociology, across social science and other professional communities, and to policy audiences. The series was established in 1967 by a bequest to ASA from Arnold and Caroline Rose to support innovations in scholarly publishing.

Lee Clarke
Lauren Krivo
Paul D. McLean
Patricia A. Roos

Editors

To Alana and Jaylen, whose unconditional love fuels my commitment to making real change

Contents

List of Illustrations

About the Author

Alexes Harris is associate professor of sociology at the University of Washington.

══ Preface ══

You have among you many a purchased slave,
Which like your asses and your dogs and mules
You use in abject and in slavish parts,
Because you bought them. Shall I say to you,
"Let them be free! Marry them to your heirs!
Why sweat they under burdens? Let their beds
Be made as soft as yours, and let their palates
Be seasoned with such viands"? You will answer,
"The slaves are ours." So do I answer you:
The pound of flesh which I demand of him
Is dearly bought, 'tis mine, and I will have it.

—Shylock, *The Merchant of Venice* by William Shakespeare
(1598), act IV, scene 1, lines 90–100

After I completed graduate school and began working as a professor, my father regularly teased me, "When are you going to write that great American novel?" I explained to my dad that I was a social scientist, I did not write fiction, and besides, my research focused on stratification, inequality, race and ethnicity, and the criminal justice system—far from a story about American life. I hadn't realized until I began writing this book how "great" and how "American" is the practice of criminal monetary sanctions in this country.

This book is about a contemporary form of social control that is imposed by court systems in the form of monetary sanctions and disproportionately punishes the poor. Also referred to as legal financial obligations (LFOs), these penalties are levied in addition to jail or prison time and regularly include fines, court user fees, restitution, and collection charges. My central thesis is that the imposition of fines and fees creates a two-tiered system of punishment: one for those with financial means and one for those who are poor. Because they cannot be held fully accountable for their offending when they are unable to pay, the poor experience a permanent punishment. Nevertheless, non-elected court bureaucrats enforce this system and assess debtors' remorse for their crimes based on their own ideas about personal responsibility, meritocracy, and accountability. This book tells the story of how U.S. court officials, behind the shield of justice, are empowered to apply the laws with a paternalistic discretion that marginalizes the poor.

This is not the story I wanted to write. In many ways, my personal story is about generational success. My grandmother was an immigrant to the United States, and my grandfather was a descendant of African people forced into slavery. My father was born in 1930, in the middle of the Great Depression. He obtained a GED so that he could enlist in the U.S. Navy at seventeen years of age. He was hired by a company as its first African American employee and worked there for forty years. He married my white mother just two years after the Supreme Court decision in *Loving v. Virginia* legalized interracial marriage in the United States in 1967. My parents worked hard to ensure that my twin brother and I would have the best education and attend college. In many ways, my family has lived the proverbial American Dream. Yet we represent the few, not the many, in this country.

At a moment when the United States has experienced considerable racial progress—the reelection of President Barack Obama, the appointment of an African American woman as U.S. attorney general, and the development of a nationwide movement for a living wage—I would love to write a book about this country's progress. Yet, while things are going well for me and for my family, I am continually reminded that all is not well for many other people living in the United States. Thus, I teach my undergraduate students about the disproportionate confinement of people of color in the juvenile and adult justice systems. I assign my students readings about the racial achievement gap in education, from preschools to graduate schools. We talk in my social problems courses about health disparities and the rising rates of HIV/AIDS in African American communities, as well as about income inequality, unemployment and wealth disparities, and occupational and residential segregation.

I wanted to be a sociologist who writes success stories—stories about social mobility and overcoming the legacy of this country's historical hurdles. I wanted to write an American story about opportunity, perseverance, and progress. For my kids, I want to trace a blueprint of the legacy and triumph of our community. Over the past eight years, however, my interviews with people convicted of felonies and people who work within the criminal justice system have convinced me that another story needs to be told.

I have engaged with people in my own community who face lifelong debt as a result of criminal convictions related to their mental health struggles and drug addictions. I have observed criminal sentencing and violation hearings and analyzed court-sentencing data. I have reviewed state criminal codes and case law. And the story of my research—the story that must be told—is that our twenty-first-century criminal justice system stains people's lives forever. The permanent stain results not just from a criminal conviction and the related societal stigma but also from the financial debt, constant surveillance, and related punishment incurred by monetary sanctions.

Many people make mistakes, both in the United States and around the world. Sometimes they do things that are horribly wrong and exact enormous costs. Although the criminal justice system ensures that most people serve time for their wrongdoings to pay their debt to society, my research shows that the imposition by the criminal justice system of fines and fees ensures that the poor alone can never atone.

Early in the course of my research for this book, I was pulled over by a police officer for speeding. The officer spent more time explaining to me how I could file for what is called a "deferred finding" than he did reprimanding me for speeding. I had the option to go online and pay a fee in addition to the traffic fine, and if I did not receive any further moving violations in the next year, the ticket would not go on my record and would not affect my insurance rate. Because I had the means, I paid for my deferred finding, was careful not to receive any more speeding tickets, and, with the violation kept off my record, managed to avoid a hike in my insurance rate. I was able to avoid entanglement in the justice system. Had I not been able to pay the ticket, I could have eventually lost my driver's license, received warrants, and even been arrested and incarcerated. People like me are able to take advantage of such "deferred" circumstances, but far more people are not. I am compelled to write this book because I have observed and learned that there is no "redemption," or assumption of "youthful indiscretion," or belief in "the land of opportunity" for poor people who come into contact with the U.S. justice system.

For his inability to make payments to the moneylender Shylock, Antonio in Shakespeare's *Merchant of Venice* is brought before a court, which decrees that his punishment will be "a pound of flesh." Early in my research for this book, a prosecutor used this phrase in describing monetary sanctions as a tool for getting his "pound of flesh" from a defendant; he said that he wanted to "screw" the defendant, whom he believed had caused grave harm to the victim. In the American criminal justice system, this prosecutor is not alone in using monetary sanctions as additional punishment for defendants viewed as deserving of extra sanctions beyond the basic sentence. "A pound of flesh" is a powerful metaphor for the study of legal financial obligations.

"A pound of flesh" also captures symbolically the actual indebtedness of many people who are convicted. Reminiscent of the days of slavery, poor people convicted today face fiscal servitude to the court. For them, the average $1,300 monetary sentence per felony conviction represents the difference between being housed or unstably housed, taking daily AIDS medication or going untreated, accessing or failing to access a public shower if homeless, and being free to move forward someday into a healthier relationship or remaining in an abusive one. Given that race and class are so highly correlated in U.S. society and that the criminal justice system has consistently managed people of color in this country in disproportionate and disparate ways, the system of monetary sanctions has become a key way in which racial and class inequalities in the United States are reproduced and reinforced. Even though much of the story told here is about class, my evidence points to the unique challenges of monetary sanctions not only for economically disadvantaged people but also for the racially marginalized; thus, this story is inescapably related to race as well.

My primary research objective was to understand the use of monetary sanctions in today's criminal justice system. Who receives fines and fees as punishment? How are offenders monitored for payment? What consequences of contact with the criminal justice system are related to monetary sanctions? And more theoretically, what role do monetary sanctions play in the administration of punishment in the contemporary United States? In what follows, I detail how monetary sanctions are levied and enforced and illustrate how impoverished debtors experience this punishment as "a pound of flesh." The poor and convicted constantly worry about LFOs, which are a painful punishment they can do nothing to address because of their marginalized position, economically or otherwise, in society.

While contemporary systems of social control may no longer be as physically brutal as systems of the past, in this book I reveal that the imposition of monetary sanctions is consistent with prior forms of American "justice." Like the colonization of the indigenous peoples, the enslavement of people from Africa, the Black Codes and Jim Crow laws that managed and isolated nonwhites, and convict leasing and forced labor camps for prisoners, the contemporary use of monetary sanctions is disproportionately imposed on the impoverished and socially isolated. These sanctions keep poor and racially marginalized people under constant surveillance and living in poverty and perpetual punishment. Thus, the contemporary criminal justice system remains essentially unchanged from earlier incarnations, which were understood to be necessary to control populations deemed in need of management and punishment. As a system that uniquely disadvantages people in poverty, the American criminal justice system generates and sustains inequality and closes off successful societal integration for many people it touches.

I guess my dad was right: I do indeed have a great American story to write, but not a novel. Instead, I have written an empirically grounded analysis of a system of social control that manages, punishes, and marginalizes a subset of the U.S. population because of their poverty status. Although specific names of people and places have been changed, *A Pound of Flesh* is a true story about class, punishment, and retribution in the contemporary U.S. criminal justice system and about the lives of the poorest Americans who encounter it. And in this true story, court officials impose LFOs as adamantly as Shylock: "'Tis mine, and I will have it."

Acknowledgments

We frequently cite the African proverb that "it takes a village to raise a child." Well, I have learned that it takes a village to support the writing of a book and one's career in academia. I have a great deal of gratitude for a number of family members, friends, colleagues, and mentors who have read drafts, talked through ideas, and encouraged me during the last nine years of data collection, analysis, and manuscript development.

Research for this project began in 2007 with two collaborators, Katherine Beckett and Heather Evans. Our collaboration provided a space where we could share our excitement about tackling a little-understood research puzzle. Katherine's mentorship and insight were extremely helpful, and Heather's ideas about pursuing various analytic avenues inform the book throughout. Over the last several years, I have had the good fortune to work with a number of graduate and undergraduate students who are cited throughout the book. In particular, the research support by Heather Evans, Jorge Martinez, and Ferdose Idris was invaluable. I am grateful for your ideas, your hard work, and your enthusiasm for the project.

After completing the initial research with my collaborators, I decided that in order to really understand the process of monetary sanctions, I needed to return to my ethnographic training and conduct observations and interviews in courthouses across the state of Washington. I am forever grateful for the training and theoretical insight of Bob Emerson, my graduate adviser at UCLA. I hope my data and analysis carry forward the tradition of his scholarship and training.

Completing the initial draft of the manuscript was a task in itself, and digging in and struggling with multiple revisions to develop, clarify, and strengthen my analyses was tedious. I am appreciative to the anonymous reviewers for their insight, suggestions, and pushback, as well as to the Rose Series editors, particularly my lead editor, Laurie Krivo, for believing in the project when it was just an underdeveloped and initially rejected book proposal. Your honest and critical, but always supportive, feedback sustained my commitment to the project and helped remind me of the importance of my scholarship.

I am thankful for my colleagues in the Sociology Department at the University of Washington. Whenever I needed a break or wanted to talk through an idea, I knew I could walk down the hallway and find encouragement from Bob Crutchfeld, Hedy Lee, Aimee Dechtor, Sarah Quinn, and Jerry Herting. I especially appreciate Stew Tolnay's reading of several early drafts of chapters and his helpful suggestions. I am also thankful to the women of WIRED (Women Investigating Race, Ethnicity, and Difference) at the University of Washington for their support, insight, and advice in navigating academia and the publishing process over the past several years.

Every village needs a team of mentors, and I am fortunate to be able to say that I have a dream team. I will always be indebted to my three lifelong mentors: Walter Allen of UCLA, for his constant support and encouragement and for always answering my phone calls when I need advice; Larry Gossett, my political mentor, who continually reminds me that I am here to make a difference; and Bob Cratchfeld for his mentorship over the last twenty years. I wrote this book with the encouragement and lessons of you three in mind, and I hope that it will serve as a small piece of your legacies. Throughout my career, Ruth Peterson has provided me with guidance, advice, and an example of a balanced academic who produces important scholarship but finds the time to mentor and create invaluable intellectual communities. Along with Laurie Krivo, she developed the Racial Democracy Crime Justice Network (RDCJN), a network of primarily scholars of color who teach and produce scholarship on issues related to race and ethnicity and the justice system. Thank you to my fellow RDCJN members for providing an encouraging intellectual space to do the work that we do.

I am indebted to Becky Pettit, who spent countless hours reading several versions of the manuscript, provided me with edits and suggestions for clarifying my ideas, and encouraged me to push forward. Thank you for helping me find my voice and create a manuscript that integrates my academic side with my desire to create real change, and for reminding me that my multiple identities are needed in this crazy world of academe.

Several people supported me personally and professionally during the writing of this book. Thank you to Nick Allen at Columbia Legal Services and Joel McAllister for always taking my phone calls when I had random, nuanced legal and financial questions; to Washington State Supreme Court Justice Mary Yu for your ideas, commitment, and passion; to Cecelia Gregson for your longtime friendship and legal insight; and to Michelle Majors, Hedy Lee, LaShawnDa Pittman, Joy Williamson-Lott, and Janine Jones, who always allowed time to bounce around ideas and provide encouragement. To my dear friend and colleague Leslie Paik, thank you for reading multiple versions of the manuscript, talking through ideas for framing, and encouraging me along the way.

My family is the crucial part of my village that has sustained me. I could not be the scholar, mother, partner, and person I am, nor could I have finished this book, without the love and support of my parents, Herb and Kathie Harris. Most importantly, my village would not be complete without my lifetime partner and husband, Eric Hampton. From the beginning, you have always supported and encouraged me to live my passions and be 100 percent me. Thank you.

Finally, this book would not have been possible if not for the fifty-five individuals who shared their criminal justice experiences, their humiliations, and their fears. Because of the public nature of our criminal justice system, many other people who had had criminal justice contact—and whom I describe in this book—were not able to consent to participating. As such, I tried to detail my observations of their interactions with judges and courtroom officials as accurately and respectfully as possible. My ultimate hope is that by shedding light on your experiences, we can bring change to a system that has permanently marginalized you.

═ Chapter 1 ═

The Criminal Justice System and Monetary Sanctions

Oh my God, I'm going to get emotional. . . . I really feel like it's time for me to move on. I'm going to be fifty years old next year, it's just time for me to have my own life again. And the financial obligations are, I mean it's something I think about every single day. I mean there's not a day that goes by that I don't think, *Okay, what can I do today to try and figure this out?* And then there are days that I do everything in my power, *Okay, it's there, but I have other things to focus on today.*

—Kathie, legal debtor

A t the time of our interview in 2009, Kathie owed over $20,000 in monetary sanctions to the Washington State Superior Court.[1] She was disabled and living with her three children, ex-husband, and father-in-law in a three-bedroom apartment because she was unable to secure her own home. Kathie's experience was similar to that of many of the defendants I interviewed and observed for this study. Washington State statutes allow judges to sentence people involved in the criminal justice system to fines, fees, restitution, and surcharges. Statutorily, monetary sanctions are viewed as a mechanism to recover the costs of the criminal justice system; like tolls and park fees, they are a product of our fee-for-service culture. And besides being imposed on defendants to obtain restitution for the victims of crimes, they are also symbolically important: in an era of increasing attention to crime and punishment, they are meant to hold offenders accountable for their offending.

Because so many defendants are poor and will face further financial hardship after they have been convicted and served time in jail or prison, criminal monetary sanctions are both real and symbolic. People like Kathie, given the size of their debt and limited capacity to pay, will be indebted to the state for the rest of their lives. For most poor, unemployed, undereducated, and physically and mentally disabled individuals who have contact with the criminal justice system, monetary sanctions are insurmountable. The legal, economic, and social consequences of legal debt often further inhibit their participation in "free" society.

Legal debt is analogous to being sentenced, like Antonio, to give "a pound of flesh." Impoverished defendants have nothing to give. For them and others barely getting by at or near the margins of economic self-sufficiency, monetary sanctions amount to perpetual punishment.

The Significance of Monetary Sanctions

Author: Do you think you should have to pay this money?

Reuben: Yeah, absolutely . . . it was a part of the judgment and sentence, and I have no qualms about it. I'm willing to pay it, every single dime. Unfortunately, you know, [the criminal justice system] took the opportunity, that opportunity, and made it a capital opportunity for themselves. They knew my situation. You know, I was broke, that's the reason I did what I did, and I was still broke in the prison system, so uh, they basically took advantage of the situation and said, "If you can't pay, we're going to put interest on it.". . . I don't blame them, I really don't . . . they have to live with themselves, if they want that amount of money, then they can have it.

Author: This is really interesting that you talk about the debt while you were locked up, that it's on people's minds.

Reuben: It's one of the only things that we are worried about. You know, they give us this opportunity with a release date, you know, to start a whole new chapter, with your debt to society, as far as serving time, but uh, a lot of people get scared. For one, the economy is going bad. Two, they can't, they know they don't have no job lined up for them because they got their . . . [criminal] history. And uh, a lot of them don't have the work background like myself. I've been locked up since I've been sixteen. So I definitely have the record against me and the [lack of] experience. So you have a lot of people like myself getting out, you know, with debts that are more than $6,000, somewhere up to the tens, hundreds, and fifty thousands of dollars, and uh, it's very prevalent on their minds that they will fail if they cannot find a job, and so a lot of them be stressing. Writing lawyers. Trying to get some legal remedies, and uh, most of the time you have to pay a, uh, what you call it, a fee?

In all states, most defendants like Rueben receive monetary sanctions as part of their sentence. Rueben had spent all of his teenage years and his entire adult life in juvenile and criminal facilities. At the time of our interview, he was twenty-four years old, enrolled in a work release program while living at the local county jail, and awaiting his full release. He had been transferred to the adult criminal system at the age of fourteen and convicted of a violent offense that included assault and burglary. In addition to the initial fines, fees, and restitution, Reuben had also been assessed surcharges, interest, and collection costs.

Many states impose these additional costs after the initial sentence. Legally, monetary sanctions are equivalent to court sentences such as jail or prison and community service or probation, and sanctions are often levied in addition to these other punishments. People with outstanding legal fees who do not make regular payments toward their monetary sanctions are regularly called to attend court hearings on the matter. If they do not respond to the court summons, warrants can be issued for their arrest and they can be put in jail for violation of court orders. Furthermore, if a judge labels a person as *willfully* not making payments toward his or her legal debt, the judge may impose further sanctions, including incarceration.

As a result of the rise in monetary sanctions—also called legal financial obligations (LFOs)—indigent defendants, who comprise the vast majority of criminal defendants in the United States, remain under criminal justice supervision, paying per-payment and collection costs and interest on the initial sentence for the remainder of their lives. Long after they complete their custodial sentence or sentenced community supervision, "legal debtors," as they are commonly known, are required to report regularly to the court, explain their living and employment circumstances, and give court clerks and judges the details of their budgets. Debtors cannot regain certain rights lost upon conviction, such as the right to vote, carry a weapon, serve on juries, or run for elected office, until their account is paid in full. Debtors are unable to receive certificates of discharge from the court, to have their records sealed, to receive pardons, or to request deferred prosecutions.[2] Since employers, banks, and apartment managers frequently search applicants' credit and legal backgrounds, legal practices that suppress convictions from the public are essential for those applying for jobs or loans or trying to rent an apartment or purchase a home. Furthermore, LFOs cannot be cleared through bankruptcy.[3] Thus, criminal monetary sanctions trigger a long series of consequences and barriers to full societal integration for poor people that are very different from the effects of monetary sanctions on defendants with financial means.

The Justification for Monetary Sanctions

Monetary sanctions arose as a way to recoup the expenses associated with the criminal justice system for both victims of crimes and the broader society. The legal reasoning of policymakers for imposing these sanctions is threefold: (1) to reimburse victims for lost wages, the cost of hospitalization, and damage done to their property (restitution); (2) to require people involved in the criminal system to help reimburse the state for the costs resulting from their criminal behavior, including the costs of arresting, prosecuting, and punishing them (fines and fees); and (3) as a means beyond the original sentence, to hold offenders accountable for their behavior and seek societal retribution (additional punishment).

A great deal of judicial discretion goes into deciding the type and amount of the LFOs imposed on defendants, and whether to impose them at all. Each state has its own statutes detailing the types of fines, fees, costs, interest charges, surcharges, and restitution costs that judges can impose as punishment for felony convictions. Within each state, counties implement their own formal policies as legally prescribed by county or parish code. In county courthouses across the United States, judges exert unfettered discretion in sentencing defendants to a wide array of monetary sanctions; monitoring, with court clerks, their payment of LFOs; and imposing additional sanctions on those they deem as *willfully* not making payments.

The Revised Code of Washington (RCW) establishes which LFOs are always assessed. Since courts across the state generally interpret the code's definition of LFOs as mandatory sanctions, judges impose a $500 victim penalty assessment (VPA) and a $100 DNA collection fee as the mandatory minimums. Thus, just as state sentencing guidelines set mandatory minimum custodial sentence lengths for particular offenses, the total mandatory minimum fiscal penalty for any felony conviction in Washington is $600. In addition to these mandatory minimum sanctions, the code also lists sanctions that "may be" assessed, and these are routinely interpreted by judges as discretionary. A number of other discretionary sentences in the form of fines, fees, and restitution can also be imposed. As a consequence, the mean sentenced LFO in Washington is $1,300—more than two times the statutory minimum.[4]

Monetary sanctions are a routine part of sentencing practices in most states, though the mandatory minimum amounts vary. In Louisiana, at the time of sentencing, indigent defendants are assessed an up-front fee of $40 for their criminal public defender and then a $300 fee for the "Judicial Expense Fund." All felony defendants in North Carolina are assessed a general "cost of justice fee" in the amount of $154.50. In all states, LFOs are imposed per felony conviction; thus, costs multiply for someone who is convicted of multiple offenses at one time. States can—and often do—charge interest on unpaid LFOs. Washington State charges 12 percent interest that begins accruing from the day of sentencing, as well as a $100 annual collection surcharge per felony conviction.[5]

Although monetary sanctions have been a feature of the formal American criminal justice system ever since its beginnings, the practice ballooned in the early 1990s, when states began to formally codify their financial penalties. The number and types of fees and surcharges have expanded ever since. As a result, the majority of people convicted of misdemeanor and felony crimes in the United States receive some type of monetary sanction. All fifteen states in one recent study imposed fees upon conviction, all imposed parole, probation, or other supervision fees, and all had laws authorizing the imposition of jail or prison fees.[6] Further evidence indicates that in most jurisdictions monetary sanctions are levied in addition to the other common sentencing options, such as community service, probation, and incarceration.[7]

Even seemingly small LFOs are of inordinate significance in the lives of poor defendants who have virtually no access to income or wages while incarcerated. Most defendants are not able to make payments toward their LFOs while incarcerated, and thus their financial situation is already precarious when they are released from jail or prison. Because of this debt, people remain subject to the surveillance and sanctioning of criminal justice agents, as well as the stigmatizing effects of their felony conviction, for long periods of time. Moreover, the added interest and surcharges expand their debts at a time when their earnings prospects, already dismal for many of them, are further diminished. As a result, the monetary sanctions associated with criminal justice contact contribute to the mounting disadvantage of poor defendants by reducing their income and creating long-term debt.

Mass Conviction, Incarceration, and Collateral Consequences

Today the number of people who have been convicted and incarcerated and are currently under surveillance by the U.S. criminal justice system is unprecedented: after forty years of expanding conviction and incarceration rates, 2.25 million Americans are incarcerated and 7.1 million are under some form of criminal justice supervision through incarceration, probation, or parole.[8] Figure 1.1 illustrates the rise in state and federal imprisonment rates since 1925. One in thirty-seven U.S. adults have spent time in state or federal prisons,[9] and more than 700,000 peo-

Figure 1.1   State and Federal Prisoners in the United States, 1950–2014

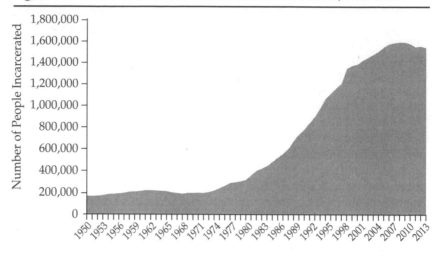

Source: Author's calculations based on data from the Bureau of Justice Statistics, National Prisoner Statistics Program.

ple leave prison each year.[10] A much larger number of people have experienced a felony conviction in their lifetime. Estimates suggest that in 1976, 1.17 million U.S. adults had received a felony conviction in their lifetime; in 1996 the number had grown by 285 percent, to 3.34 million, and in 2010 the number of adults living with a felony conviction had increased by 500 percent, to 5.85 million.[11] Across the United States today, 2.5 percent of the adult population—one out of every forty adults—have been convicted of a felony.[12]

No national data sets are available that count how many people have been sentenced to monetary sanctions. But given the increase in the number of statutes that allow for monetary sanctions, it is reasonable to suspect that a large portion of the population with felony convictions have received monetary sanctions, thus incurring legal debt.

At the center of the American criminal justice system expansion is a particular subset of the U.S. population. Over half of the people living in prison are people of color (60 percent). Among African American men in their thirties, one in ten are living behind bars. If recent incarceration trends continue, one in three African American males born today may live in prison at some point in their lifetime, as may one in six Latino males, in contrast to one in seventeen white males. Observing that criminal defendants tend to be undereducated and that the odds of being incarcerated are much higher for those without a high school diploma or GED, Becky Pettit and Bruce Western have concluded that "imprisonment now rivals or overshadows the frequency of military service and college graduation for recent cohorts of African American men."[13] The same disproportionate pattern prevails among those with felony convictions living in the United States. One out of thirteen African American adults have experienced a felony conviction (7.7 percent), while one out of fifty-six non–African Americans have been convicted of a felony (1.8 percent).[14] With disproportionately high rates of criminal conviction, African Americans are disproportionately burdened by monetary sanctions.

Poor people are also disproportionately shouldering the weight of monetary sanctions. People convicted of felonies tend to be financially worse off before arrest and conviction than those not connected to the criminal justice system, and defendants tend to have higher unemployment rates than nondefendants: estimates suggest that between 30 and 36 percent of jail and state prison inmates did not have a job prior to their arrest.[15] Among state prison inmates who had a job, 26 percent were working part-time.[16] Of those working in the month before arrest, nearly one-quarter (23 percent) reported monthly earnings of $600 or less, and one-half reported a monthly income of $1,200 or less. Nationally, the earned annual income of two-thirds of jail inmates was under $12,000 in the year prior to arrest.[17] Clear majorities of criminal defendants are poor, and they face a variety of financial hurdles even in the absence of monetary sanctions.

In addition to low levels of education and high rates of unemployment, people involved in the criminal justice system experience more physical and mental health issues than the general population. In 1996, one-third of jail inmates reported physical or mental health problems, almost half (48 percent) of women in jail reported being physically or sexually abused, and 27 percent reported being raped prior to jail admission.[18] Data from the same period on adults who were on probation for both felony and misdemeanor offenses illustrate other social dislocations: 37 percent were undergoing drug or alcohol treatment, 65 percent were unemployed, and 84 percent had been sentenced to fines, fees, and court costs.[19] Another 42 percent had less than a high school diploma at the time of their arrest.[20] A 2004 court survey of inmates in New York found that, "of the people released on parole in . . . New York State, 49% were unemployed, 81% needed services for drug abuse, and 15% had only a grade school education."[21] The numbers illustrate that prior to even entering the criminal justice system, defendants experience a host of health, economic, and social challenges.

Conviction only compounds the problems of the poor. Convicted felons in many states are politically disenfranchised, face unemployment or underemployment as well as reduced income and wages, suffer poor health, and have difficulty reintegrating into their families and communities after release. In many states, convicted felons lose the right to vote and to serve on juries.[22] They can be legally discriminated against in hiring decisions by employers who see them as a liability.[23] Convicted felons can also lose custody of their children and be required to pay child support.[24] They can become ineligible for several types of federal benefits, such as Temporary Assistance for Needy Families (TANF), the Supplemental Nutrition Assistance Program (SNAP, formerly known as food stamps), and educational loans.[25] Several jurisdictions have "one-strike" housing prohibitions that disqualify convicted felons from living in certain areas.[26] And those who are not U.S. citizens may face deportation when convicted of a felony. Felony convictions leave people in a liminal legal space where they cannot exercise their full rights as citizens and are marked as qualitatively different from others in society.

Incarceration has a tremendous influence on children and families. Over 2.7 million minor children, or one in twenty-eight, have a parent in jail or prison. A recent study found that among children born in 1990, one out of every twenty-five white children and one out of every four black children had a parent imprisoned.[27] In fact, having an incarcerated parent has become such a common experience that the long-running children's television program *Sesame Street*, in an effort to teach children and caregivers how to talk about incarceration and its effects on children, developed a character named Alex who has a father living in prison.

The criminal justice system reinforces the U.S. system of social stratification. Felony conviction is now directly linked to the generation and maintenance of inequality. People who are poor, undereducated, and of color disproportionately make contact with the criminal justice system. They are arrested, detained in jail, prosecuted, convicted, and sentenced at higher rates than their peers who are wealthy, more educated, and white.[28] When people are released from court with a criminal conviction, they face a myriad of social, legal, and financial problems that exacerbate the dislocations they may have experienced prior to their contact with the criminal justice system.[29]

Although all U.S. states now allow the imposition of fiscal penalties on people convicted of felonies, suggesting that monetary sanctions have become widespread, data are not currently available with which we could directly estimate the prevalence or ubiquity of monetary sanctions. What evidence we do have indicates that LFOs are widespread and consequential for race and class inequalities. I begin by asking two central questions: How are monetary sanctions legally structured and imposed? And what are the consequences of LFOs for people convicted of felonies?

The American Culture of Punishment

In their classic Marxist analysis of punishment systems, Georg Rusche and Otto Kirchheimer suggest that "punishment must be understood as a social phenomenon freed from both its juristic concept and its social ends."[30] This study's dissection of the contemporary culture of punishment embodied in the U.S. criminal justice system is one way to understand the exceptional U.S. criminal justice practices. Moreover, this study provides a window through which the unique reliance on the criminal justice system in the United States can be compared to practices in other nations.

Societal values and morals can be viewed as embedded in the laws and policies that guide justice practices and outcomes. Thus, the criminal justice system shares, and is infused with, the aims, values, priorities, and goals of the broader U.S. society and can be studied not only for the outcomes it produces—such as the number of people who are convicted and incarcerated—and related consequences, but also for the culture it represents. Past and current iterations of the U.S. criminal justice system reflect this society's conceptions of justice, fear, and punishment. As such, I use the term "punishment culture" as a framework to understand why and how the system of monetary sanctions is implemented across the United States—and more specifically in my case study, how monetary sanctions operate in Washington State.

The Expanding Costs of the U.S. Criminal Justice System

The study of monetary sanctions also offers insight into the practical costs associated with the expansion of the U.S. criminal justice system and the ways in which those costs have become an additional punishment for defendants. Local, state, and federal jurisdictions face enormous expenditures related to increased conviction, supervision, and incarceration rates. The criminal justice system includes police, courts, community-based supervision, and jails and prisons, and each of these arms of the system has grown, as have personnel and management costs. State corrections spending totaled $47 billion in 2013, and state and local jurisdictions have attempted to pay for the rising costs of their criminal justice systems brought on by the unprecedented growth in conviction and incarceration rates by shifting their budget priorities. Between 1986 and 2013, states increased spending on K–12 education by 69 percent, on higher education by less than 6 percent, and on corrections by 141 percent.[31] In other words, some state legislators and local politicians have increased spending on criminal justice at the expense of educational programming.

It is important to note that many more costs are associated with the rise in conviction rates than just corrections. A recent study of prison costs in forty states found that total corrections budgets came to $33.5 billion, but the actual total costs to taxpayers for the prison system was $39 billion. The report highlighted the fact that, above and beyond the costs related to corrections management—which are extraordinary in their own right—several other expenses not normally included in corrections budgets result from the massive rise in conviction rates, including employee benefits and taxes, pension contributions, retiree health care contributions, capital costs, legal judgments and claims, and statewide administrative costs, as well as the costs associated with having private businesses provide hospital care and education and training. Thus, in addition to the expense of housing, securing, feeding, and clothing inmates, billions of dollars are paid to state employees to process and manage inmates. The average total per-inmate cost across the United States in 2010 was $31,286. Per-inmate expenditures ranged from $14,603 in Kentucky to $60,076 in New York. In contrast, per-pupil spending for K-12 education averaged $12,608 across the United States.[32]

In the face of rising criminal justice–related costs, many states have come to rely on private for-profit entities to manage their criminal justice system. Such strategies include the use of private business to oversee community supervision and probation (including electronic monitoring); to operate work release programs, halfway houses, and for-profit residential treatment centers; and to manage local jails and prisons and the people living in them. Private industries also are contracted by state corrections agencies to provide services within corrections facilities such as health care, email and phone systems, and inmates' payments and accounts.[33] It is unclear whether such reliance on private businesses reduces criminal justice costs for jurisdictions or instead creates another layer of punishment for people who are unable to pay for services rendered while they are under criminal justice supervision.

The exponentially increasing costs associated with mass conviction and incarceration, combined with the effects of the 2008 economic recession, have compelled states to explore strategies for reducing criminal justice costs and generating financial resources. California has experienced a highly public struggle over the management of its criminal justice–related expenses. In 2011 the U.S. Supreme Court, in *Brown v.*

Plata, established a limit for prison populations. The Court determined that a prison population at 137.5 percent of a prison's design capacity was the limit of crowding that a state could impose. Any further over-crowding would be considered cruel and unusual punishment and thus constitute a violation of a person's Eighth Amendment rights. In the same year as the *Plata* decision, California's legislature passed the Criminal Justice Realignment Act, which shifted the management of lower-level offenders, at the state's discretion, from the state to the counties. Although the act did not lead to the release of any prisoners, it gave local law enforcement the flexibility to give low-level offenders community-based, less costly, noncustodial sentences. In its first two years, the act allocated more than $2 billion to local programs, includ-ing alternative community-based sentences for more than 100,000 pris-oners. What has been called the "biggest penal experiment in modern history" was intended, as stated by California governor Jerry Brown, to address "the costly, ineffective and unsafe 'revolving door' of lower-level offenders and parole violators through [California's] state pris-ons."[34]

State legislatures and county courts have also decided to shift crimi-nal justice costs directly onto defendants. Sentencing defendants to pay the costs related to their own court processing and incarceration has been identified as a way to recoup criminal justice expenditures. This study of monetary sanctions sheds light on the practical financial costs associated with contemporary U.S. criminal justice practices and exam-ines the blurred line between punishment and fiscal management.

The Study of Monetary Sanctions and Social Inequality

Political rhetoric is partly responsible for the aggressive law enforce-ment and criminal justice policies and procedures that have produced the current state of mass conviction and incarceration.[35] Policies such as "three strikes," mandatory minimum sentences, and sentence enhance-ments have extended sentencing ranges and led to compulsory incar-ceration for people convicted of a wide range of offenses. Meanwhile, the stigma attached to felony conviction and incarceration stunts indi-viduals' ability to reenter society and move forward with their lives after contact with the criminal justice system. We know that felony con-victions reduce wages, stigma perpetuates inequality among African American and Latino men and among high school dropouts in the em-ployment market, and the aggregate effect of the loss of voting rights on convicted felons is profound.[36]

Despite this large body of research, little attention has been devoted to understanding how policymakers and practitioners define, interpret, and apply policies *within* the criminal justice system that allow it to act as a social stratifying institution. Nor has any significant amount of scholarly attention been focused on the ongoing nature of contemporary punishment: for many defendants, criminal justice contact continues well beyond the one discrete moment of conviction or the period of incarceration. Little research has detailed the practice of monetary sanctions, much less the practical significance of such debt for community reentry.[37]

The complex context of monetary sanctions includes not only the forty-year rise in U.S. conviction rates but also the punitive culture of punishment now prevailing in the United States. Justified by the increasing costs of criminal justice processing, monetary sanctions practically represent a sentence for cost recoupment, but symbolically they also represent a sentence of accountability. In addition, the criminal justice system plays an important part in the reproduction of social inequality.

Because of the complexities and legal variations in the amounts and types of monetary sanctions that can be imposed nationally and within states, I decided to focus this study on the monetary sanctions imposed on people convicted of felony offenses in state superior courts, especially in Washington State. I should note, however, that multiple types of legal monetary sanctions are imposed at numerous court levels, with similar outcomes for debtors. In addition to felony adult court, additional sites of debt include court-related services, private debt management, privatized probation, child support costs, fines for parents with truant children, and the legal monetary sanctions resulting from involvement in misdemeanor and traffic courts, juvenile courts, district courts, and the federal courts. Furthermore, just as with criminal debt, the state can sanction debtors in most arenas through both publicly and privately administered court summonses, warrants, and even incarceration. The imposition of felony legal debt may be the focus of this book, but it is important to understand the wider context in which legal debt is imposed and the ways in which the state controls and sanctions debtors.

Why Washington State?

To better understand the system of monetary sanctions, I selected one state, Washington, and five counties within it for an analysis of the mechanisms and outcomes related to the imposition of monetary sanctions. Washington is an ideal case study for several reasons. All U.S.

states have statutes governing the use of fines and fees for the punishment of felons, but Washington has a clearly articulated and detailed statute that outlines "legal financial obligations."[38] As a result, the legal climate surrounding the use of monetary sanctions has developed with the passage of multiple supplementary statutes and been the focus of legal and political discourse over the past twenty-five years in both case law and the state legislature. Such an environment provides an interesting case study for understanding monetary sanctions, as well as a unique opportunity to examine how policymakers and practitioners understand the sanctions, the various ways in which the policies are imposed in the state, and the resulting legal outcomes and contestations.

I obtained access to a sample of court data from Washington that allows a statistical analysis of both state- and county-level decision-making. The data raise important questions about the county- and individual-level differences in assessment and sanctioning norms and thus provide an important context for my qualitative research. These analyses in Washington are particularly illuminating about the different ways in which county officials interpret the legislation governing the assessment of monetary sanctions and the various mechanisms they use to sanction nonpayers. Thus, future research on the uses and consequences of monetary sanctions in other states should benefit from my analysis of the legal and political culture surrounding monetary sanctions in Washington, the types of mechanisms used to impose sanctions, and the consequences for legal debtors. The continuum of punishment in this state is a valuable starting point from which to understand the parameters of varying cultural orientations toward punishment on the national scale. My analysis sketches the various policies and practices used to interpret and apply state monetary sanction statutes as well as the various ways in which debtors are sanctioned and monitored.

A growing segment of Washington's judiciary, legislators, practitioners, and citizens have become interested in changing the state's use of monetary sanctions: some want to broaden the use of monetary sanctions, while others seek to curtail their use.[39] This environment has generated a field site with informants who want to discuss the uses, policies, practices, and outcomes associated with monetary sanctions. The legal context, the availability of quantitative and qualitative data, and the widespread attention to this practice make Washington State a prime setting for investigating the interactions of the political, legal, and social dimensions of monetary sanctions with court officials' interpretations and applications of state law.

The Logic of Monetary Sanctions

In many ways it may seem rational to sentence defendants to repay the costs resulting from their own criminal offending, processing, and punishment. Further, the payment of monetary sanctions could be a useful tool for offenders in expressing their accountability to their victims and remorse for their offending. With the expansion of the criminal justice system and the disparate ways in which poor and racialized communities are harmed, however, it is important to understand how this system operates. My analysis and discussion here are guided by two sets of questions.

First, how do monetary sanctions operate, both nationally and within one specific state, and with what consequences? In this line of inquiry, I investigate the similarities and differences between the fifty state statutes governing monetary sanctions and the effects of these laws on the criminal justice system as an institution and on individual offenders. From this analysis the second set of questions emerges: How do practitioners interpret and apply the statutes governing monetary sanctions? What are the local cultural and organizational contexts within which people are labeled "legal debtors," and how are they subsequently monitored and sanctioned for incomplete payment or nonpayment?

In answering these questions, I tell a modern-day American story about crime and punishment that relies on quantitative and qualitative data and analyses to give a contextualized and detailed account of monetary sanctions. I have relied on eighty-nine interviews—with judges (fifteen), clerks (eight), prosecutors (four), defense attorneys (four), state representatives (three), and felony defendants (fifty)—as well as on five case studies of persons convicted of felonies and 140 observations of LFO sentencing and sanctioning hearings.[40] My detailed review of state statutes has enabled me to compare and contrast monetary sanction policies and practices across the United States. The book is also informed by my statistical analysis of a sample of 2004 criminal court data from the Washington State Administrative Office of the Courts (AOC).

Using this mixed-method approach, I present empirical evidence to support two arguments. First, *monetary sanctions imposed by the criminal justice system create and sustain inequality in the United States.* The sentencing of fines and fees generates financial hardship for defendants, and because LFOs are disproportionately imposed on impoverished defendants, they reinforce inequality. Further, monetary sanctions contribute to the social and emotional marginalization of defendants through continual court monitoring of payments and sanctions for nonpayment and the emotional stress from related economic hardships.

Monetary sanctions represent a class-based punishment scheme that differentially affects poor defendants.

Second, *the system of monetary sanctions is enforced by criminal justice bureaucrats whose discretion is shaped by a culture of accountability.* Relying on cultural ideas about personal responsibility, meritocracy, and paternalism, court officials translate the seemingly rational system of monetary sanctions aimed at recouping expenses related to offending into perpetual punishment for those defendants who have little to no economic means and are viewed by these officials as having poor moral character. As a result of officials' reliance on personal beliefs and values to guide their imposition of policy and their practice, monetary sanctions have become inherently localized, with extreme variability in the sentencing, monitoring, and sanctioning of legal debtors. Monetary sanctions amount to a two-tiered system of justice imposed by street-level bureaucrats with little governmental accountability and oversight.

The Outline of the Book

The remaining six chapters of this book present support for these two arguments. To begin my analysis of the broad system of monetary sanctions in chapter 2, I ask the simple question: what does the system of monetary sanctions look like across the United States? I review related research on monetary sanctions, outline the consequences of legal debt, and describe the shared set of legal practices that provides the framework for monetary sanctions across all fifty states. I then outline the similarities between the states in their monetary sanction statutes—including fines, user fees, costs for incarceration, community supervision, treatment, and indigent public defense—and describe the legal contexts and justifications for the imposition of such costs on defendants. This chapter reveals that monetary sanctions have become an increasingly common national sentencing practice, with indeterminate and unending legal consequences for indigent defendants.

In chapter 3, I explore the experiences of people sentenced to monetary sanctions and provide amortization tables to show how debt increases as a result of interest and collection costs. Using interview data, I examine the sense of marginalization among convicted felons caused by debt-related frustration, the difficulty they experience in moving forward with their lives because of LFOs, and the strain that legal debt creates in other areas of their lives. I also outline the ways in which monetary sanctions serve as perpetual punishment and both emotionally and structurally marginalize indigent defendants, who remain tethered to the criminal justice system and cannot take advantage of deferred prosecutions and avoid the court expenses related to subsequent sanctions.

Chapter 4 interrogates the legal justifications for and outcomes of monetary sanctions. I trace the legal statutes in Washington that govern LFOs and present the conceptualizations of LFOs held by legislators and court officials. In the interviews, they commonly talked about LFOs as a mechanism to provide restitution to victims, to recover the costs of using the criminal justice system, to impose further punishment, and to hold offenders "accountable" for their criminality. My examination of data on LFOs from Washington reveals, however, that most defendants can pay only very little of the amount they owe and that victims receive little, if any, restitution in many jurisdictions. In fact, some jurisdictions prioritize paying for the cost of collection over paying restitution to victims. Monetary sanctions have become a marginally self-sustaining system: just enough is collected to pay for the maintenance of the system. Monetary sanctions may have initially been created to recoup costs, but they are now embedded in a system under which poor defendants receive sentences that they can never complete. Condemned to a life sentence of criminal justice monitoring, they remain subject to continual assessment according to the amorphous standard of "accountability."

In chapter 5, I move from an examination of the structure of monetary sanctions in the state of Washington to a consideration of how the system operates on the ground level. My examination of court data, interviews, and observations reveal wide variability in Washington's sentencing, monitoring, and sanctioning practices, thus supporting the concept of a punishment continuum. Sentencing and monitoring range from less to more punitive across counties within the state, but county-level characteristics do not explain all of the variation in LFO amounts to which offenders are sentenced. Interview and observational data illustrate that local court officials translate the legal intent established at the state level to fit local norms and assumptions about criminality and punishment.

In chapter 6, I consider more closely the alternative explanations for the sentencing, monitoring, and sanctioning decisions of judges, prosecutors, and clerks. The chapter shows that how these officials understand crime—whether as a social problem resulting from structural inequalities and lack of opportunities or as an individual problem resulting from character flaws and personal choice—helps explain the variability among them in how they sentence, monitor, and sanction legal debtors. In other words, their orientation toward "American values" shapes and informs officials' use of discretion, and their decisions can be understood in relation to both individual and collective adherence to ideas of personal responsibility, meritocracy, and paternalism.

In the final chapter of the book, I consider the implications of monetary sanctions for social stratification and inequality. Effectively serving as permanent punishment, LFOs reinforce poverty, destabilize community reentry, and relegate impoverished debtors to a lifetime of punishment because their poverty leaves them unable to fulfill expectations of accountability. Disproportionately imposed on economically and marginalized citizens, LFOs permanently tether poor criminal defendants to the criminal justice system and lead to lifelong—and bitter—relationships with justice agents. My institutional analysis, drawing attention to monetary sanctions as a method of social control that symbolically, physically, and perpetually punishes the poor, thus has even greater significance for the scholarly study of inequality and critiques of the American Dream.

=== Chapter 2 ===

Criminal Monetary Sanctions in the United States

For count one: 12 months plus one day [in prison], counts two and four: 365 days each, suspended for two years. For all three counts: domestic violence evaluation, 12 months' community supervision. Under count one: $500 Victim Penalty Assessment, $200 in court costs, $400 defense costs, $100 DNA fee. I don't know if there is any restitution. "If we need to we can set at a later date."

—Field notes from observations of the sentencing of a male defendant in Alexander County, Wash., 2012

S entencing criminal defendants to monetary sanctions is not new. Charging people money as part of their punishment has long been included in Western systems of justice. Georg Rusche and Otto Kirchheimer discuss the use of fines in criminal cases in the Middle Ages.[1] Most state penal statutes have included references to fines and fees as far back as the nineteenth century, when American legal codes were first designed, using the model of European penal codes. As David Oshinsky documents, a free black man in Mississippi in the late 1800s was fined $5.00 for being a "tramp" and assessed other costs totaling $9.95.[2]

Across the United States, however, states have recently formalized the imposition and enforcement of monetary sanctions in state laws and expanded the types of fines, fees, and surcharges imposed on felony defendants at the time of conviction. For at least the past twenty-five years, states have added statutes to their criminal codes that allow judges to assess a wide range of financial penalties, many of which are now viewed by judges as mandatory. Although monetary sanctions are not custodial sentences, they are similar in that, until a defendant's financial sentence is paid in full, he or she remains under the supervision of the criminal justice system. Furthermore, state legislatures have developed statutes to allow legal debt to accumulate over time with interest and to allow for the incarceration of nonpaying debtors. Thus, unlike a determinant sentence of confinement, which allows a person to anticipate a release date, LFOs can drag on over the course of an entire life.[3]

This chapter explores the legal landscape governing the use of monetary sanctions across the United States. There are striking similarities across the states in the types of fines, fees, and surcharges imposed on felony defendants, including court costs, fees for incarceration, treatment, and supervision, and surcharges that are unrelated to criminal justice. States regularly allow courts to incarcerate people as punishment for "willfully" failing to make regular payments toward their legal debt, even when defendants may be financially unable to pay. Monetary sanctions have become a common punishment tool in the United States guided by a consistent set of sentencing and sanctioning guidelines that control and monitor criminal offenders.

The Evolution of Monetary Sanctions

Neither slavery nor involuntary servitude, except as a punishment for crime where of the party shall have been duly convicted, shall exist within the United States.

—U.S. Constitution, Thirteenth Amendment (1865)

Sentencing people to prison for nonpayment of debt was a common practice around the world until at least the 1800s. From the Middle Ages through the mid-nineteenth century, European courts commonly imprisoned people who could not or did not pay their civil debts. Although the appropriateness of imprisonment as a sanction for people declared bankrupt had been debated since the mid-sixteenth century, debtors were nevertheless regularly found on prison rosters. London even had an entire prison dedicated to indigent debtors.[4] This practice carried over to the United States, where many of the early settlers were debtors escaping Europe. Indeed, one scholar has called the early American cities "Debtors' Asylums" because nearly two-thirds of the Europeans in the American colonies were debtors.[5]

On the heels of the first American stock market crash in 1792, a new ideology began to emerge about the character of debtors, including general beliefs about debt and forgiveness.[6] Debt became a common experience for both poor *and* formerly wealthy people. In 1831 legislatures in New York, Maine, and Tennessee abolished the practice of imprisoning people for debt. Soon all other states followed. After this national movement to abolish the practice of incarcerating debtors in the 1830s, every state amended its constitution to define as unconstitutional the incarceration of debtors who had no means with which to make payments toward their obligations. Even as state constitutions disallowed the incarceration of civil debtors, however, many still allowed for the incarceration of people who were labeled "absconding debtors," or those who had not paid "fines and penalties imposed by law."[7]

Legal challenges to the incarceration of debtors have affirmed that constitutional protections against debtors' prisons protect *civil* debtors, not *criminal* debtors. The Washington State Supreme Court found in *State v. Barklind* (1976) that:

> We believe the constitutional prohibition against imprisonment for debt relates to run-of-the-mill debtor-creditor relationships arising, to some extent, out of tort claims, but principally, out of matters basically contractual in nature. In such cases, the judgment of the court is merely a declaration of an amount owing and is not an order to pay.[8]

Most courts view the imprisonment of legal debtors—that is, the imprisonment of persons with outstanding debt from LFOs—as legally allowable because such debtors are being incarcerated because they are failing to comply with court orders, not because of their inability to pay. Rulings have affirmed that legal debtors can be held in contempt of the court (and thus incarcerated) for not fulfilling their criminal sentence, which often includes monetary sanctions. In *Williams v. Illinois* (1970), the defendant, Sandy Williams, was sentenced to the maximum penalty for petty theft under Illinois law, which at the time was one year in jail and $505 in legal fines and court fees. At sentencing, he was told that if he did not pay the total amount by the end of his one-year sentence, he would remain in jail and his delinquent account would be credited $5 a day until the debt was paid in full. Williams challenged his sentence, arguing that he was denied equal protection under the Fourteenth Amendment of the U.S. Constitution. His indigence would compel him to remain confined for an additional 101 days past the maximum allowed sentence for his crime. The Supreme Court concluded that

> a State may not constitutionally imprison beyond the maximum duration fixed by statute a defendant who is financially unable to pay a fine. A statute permitting a sentence of both imprisonment and fine cannot be parlayed into a longer term of imprisonment than is fixed by the statute, since to do so would be to accomplish indirectly as to an indigent that which cannot be done directly.[9]

Tate v. Short (1971) prohibited states from imposing a fine as a sentence and then automatically converting the fine into a jail term solely because the defendant is indigent. In *Tate*, the court held that other constitutional means are available to serve the state's valid interest in enforcing the payment of fines. However, the decision permitted the incarceration of a legal debtor if a court determines that this person has means to make payments and can be labeled a "willful nonpayer."

Determining defendants' ability to pay became the focus of the courts' analyses. *Bearden v. Georgia* (1983) established the precedent for "willfulness." The defendant, Danny Bearden, was convicted of burglary and theft and sentenced to probation and $750 in fines, fees, and restitution. He was ordered to pay $200 within two days of his sentencing and the remaining $550 within four months. Bearden secured a loan from his parents for the first $200, but soon thereafter became unemployed. After he informed his probation officer that he would be unable to make the subsequent payment, a hearing was held at which his unemployment and lack of income and assets were established. Nonetheless, his probation was revoked and he was incarcerated for contempt.

The primary issue in *Bearden* was equal protection. Was the defendant treated differently than someone who would have had the means to pay the monetary sanctions? The Supreme Court ruled in favor of Bearden, finding that the trial court erred in revoking his probation without determining whether he had made "sufficient bona fide efforts" to pay his monetary sanctions and whether alternative forms of punishment were available.

The Supreme Court indicated that the sentencing judge should have asked whether Bearden attempted to find the resources to make his payments. In a hearing, Bearden and his wife explained that they were unemployed, had no income or assets, and had tried to find work. The judge, in turn, told them that odd jobs, such as lawn mowing, were always available to generate money. The Supreme Court found the sentencing judge's statement to be insufficient evidence that the court had considered Bearden's reasons for nonpayment. Instead, the Supreme Court ruled, the sentencing court had to have found that the defendant "willfully" refused to pay or failed to make sufficient efforts to acquire the resources to pay. The Court further ruled that if a defendant cannot pay, despite sufficient efforts to do so, the trial court should consider measures other than imprisonment before incarcerating the defendant for contempt.[10] In addition to equal protection, *Bearden* was important for its consideration of due process. It stipulated that judges must hold hearings and make inquiries as to whether or not defendants have the ability to make payments.

As a result of the decisions in *Williams v. Illinois, Tate v. Short,* and *Bearden v. Georgia,* the concepts of "willful" nonpayment and "bona fide efforts" have become more important in state laws and in courts' determination of the status of nonpaying defendants and whether or not they can be sentenced to incarceration. In the language of these court decisions, defendants who have made "reasonable," "sufficient bona fide," or "good faith" efforts to pay cannot be held in contempt for nonpayment. Yet defining such efforts can be difficult, and courts and court officials vary in how they go about measuring them. Courts have determined that prior to incarcerating a defendant a judge must, at the very least, hold hearings to determine not only whether the defendant has failed to make payments but also whether he or she has "willfully" chosen not to make payments. Significant debate continues on how to establish that nonpayment has been "willful" and what constitutes a "good faith" effort, and state courts continue to struggle with these issues, which I discuss in greater detail in chapters 4 and 5.

Determinations of good faith and willfulness are tightly linked to conceptualizations of worthiness and accountability. *Washington v. Bower* (1992) attempted to challenge the practice of penalizing people who say that they are unable to pay monetary sanctions. Robert Wayne Bower contended that the state could not incarcerate him for his inability to make regular payments toward his LFOs. The Washington Court of Appeals, Division I, determined that, while the state needed to establish noncompliance with the sentencing conditions of the court, it was the defendant's burden to present evidence of his inability to pay and reasons why he should not be sanctioned. Thus, while prosecutors had to prove to courts that debtors missed payments, discretion was left to judges to assess whether defendants had presented enough evidence that they were too impoverished to make minimum monthly payments.

More recently, *Washington v. Nason* (2010) questioned the constitutionality of incarcerating nonpaying defendants. James Robert Nason contended that his county's "auto-jail" policy, which mandated that he report for jail on a specific day and time without a hearing once he failed to make a monthly payment, violated his due process rights. Relying on *Bearden,* the court partly struck down the auto-jail policy, finding that the court did not hold hearings to allow the defendant to present his reasons for nonpayment. The court also found, however, that jailing for nonpayment is permissible when the court determines that a defendant has willfully refused to pay.

Washington v. Stone (2012) addressed due process rights in Washington State. The defendant, James Michael Stone, had been denied a defense attorney in a show cause hearing to determine how willfully he was not paying his LFOs. The Washington Court of Appeals found that

Table 2.1   Legislative History of the Arizona Felony Surcharge, 1994–2012

Year	Felony Surcharge
1994	57%
1995	59
1996	60
1999	70
1999	77
2002	80
2007	84
2012	83

Source: Arizona Revised Statutes (ARS), sections 12-116.01(A, B) ("Surcharges: Fund Deposits"), 12-116.02(A) ("Additional Surcharges: Fund Deposits"), and 16-954(A) ("Disposition of Excess Monies").

the court violated Stone's fundamental due process rights by failing to inquire about his ability to pay and denying him the right to an attorney prior to incarcerating him for willful nonpayment. As it stands, the vast majority of states allow the incarceration of nonpaying defendants. The U.S. Supreme Court and state courts have established the constitutionality of imprisoning debtors if sentencing judges hold hearings to determine the reason for their nonpayment and find that their nonpayment is "willful."

The Expansion of Monetary Sanctions

In recent years, there has been dramatic expansion across the United States in the types of LFOs that can be levied. Inmate surveys reveal a swift rise in the number of people who have been sentenced to monetary sanctions: 25 percent of inmates reported receiving LFOs in 1991, but that number had risen to 66 percent by 2004. The increase was the greatest for court fees, compared to other types of LFOs.[11]

The expansion of LFOs has followed from relatively recent changes to state penal codes, which have added new types of monetary sanctions and modified existing sanctions to increase the amounts that can be assessed. Arizona's statute change is representative of such modifications. That state's felony surcharge, which is levied in addition to the other monetary sanctions imposed on a defendant, was created in 1994, when it was initially set at a rate of 57 percent of the combined total of other LFOs. For example, if a defendant was assessed $1,000 for fines and fees, the surcharge would add $570 to create a total monetary sanction of $1,570. The state legislature gradually increased the amount of felony surcharges throughout the 1990s and 2000s (table 2.1), to a peak

Table 2.2   Legislative History of the Washington Victim Penalty
Assessment for Felonies, 1977–1996

Year	Victim Penalty Assessment
1977	$25
1982	$50
1985	$70
1989	$100
1996	$500

Source: Revised Code of Washington (RCW) 7.68.035 ("Penalty Assessments in Addition
to Fine or Bail Forfeiture . . .").

Table 2.3   Legislative History of the Jury Fee for a Felony-Related Twelve-
Person Jury in Washington, 1961–2005

Year	Jury Fee
1961	$12
1977	$25
2002	$150
2005	$250

Source: RCW 36.18.016 ("Various Fees Collected . . .").

of 83 percent in 2012—a 26 percent increase over a span of eighteen
years.[12] The Washington State Legislature similarly expanded monetary sanction statutes (table 2.2): in 1977 the legislature stipulated a
mandatory victim penalty assessment (VPA) for criminal defendants of
$25 per felony conviction, and over the next twenty years the fee grew
from $25 to $500 per felony conviction.

The cost of choosing to have one's case adjudicated by a jury has also
increased, in similar fashion (table 2.3). In Washington, defendants are
assessed a fee for the use of a jury. Since the inception of the criminal
code in 1869, there has been a provision for a jury fee, but no fee was
stipulated until 1961, when the criminal code was amended to allow for
the assessment of a $12 jury fee. In 2005 Senate Bill (SB) 5454 raised jury
fees to the current levels of $150 and $250 for a six- or twelve-person
jury, respectively.[13]

The expansion of monetary sanctions is also evident in the number
of open accounts held by state superior courts. These accounts represent each conviction with sentenced monetary sanctions. An individual
can have multiple open accounts if he or she has received multiple convictions. In 2012 Washington had just under half a million court-ordered
LFO accounts (483,725), an increase of 33 percent over the number of

accounts in 2006 (363,875). In Alexander County, one of the largest counties in Washington, just under 19,000 new LFO accounts were opened annually between 2007 and 2012.[14] In 2014 a total of $740,716,759 was owed on LFO accounts in Alexander County. The average arrear was $4,713. In the same year, 123,198 people—8 percent of the adult population—were in legal debt to Alexander County.[15]

Unpaid legal debt is accruing in other jurisdictions too. In an analysis of eleven states, Rachel McLean and Michael Thompson estimated that $178 million in court costs—fees, fines, and restitution—was owed in each state.[16] Courts have responded by establishing collection units, and some have enlisted private agencies to collect on LFOs. With the expansion of monetary sanctions, a new bureaucratic arm of the criminal justice system has emerged, with its own costs and priorities that may or may not align with other aspects of the system.

National Laws and Procedures for Imposing Monetary Sanctions

Case law has established the constitutionality of imposing legal debt on defendants and sanctioning them, even with incarceration, for inadequate payments. Judges impose a variety of monetary sanctions at criminal hearings, including fines, fees, costs, interest, surcharges, and restitution. Just like confinement, community service, or supervision, LFOs are listed on every state superior court's "judgment and sentence" (J and S) forms. Judges need only check a box to impose an LFO.

Although research on the prevalence of LFOs is limited, monetary sanctions are used in all states, and their imposition by judges is also widespread. Surveys from the mid-1980s found that more than 80 percent of judges imposed LFOs, and judges themselves reported imposing LFOs on more than 80 percent of the criminal defendants they sentenced.[17] Fines and fees have long been common even in misdemeanor cases: data from the late 1980s indicate that fines and fees were assessed in 60 to 80 percent of misdemeanor cases.[18]

Most of the studies on monetary sanctions have examined the relationship between LFO amount and recidivism. Research is mixed on how the size and amount of LFOs affect criminal justice contact after conviction. Margaret Gordon and Daniel Glaser have found that the size of penalties is not related to postsentencing arrests or reincarceration. Yet the imposed amount increases the likelihood of probation revocation—that is, the higher the LFO sentence the more likely defendants are to be found in violation of their probation. They also find that those sentenced to lower monetary sanctions are more likely to pay back the amount in full, and that defendants who pay more toward their owed

restitution have lower rearrest rates.[19] Other research finds higher pay-
back rates among misdemeanants than felony probationers.[20]

Judges exercise their discretion in deciding when and on whom they
will impose monetary sentences during the sentencing process. Social
demographic characteristics and type of crime partly explain the variability in whether they impose monetary sanctions and in the amounts
when they do. In some jurisdictions, defendants' racial and ethnic characteristics significantly influence the amounts imposed by judges. For
example, data from Washington indicate that Latinos are assessed
higher financial sentences than non-Latinos, even when controlling for
prior convictions and offense type.[21] Other studies confirm that age,
gender, and occupational status affect the imposition of higher monetary sanctions in both misdemeanor and felony cases.[22]

Types of Monetary Sanctions

LFOs exist in some form in all fifty states and the District of Columbia
and are primarily governed by state law; federal statutes govern the use
of LFOs in federal courts (see table A2.1). Legislators have designed
LFO policies in remarkably similar ways, and I commonly refer to the
myriad types of LFOs collectively, but it is important to distinguish
between the several different types. *Fines* are fixed financial penalties
attached to conviction for given offenses. *Fees* are charges for the costs
of using the justice system, including the cost of a public defender,
court costs such as paperwork and filing fees, probation supervision
fees, and incarceration costs. Rates for the *interest* charged on LFOs are
either fixed or variable and are based on either the total amount or a
portion of the unpaid debt. *Surcharges,* which are commonly used to
support court- and state-related functions, are levied on top of fines and
fees and calculated as a percentage of the total LFO. *Restitution* is a
monetary sentence assessed to compensate victims for lost wages, hospital bills, or loss of property. Finally, many states charge *collection fees,*
which may be handled through the court or through a court-contracted
private collection firm.

Many jurisdictions have mandatory minimum sentences for LFOs.
In Washington, for example, each felony conviction carries a minimum
financial sentence of $600. The mandatory minimum financial sentence
for a felony conviction in Texas is $564. Table 2.4 illustrates the key di-
mensions of these policies. In the following sections, I summarize the
characteristics of monetary sanction statutes across the United States.[23]

Fines All fifty states, the District of Columbia, and federal courts
allow—and in some cases require—that fines be levied upon criminal

conviction. States vary in whether and how they assess fines. Some states assess fines for each type of conviction, such as felony class A or felony class B. Others assess fines for each specific offense, such as a sex offense or driving under the influence. Fines are considered mandatory when the statute language indicates that fines "shall" be sentenced. However, legislation typically allows for judicial discretion in applying fines; judges can consider the indigent status of defendants when determining whether to assess fines.

The maximum fine per felony conviction ranges widely across states. In Massachusetts, defendants convicted of a felony can be fined $500. In Arkansas, class A and B felonies carry a fine of up to $15,000. Defendants found guilty of murder, attempted murder, or sexual assault in Alaska or guilty of "off-grid" felonies or level 1 drug crimes in Kansas can be fined up to $500,000. In many jurisdictions, the maximum fine does not include other monetary sanctions such as restitution, assessments, incarceration costs, and surcharges.[24]

Defendants have challenged the imposition of "mandatory" fines or fees, but state supreme courts have affirmed the right of states to impose them. *Washington v. Curry* (1992) challenged the right of the state to impose a mandatory victim penalty assessment on indigent defendants.[25] Defendants have argued that the state cannot impose monetary sanctions without first determining a defendant's ability to pay. The Washington State Supreme Court found that the blind imposition of LFOs on all convicted felony defendants was constitutional, ruling that courts need only to determine ability to pay when setting the amount of minimum monthly payments. A recent case, *Washington v. Blazina* (2015), continues to allow LFOs but requires judges to explicitly consider defendants' current and future ability to pay nonmandatory monetary sanctions at the time of sentencing.

"User" Fees   In addition to fines, states also allow criminal defendants to be charged fees or additional surcharges. Each county exercises a great deal of discretion in implementing its own fees and cost reimbursements to be imposed as part of a defendant's LFO at the discretion of county judges. For example, in Pennsylvania there are 2,629 types of monetary sanctions. Of allowable LFOs, only 79 are fines and 2,371 (or 90 percent) are fees and costs. The remainder are various criminal justice–related fees.[26] Some statutes specifically note that defendants can be assessed the "actual court costs" and fees related to their prosecution. These fees can include charges related to court and prosecution time, juries and witnesses, warrants, and criminal laboratory costs.

Like Pennsylvania, other states and counties can exercise a great deal of discretion in how they design and implement user fee policies in the

(Text continues on p. 42.)

Table 2.4   Federal and State Monetary Sanction Statutes and Related Consequences, 2014

State	Example of LFO Statute (Fine or Fee) Citation	Felony Fines Maximum	Example of Fees and Surcharges for Felony Convictions
Alabama	Alabama (ALA) Code, Title 13A, Criminal Code—Section 13A-5-11	$60,000	$397.50 felony cost; $497.50 drug fee; $21 solicitor's fee (Baldwin County)
Alaska	Alaska Statutes (AS), Title 12, Section 12.55.035	$500,000	$100 felony surcharge; $50 misdemeanor surcharge
Arizona	Arizona Revised Statutes (ARS), Title 13, Chapter 8, Section 13-801	$150,000	83 percent surcharge for each charge
Arkansas	Arkansas (AR) Code, Title 5, Section 5-4-201	$15,000	$10 to $100 for public defense
California	California Penal Code (CPC), Section 1170	Offense-specific	20 percent surcharge added to base fine; $40 court security fee per felony conviction
Colorado	Colorado Revised Statutes (CRS), Sections 18-1.3-401 and 16-11-101.6	$100,000	$50/month supervision cost; other fees vary with level of felony/misdemeanor
Connecticut	Connecticut General Statutes (CGS), Title 53a, Chapter 952, Section 53a-41	$20,000	$100 pretrial alcohol education program application fee

Charge for Public Defense?	Example of Financing Charges (Additional Costs for Inability to Pay Debt in Full)	Community Service Provision?	Incarceration for "Willful" Nonpayment?	Can Debtors Vote?
Yes	12 percent collection fee, 30 percent fee if ninety days overdue	Yes	Yes	No
No	Department of Law is authorized to contract out collection procedures and seek reimbursement for cost of collections	Yes	Yes	No
Yes	A $20 time payment fee for legal debt not paid in full on the day of imposition cannot be waived or suspended; $20 to set up payment plan	No	Yes	No
Yes	$5 per month for participating in payment plan	Unknown	Unknown	Provisional
Yes	$300 surcharge for failure to pay; $50 to establish a payment installment account (Riverside County)	Yes	Yes	Yes
Yes	$10 late penalty fee; $25 time payment fee (can be assessed annually)	Yes	Yes	Yes
Yes	8 percent legal interest rate of judgment	Unknown	Yes	No

(Table continues on p. 30.)

Table 2.4 *Continued*

State	Example of LFO Statute (Fine or Fee) Citation	Felony Fines Maximum	Example of Fees and Surcharges for Felony Convictions
Delaware	Delaware (DE) Code, Title 11, Chapter 41, Section 4101	Undefined	Surcharges: 50 percent of the fine for the Transportation Trust Fund, 18 percent for crime victim fund, and 15 percent for rehabilitation fund (drug offenses)
District of Columbia	District of Columbia (DC) Code, Section 4-516	$5,000	Felony assessment between $100 and $5,000 to crime victim fund; DNA test fee (nonspecified amount)
Florida	Florida Statutes (FS), Sections 775.082 and 775.083	$15,000	$100 cost of prosecution; 5 percent surcharge on imposed fines and costs
Georgia	Official Code of Georgia Annotated (OGCA), Title 17, Section 17-10-8	$100,000	$50 crime lab fee; 5 percent of fine over $101 for Peace Officers Annuity Benefit; $1.75 per fine for superior and state court judges' and clerks' retirement funds; 10 percent of criminal fine for indigent defense fund
Hawaii	Hawaii Revised Statutes (HRS), Title 37, Chapter 706, Section 706-640	$50,000	$150 probation service fee for those sentenced to probation over one year, $75 for those sentenced to less than one year
Idaho	Idaho Statutes (IS), Title 18, Section 18-112	$50,000	$10 administrative clerk fee; $10 technology fee; $100 surcharge fee for each felony offense after 2010
Illinois	Illinois Compiled Statutes (ILCS), 730 ILCS 5/5-4.5-50(b)	$25,000	$250 jury fee; $15 court automation fee; $15 document storage fee (Cook County)

Charge for Public Defense?	Example of Financing Charges (Additional Costs for Inability to Pay Debt in Full)	Community Service Provision?	Incarceration for "Willful" Nonpayment?	Can Debtors Vote?
Yes	None	Yes	Yes	No
Unknown		Unknown	Yes	Yes
Yes	40 percent collection fee surcharge; $10 to $20 late payment fee; $25 to enroll in payment plan; 4.75 percent interest on monetary sanctions; $50 application fee for public defender	Yes	Yes	No
Yes	7 percent interest on unpaid sanctions	Yes	Yes	No
No	None	Yes	Yes	Yes
No	Up to 33 percent private collection fees; $2 handling fee per monthly installment toward debt	Yes	Yes	No
Yes	40 percent collection fee; 15 percent judgment of delinquency	Provisional	Yes	Yes

(Table continues on p. 32.)

Table 2.4 *Continued*

State	Example of LFO Statute (Fine or Fee) Citation	Felony Fines Maximum	Example of Fees and Surcharges for Felony Convictions
Indiana	Indiana Code (IC), Section 35-50-2-4	$10,000	$100 criminal cost fee; $2 document storage fee; $5 public defense administration fee; $2 DNA sample processing fee; $120 deferred prosecution fee
Iowa	Iowa Code (IC), Section 909.2	$10,000	Criminal penalty surcharge of 35 percent of fine; $125 law enforcement initiative surcharge
Kansas	Kansas Statutes Annotated (KSA), 21-6611	$500,000	$193 felony docket fee and surcharge; $119 fee for expungement (either conviction or arrest)
Kentucky	Kentucky Revised Statutes (KRS) (annotated), Section 534.030	$10,000	$47 district court costs; $10 correctional facilities authority costs; offense-specific fee for crime victim fund
Louisiana	Louisiana Revised Statutes (LRS), Title 15; Louisiana Code of Criminal Procedure (CCRP), 890.2, 884, and 885.1	Undefined	$75 special court cost
Maine	Maine Revised Statutes (MRS), Title 17-A, Chapter 53, Section 1301(1)a	$50,000	$300 jury trial fee; $400 surcharge for drug crimes
Maryland	Annotated Code of Maryland (ACM), Title 7, Chapter 5, Sections 7-503 and 7-504	Offense-specific	$80 filing fee

Charge for Public Defense?	Example of Financing Charges (Additional Costs for Inability to Pay Debt in Full)	Community Service Provision?	Incarceration for "Willful" Nonpayment?	Can Debtors Vote?
Yes	$25 late payment fee	No	Yes	Yes
Yes	None	Yes	No	No
Yes	$100 application fee for public defender	Yes	Yes	Yes
Yes	Defendants receive daily credit against fine or court costs for time served; option to choose jail or community service in lieu of LFOs	Yes	Yes	Provisional
Yes	$100 to enter into payment plan (Orleans District)' late payment fee of $100	Yes	Yes	No
No	Late payment fees ranging from $25 to $100	Yes	Yes	Yes
No	None	No	Unknown	Yes

(Table continues on p. 34.)

Table 2.4 *Continued*

State	Example of LFO Statute (Fine or Fee) Citation	Felony Fines Maximum	Example of Fees and Surcharges for Felony Convictions
Massachu-setts	Massachusetts General Law (MAGL), Part IV, Title II, Chapter 280, Section 6B	$500	
Michigan	Michigan Code of Criminal Procedure (MCCP), Act 175, Section 769. 1J	Undefined	$130 crime victim rights fee; $68 cost for felony; up to $700 in court costs
Minnesota	Minnesota Revised Statutes (MNRS), Chapter 609, Section 0341	$50,000	$100 jury trial fee; $75 surcharge for felony conviction
Mississippi	Mississippi (MS) Code, Sections 99-19-20 and 32	$10,000	$150 state assessment fee for felony (applied to, for example, crime victim fund, criminal justice fund, and law enforcement officers' training fund)
Missouri	Missouri Revised Statutes (MRS), Title 39, Chapter 560, Section .011	$5,000	$68 fee for class A or B felony; $46 fee for class C or D felony
Montana	Montana Code (MC), Section 46-18-231	$50,000	$100 per felony or cost of prosecution, jury, and community supervision, whichever is greater; $10 per month while under community supervision
Nebraska	Nebraska Revised Statutes (NRS), Chapter 28, Section 105	$25,000	$6 tax for judges' retirement fund; $42 district court docket fee; $8 court automation fee
Nevada	Nevada Revised Statutes (NRS), 176.064	$10,000	$25 assessment for each felony; collection agency fees; $6 judges' retirement fee; $5.25 legal services fee; total fees added: $86 (adult) and $67 (juvenile)

Charge for Public Defense?	Example of Financing Charges (Additional Costs for Inability to Pay Debt in Full)	Community Service Provision?	Incarceration for "Willful" Nonpayment?	Can Debtors Vote?
No	None	Provisional	Yes	Yes
Yes	$45 to begin payment plan; 20 percent fee after fifty-six days late	Yes	Yes	Yes
Yes	If a collections agency is used, the costs of collections may be added to the amount due	No	Unknown	Provisional
No	$25 per day "payback" rate on accounts of indigent debtors in prison	Yes	Yes	No
Yes	$25 late fee; 20 percent added to debt if it is delinquent; probation extended if debt is unpaid	Yes	Yes	No
No	None	Unknown	Unknown	Yes
Yes	None	Yes	Yes	Provisional
No	Additional fine of 10 percent of amount for delinquent payments; $5 garnishment fee; variable 12 percent interest rate	Yes	Yes	Provisional

(Table continues on p. 36.)

Table 2.4 *Continued*

State	Example of LFO Statute (Fine or Fee) Citation	Felony Fines Maximum	Example of Fees and Surcharges for Felony Convictions
New Hampshire	New Hampshire Statutes (NHS), Title LXII, Chapter 651, Section 2(9)a	$4,000	Prisoner transportation costs up until arraignment may be imposed on defendant
New Jersey	New Jersey Revised Statutes (NJRS), Section 2C:43-3 (2013)	$200,000	Offense-specific surcharges and penalties: sex offenders programs, computer crimes fund, mandatory drug enforcement fund
New Mexico	New Mexico Statutes (NMS), Section 31-18-15(E)1	$17,500	$100 DNA fee; in addition to fine, defendant may be ordered to reimburse conviction costs
New York	New York Penal Law (NYPL), Title E, Article 80.00	$100,000	$300 felony surcharge; $50 DNA data bank fee
North Carolina	North Carolina General Statutes (NCSC), Sections 15A-1340.17 and 15A-1362	Undefined	$102.50 General Court of Justice fee; $262 felony fee; $200 to undertake community service in lieu of debt
North Dakota	North Dakota Century Code (NDCC), Chapter 12, Section 12.1-32-01	$20,000	In addition to felony fine, defendant may be fined the cost of prosecution; $50 for presentence investigation
Ohio	Ohio Revised Code (ORC), Title 29, Chapter 2929, Section 18(B)3, 2947.09	$20,000	$85 criminal reparation fee; $30 for felony to funds covering court costs and bail
Oklahoma	Oklahoma Statutes (OS), Section 2164	Undefined	$150 lab fee (DNA); $103 surcharge per felony conviction; $50 to $10,000 for crime victim fund

Charge for Public Defense?	Example of Financing Charges (Additional Costs for Inability to Pay Debt in Full)	Community Service Provision?	Incarceration for "Willful" Nonpayment?	Can Debtors Vote?
No	$25 fee added to the fine in any deferral or order of periodic payment	No	Yes	Yes
Yes	$2 transaction fee for each payment made if not paid in full	Yes	Yes	Provisional
Yes	None	Yes	Yes	Provisional
No	None	No	Yes	No
Yes	$20 charge to set up payment plan; $50 fee for indigent defense	No	Yes	No
Yes	Court may stipulate that defendant pay for public defender and probation costs as condition of probation	Yes	Yes	Yes
Yes	$25 payment plan fee (Franklin County)	Yes	Yes	Yes
Yes	$15 fee for payment plan; $25 to $250 for community service assessment	Yes	Yes	Provisional

(Table continues on p. 38.)

Table 2.4   *Continued*

State	Example of LFO Statute (Fine or Fee) Citation	Felony Fines Maximum	Example of Fees and Surcharges for Felony Convictions
Oregon	Oregon Revised Statutes (ORS), Section 161.625	$375,000	$100 clerk fee for court supervision
Pennsylvania	Pennsylvania Consolidated Statutes (PCS), Title 18, Chapter 11, Section 1106; Pennsylvania Sentencing Alternatives (PACSA), Title 42, Section 9728	$50,000	$50 sheriff costs; $200 drug fee; $200 special administration fee; $26.80 county court cost; $18.40 commonwealth cost
Rhode Island	Rhode Island General Laws (RIGL), Sections 12-19-23.2 , 12-21-20, and 12-20-10	Undefined	$400 drug charge; $118 DNA fee; $300 or 10 percent of fine surcharge for felony; $300 for probation and parole fund
South Carolina	South Carolina Code of Laws (SCCL), 17-25-350	Offense-specific	Additional $2,000 for felony offenses with guns
South Dakota	South Dakota Codified Laws (SDCL), Title 22, Chapters 22-6-1 and 23A-27-25.2	$50,000	Potential fees include statutory sheriff's fees incurred in connection with the prosecution, witnesses' fees and mileage paid or ordered paid by the county, cost of transcripts, court-appointed counsel fees, filing fees, Breathalyzer test fees, blood test fees, and other chemical test fees
Tennessee	Tennessee Code Annotated (TCA), Sections 40-35-111 and 40-24	$50,000	County jails may charge $60 a day for incarceration; $300 clerk's fee per felony case; $100 for expungement
Texas	Texas Code of Criminal Procedure (TCCP), Chapters 42.15 and 43.03	$10,000	$40 clerk's fee for felony; $133 court cost; $250 DNA testing; $50 drug court program fee; $2 for indigent defense fund

Charge for Public Defense?	Example of Financing Charges (Additional Costs for Inability to Pay Debt in Full)	Community Service Provision?	Incarceration for "Willful" Nonpayment?	Can Debtors Vote?
Yes	25 percent of fine collection fee; $50 to $100 added to unpaid balances after thirty days (for nonprobation)	Yes	Yes	Yes
No	Driver's license suspended for late payment or non-payment; $60 fee before being released on parole or community service	Yes	Yes	Yes
No	None	Yes	Yes	Yes
Yes	$40 indigence application fee	No	Yes	Provisional
No	Unknown	Yes	Yes	Yes
Yes	$15 clerk's fee for setting up payment plan	No	Yes	No
Yes	4 percent credit card convenience fee; $25 time payment fee	Yes	Yes	Provisional

(Table continues on p. 40.)

Table 2.4 *Continued*

State	Example of LFO Statute (Fine or Fee) Citation	Felony Fines Maximum	Example of Fees and Surcharges for Felony Convictions
Utah	Utah Code (UC), Title 76-3-301	$10,000	90 percent surcharge on fine for felony
Vermont	Vermont Statutes Annotated (VSA), Title 13, Section 7252	Offense-specific	$12 court technology special fund; 15 percent of fine for victim's restitution special fund; $100 surcharge for specialized investigative units
Virginia	Code of Virginia (CV), Title 18, Section 18.2-10; Title 19.2, Section 19.2-340.1	$100,000	As much as $1,235 per count for certain felonies
Washington	Revised Code of Washington (RCW), Sections 9.94A.760 and 9.94A.550	$50,000	$500 victim penalty assessment; $100 DNA; $200 court costs; $450 for public defense
West Virginia	West Virginia (WV) Code, Section 62-5-7	Offense-specific	$75 fee for each felony count; a supervision fee, in an amount determined by the judge, if given a period of community corrections supervision
Wisconsin	Wisconsin Statutes (WS), Chapter 973, Section 973.05	$100,000	Offense-specific surcharges, such as $250 DNA surcharge; $92 victim surcharge for each felony; and $10 per conviction drug surcharge
Wyoming	Wyoming Statutes (WY), Section 6-10-102	$10,000	$10 fee if found guilty; prosecution costs; $20 fee for judicial systems automation account and indigent civil legal services account
United States (federal)	Title 18, Sections 3571 and 3013(A)(2)(A)	$250,000	$100 per felony fee

Source: Author's review of national state statutes; see table A2.2 for specific sources.

Charge for Public Defense?	Example of Financing Charges (Additional Costs for Inability to Pay Debt in Full)	Community Service Provision?	Incarceration for "Willful" Nonpayment?	Can Debtors Vote?
Yes	Unknown	Yes	Yes	Yes
Yes	$50 minimum public defender charge (unless found indigent)	Yes	Yes	Yes
Yes	$100 initial mandatory fee for payment plan; minimum $50 per month; interest on fines added forty days after judgment; 6 percent annual payment plan fee	Yes	Yes	No
Yes	12 percent interest on LFO. accruing from day of sentencing; $100 annual collection fee; defendant is responsible for private collection fees	Yes	Yes	Provisional
No	Suspension of driver's license for failure to pay fines and costs; a participation fee for defendants who choose to do community service in lieu of fines	Yes	Yes	Provisional
Yes	Unknown	Yes	Yes	Provisional
Yes	Unknown	No	Yes	No
Yes	10 percent fee on the delinquent principal; 15 percent fee on the defaulted principal	Unknown	Yes	State laws apply

absence of clear federal and state guidelines. For example, in Louisiana felony defendants can be assessed a $300 fee for a "judicial expense fund" and a $50 fee for "special court costs." In North Carolina, felony defendants are assessed a $154.50 "cost of justice fee" for every felony conviction. In California, every felony conviction carries a $40 "court security fee." Cook County, Illinois, charges a $190 per felony filing fee, and Indiana charges $120 per felony conviction as a "criminal cost fee."[27] States and localities even sentence defendants for the costs of collecting, recording, and storing their DNA—$200 in Illinois, $250 in Texas, and $100 in Washington.[28]

Surcharges   States levy surcharges on top of initial fines, fees, and costs. Arizona imposes an 83 percent surcharge on all LFOs initially sentenced. Of this total amount, 47 percent is allocated to a "criminal justice enhancement fund," 13 percent to a "medical services enhancement fund," 10 percent to a "clean elections fund," 7 percent to a "fill the gap fund," and 6 percent to fund DNA collections. A fine of $100 carries an additional $83 penalty. Arizona also assesses a "probation surcharge" of $20; thus, an initial fine of $100 is actually $203. Illinois assesses a 25 percent surcharge on all fines assessed.[29]

States also levy penalties for financing in the event that defendants cannot pay their monetary sanctions on time and in full. More than half of states have statutes that allow additional costs related to late payments, incomplete payments, or nonpayment. Fees are charged to establish payment plans and make payments for late fees; annual collection fees, surcharges, and interest are also levied. Florida charges 4.75 percent interest on uncollected legal debt, Georgia charges 7 percent, and Washington charges 12 percent. States can find defendants delinquent on their payments and impose additional penalties for nonpayment.[30] Illinois allows judges to assess a 15 percent penalty on unpaid LFOs in addition to a 30 percent collection fee. Arizona charges a $35 fee and a 19 percent collection fee for delinquent payments on monetary sanctions.[31]

Costs for a Public Defender   Two-thirds of states allow judges to require defendants to pay for a court-appointed public defender (table 2.1). Defendants who rely on public defenders provided by the state definitely are already impoverished or otherwise unable to pay for legal counsel. Yet defendants can be held responsible for at least a portion of the costs related to their legal counsel and representation.[32] Twenty-four states require defendants seeking a public defender to pay up-front fees, which range from application fees for eligibility determination to attorneys' costs for representation during adjudication or sentence. Arkansas imposes a fee ranging from $10 to $100 for a public defender.[33] Some counties in Washington require defendants to pay application fees of $10 to $25 and to sign a promissory note for the use of a public defender; in 2007 the felony promissory note was for six monthly payments of $226.11. In other counties, defendants are charged between $350 and $950 for the cost of their public defender.[34] Other states allow "a reasonable cost" to be assessed for a public defender. Illinois allows felons to be charged, but not more than $5,000, for a public defender. In some jurisdictions, defendants may be liable for their own legal counsel as well as for the cost of their prosecution. In Illinois, defendants are charged $10 to $100 for the cost of prosecution, and Ohio mandates that judges include the costs of prosecution in defendants' sentences.[35]

Gideon v. Wainwright (1963) established the assistance of counsel as a fundamental right in a criminal trial. The prosecution of defendants without legal representation is a violation of the Fourteenth Amendment, specifically the Equal Protection Clause.[36] Furthermore, Miranda v. Arizona (1966) established that at the time of arrest a person must be warned of his or her Fifth Amendment right not to be compelled to self-incrimination. From these decisions, local jurisdictions have developed the required "Miranda warnings" that must be read to all arrestees.[37] The U.S. Supreme Court also found that defendants' right to the assistance of counsel is not contingent on their financial status and thus all defendants should have the right to legal representation. Further, if they cannot afford an attorney, they must be told that an attorney will be "appointed" to them. "The financial ability of the individual has no relationship to the scope of the rights involved here. . . . The need for counsel in order to protect the privilege exists for the indigent as well as the affluent."[38] However, neither opinion clarifies how the cost of "appointed counsel" will be paid; the state is not required to pay for the attorney. This disconnect—the Court has maintained that poor people have the right to an attorney yet has not identified a source of income to pay for that attorney—creates a tension between rights and justice for indigent defendants.

Charging indigent defendants attorneys' fees has been legally challenged since at least the early 1970s. In James v. Strange (1972), which challenged the legitimacy of charging a defendant for legal fees, the Supreme Court ultimately found that such costs could unfairly harm poor defendants. In this case, David Strange was appointed a public defender, who applied after the conviction to the Kansas State Aid to Indigent Defense Fund and was paid $500 for his services. As allowed under state statute, the Kansas judicial administrator requested that Strange reimburse the state for the fee within sixty days or a judgment would be made against him. If Strange failed to make payment within sixty days, 6 percent interest would begin to accrue, the debt could be enforced with a lien on his property, and his wages could be garnished. Furthermore, Strange would not be afforded the safeguards of other civil debtors who hired private attorneys: defendants with private attorneys who defaulted on payments were afforded protections under the Kansas Code of Civil Procedure. Yet debtors with public defenders were not granted similar protections. The Supreme Court noted that the importance of protecting the rights of indigents "is more important to a debtor than the exemption of his wages from unrestricted garnishment. The debtor's wages are his sustenance, with which he supports himself and his family. The average low income wage earner spends nearly nine-tenths of those wages for items of immediate consumption."[39] The Court found the practice of imposing indigent defense fees particularly egregious and punitive, stating that the imposition of the fee differentially harmed indigent defendants and thus invalidated the district court policy.[40] In this case, the Supreme Court justices found that fees should not be imposed on people deemed indigent for their public defense without determining their ability to pay.

Fuller v. Oregon (1974) posed a challenge to Oregon's statute that allowed for the imposition of counsel fees on indigent defendants. The defendant, Prince Eric Fuller, argued that it was unconstitutional for the courts to condition the completion of his probation on the requirement that he reimburse the state for the attorneys' fees and costs related to his prosecution. The Supreme Court found that the Oregon statute, unlike the Kansas code, included safeguards for defendants by stipulating that only those people who were indigent at the time of arrest but had a future ability to pay could be charged fees. Oregon state legislators had included four safeguards in the statute to protect indigent defendants when it came to assessing attorneys' fees and costs: (1) only the convicted could be charged; (2) such costs were imposed on defendants only if they were able to pay or would be able to pay in the future; (3) a defendant could petition the court for a remission of payments if they imposed a manifest hardship on the defendant or the defendant's family; and (4) no person could be held in contempt for failure to pay if he or she had not intended to avoid payment or had made a good faith effort to pay.

Citing these statutory protections of the rights of indigent defendants—which were not present in *James v. Strange*—the Supreme Court determined that the Oregon law did not infringe upon defendants' right to counsel, since defendants' knowledge that they may ultimately have to repay the costs of legal services does not affect their ability to obtain such services at the outset of the case and during its prosecution.

The Supreme Court further noted that the requirement of payment "is never mandatory."[41]

Charging indigent defendants for the cost of their public defense is both legal and common. Nationally, most states have adopted language like Oregon's, and such language has withstood constitutional challenges.

Other Charges   In addition to fines and user fees, states sentence offense-specific fees that are designed to raise funds for justice programming or special victims' funds that are directly related to certain types of crimes. In Louisiana, for instance, all defendants convicted of drug-related offenses "may be assessed" $100 as a "special cost of court." First-time offenders convicted of driving under the influence of drugs or alcohol in New Mexico can be sentenced up to $500. Dade County, Miami, imposes a surcharge of $201 on people convicted of domestic violence.[42]

Criminal defendants who serve time in jail or prison or receive probation or parole are also eligible to be charged for the costs of their incarceration and supervision. Counties establish the rates charged. Marion County, Florida, assesses those sentenced to jail or prison $50 a day regardless of the length of their sentence, their indigent status, or the type of conviction. Kentucky caps the daily jail fee at $40.[43] Some states assess "a reasonable cost of imprisonment," while others allow defendants to be assessed their incarceration costs but do not define the rate, instead leaving it to the sentencing judge to determine those costs. Washington assesses $50 for each day in prison and allows defendants to be charged the cost of confinement up to $100 for each day they spend in a local jail.[44] Inmates in state and local correctional facilities, both those adjudicated and those awaiting trial, are thus mandated to "pay to stay."

Mandated "pay to stay" programs are not all created equal. In Beverly Hills, California, convicted defendants have the option to prepay $110 per calendar day to serve their sentences in a "safe, clean, and secure environment of the Beverly Hills Police Department's Jail facility."[45] The segregated housing option is reserved for defendants who have the sentencing judge's approval to serve their jail time in a municipal facility in Los Angeles County *and* who have a doctor's note indicating that they are in "good health" and have "no infectious disease." "Pay to stay" inmates who qualify for and participate in the program in Beverly Hills are housed in separate, specially designated cells, segregated from the general population in the jail. Criminal defendants who have the ability to pay can thus serve their sentences in a "safe" and "secure" environment segregated from criminal defendants who have no such ability to pay.

Costs related to probation or community supervision usually take the form of monthly user fees. States commonly establish an amount to be collected by their Department of Corrections. Arizona charges a monthly probation fee of $65. Alabama imposes a fee that is limited to no more than 25 percent of the defendant's adjusted gross weekly income. Oregon's Multnomah County charges $35 a month for probation ordered at sentencing.[46]

Specialized courts and the use of programmatic sentences can incur additional costs. Criminal defendants sentenced to drug and alcohol treatment courts, community courts, mental health courts, or domestic violence courts can be charged for their sentences. The California Penal Code allows courts to charge convicted drug or alcohol offenders a $150 fee, which must be paid to participate in a drug or alcohol assessment program. Florida requires offenders sentenced to community residential drug treatment centers to pay fees for room and board, treatment, and random drug testing.[47]

Other Uses of Fees Imposed on Defendants

The fines, fees, costs, and surcharges that criminal defendants are assessed generate revenue not only for criminal justice systems but also for activities of the criminal justice system unrelated to criminal justice. Some fees are used to provide restitution to victims or to fund programs that target certain types of offenders, but others are applied to non–criminal justice activities and services. Arizona's 83 percent surcharge on LFOs is used for a variety of purposes, including a "clean elections" program that receives 10 percent of the revenue generated by the surcharge. Political candidates who are running for state legislature or other statewide office are eligible for money from this fund. Candidates raising small donations can qualify for clean elections money by agreeing not to accept donations from political action committees or private corporations and meeting other requirements. In 2013 just under $8.8 million was generated from court assessments alone for the clean elections program. The fines and fees collected from convicts— who are unable to vote in Arizona elections while they remain debtors— help fund Arizona's statewide election campaigns.[48]

Delaware courts impose a 50 percent surcharge on all motor vehicle violations to support the Transportation Trust Fund (TTF). This additional revenue helps to offset the operating expenses of the Delaware Department of Transportation.[49] Nebraska collects from criminal defendants to pay for a state judicial retirement fund. Judges assess convicted civil, criminal, and juvenile defendants a $6 "tax" to provide for their own retirement.[50]

Even the Young and the Innocent Pay

Statutes and case law related to monetary sanctions are difficult to document, disentangle, and understand at the national level, much less within one state. Although I intentionally decided to focus on monetary sanctions imposed on adult felony defendants, it is important to note here that minors convicted in juvenile courts are also assessed monetary sanctions—despite the fact that, almost by definition, minors have yet to finish high school and are commonly unemployed and thus have little capacity to pay. In Washington, minors convicted of felony offenses receive monetary sanctions just like adults.[51] Minors convicted of felonies can be assessed a nonrefundable bail fee; service-related costs, based on parents' ability to pay, for diversion programs; costs and fees for indigent attorney services; costs related to their "support, treatment and confinement"; and a youth court nonrefundable fee of $30. Both the minor and his or her parents can be ordered to pay a "reasonable" sum or total amount of attorneys' fees. Finally, victim penalty assessments and DNA collection fees of $100 each are mandatory for minors convicted of felonies. It is customary for debt to persist for ten years, although it can be extended for longer. Judgments can be ordered against guardians of juveniles, leaving them legally obligated to make payments on the juvenile's financial obligations. If parents are found to have willfully failed or refused to pay, they can be held in contempt and even jailed.[52]

Nonpayment of LFOs subjects juveniles to enhanced criminal justice scrutiny. Faced with the extension of court supervision and incarceration, a juvenile offender can be trailed by a youthful indiscretion long into adulthood. *NST v. Washington* (2010) established that failure to pay legal costs can prevent the expungement of a juvenile record. "NST" was a minor convicted at age fourteen of residential burglary and malicious mischief. She fought with another youth over an iPod and threw a rock through a window. NST was assessed $2,630.40 in legal financial obligations, including restitution. Allowed to enter a deferred disposition, she would have seen her conviction vacated and dismissed if she had been able to meet all the obligations of her sentence, including full payment of her monetary sanctions.[53] NST and her single mother had been paying the minimum $10 a month and had paid a total of $235 toward her LFOs, yet because the debt was not paid in full when she turned eighteen, her deferred disposition was revoked. NST appealed the court's decision but lost her appeal: the court found that she had failed to demonstrate sufficient bona fide efforts to make full payment. Because of her and her mother's inability to pay her LFOs in full, NST's charges remain on her record. Had she been able to pay all of her debt by the time she turned 18 years of age, the charges would have not been placed on her record.

Even defendants eventually found innocent are sometimes on the hook for LFOs. Jurisdictions allow criminal justice–related fees and costs that accrue prior to adjudication or determination of guilt or innocence to be imposed on defendants. Some jurisdictions charge people for the cost of their housing in jail while they await their trial. Even when they are not convicted for the arresting offense, people are charged booking fees or bond costs. The sheriff in Polk County, Iowa, charges all criminal defendants a onetime fee of $75 for pretrial detention and a daily rate of $50 for their stay in jail prior to their adjudication. Recently, Polk County raised $718,728 in just one year from its "pay and stay" practices for all defendants held in its jail. Counties also charge to have records cleared. In Louisiana, for example, even if defendants are found not guilty, they must pay $100 to have the record of their arrest removed from their legal record.[54]

It is important to note that as LFO legislation has expanded the punitive nature of monetary sanctions over the past twenty-five years in Washington and across the country by increasing the types and amounts of the fines, fees, and surcharges that can be imposed and also by extending such debt for life, state legislation, in contrast, has attempted to mitigate some of the negative consequences for legal debtors by limiting interest accrual when they are incarcerated and granting them the provisional right to vote.

Consequences of Monetary Sanctions

Monetary sanctions are commonly thought of as "intermediate," "alternative," or "less restrictive" punishments than custodial sentences; considering that monetary sanctions are commonly levied in *addition* to incarceration, however, this legal debt can have important short- and long-term consequences for criminal defendants. Research indicates that defendants sentenced to jail are assessed higher fines and fees than those who do not receive custodial sentences.[55] Perhaps more importantly, however, legal debtors remain under judicial supervision, subject to court summonses, warrants, and jail stays until their LFOs are paid in full. Monetary sanctions have particularly serious implications for people with felony convictions who are unable to pay. Their legal debt looms large in their expected earnings by contributing to their accumulating disadvantage as their available income is reduced, creating long-term debt and increasing the chances of their ongoing criminal justice involvement.[56]

The criminal justice system, including warrants for unpaid LFOs, fundamentally undermines the social fabric of urban social life. For instance, research has illustrated the impact of monetary sanctions on daily lives, routines, and the social fabric of urban life in Philadelphia, where LFO nonpayment triggers warrants and men with outstanding LFOs or warrants avoid holding down a regular job, attending school, or even visiting a hospital for fear of being arrested and sent to jail. Criminal justice surveillance leads these debtors to avoid institutions that might invoke criminal justice sanctions for nonpayment.[57] Other research using national data confirms that people who have had contact with the criminal justice system regularly avoid making contact with institutions like medical facilities, financial institutions, workplaces, and schools.[58] Clearly, legal debt is a barrier to full societal integration, and it looms especially large with respect to the loss of voting rights among those with a felony conviction and reincarceration for nonpayment of LFOs.

The Limited Rights of Legal Debtors

In over half of U.S. states, legal debtors' voting rights are curtailed. Seventeen states prohibit legal debtors from voting at all until they pay their debts in full. Thirteen other states grant persons with legal debt a "provisional" or temporary right to vote, conditional on making regular monthly minimum payments toward their debt. Being provisional, their right to vote can be revoked if they do not make regular payments.

In 2007, in *Madison v. Washington*, three defendants challenged the denial of voting rights to debtors in Washington State. Daniel Madison, Beverly Dubois, and Dannielle Garner had been barred from voting because of their outstanding LFO debt, which ranged from $610 to $1,895. They argued that debtors were discriminated against and excluded from voting because they could not pay their LFOs while otherwise similar wealthy defendants could regain their right to vote because they could reconcile their LFOs. The case likened the political disenfranchisement of debtors to poll taxes, which had been explicitly outlawed in the 1975 amendment to the 1965 Voting Rights Act. The Washington State Supreme Court ruled against Madison, Dubois, and Garner, finding that the "disenfranchisement scheme did not violate the privileges and immunities clause of the Washington Constitution or the equal protection clause of the United States Constitution." The public reaction was fierce and galvanized the legislature to revise the state statute so that people who have completed all of their sentencing requirements except the payment of their LFOs are allowed the right to vote. In Washington, people with legal debt continue to have a "provisional" right to vote, which can be revoked if they fail to make three payments in a twelve-month period.[59]

Incarceration for Nonpayment

Forty-four U.S. states and the District of Columbia allow judges to incarcerate people for unpaid or delinquent LFOs. Only two states have statutes that clearly prohibit the involuntary incapacitation of people with outstanding LFOs, and the law governing the use of incarceration for legal debtors is ambiguous or unclear in four other states. People are incarcerated not for their failure to pay directly but for violating their court sentencing conditions, which include the payment of monetary sanctions.

The notion of "willfulness" is what determines whether or not a debtor is eligible for incarceration.[60] In Arizona, upon the court finding that a defendant is a willful nonpayer, the judge shall "order the defendant incarcerated in the county jail until the fine, fee, restitution or incarceration costs, or a specified part of the fine, fee, restitution or incarceration costs, is paid." Debtors found to have intentionally not paid their fines in Kentucky can be sentenced to up to sixty days in jail for nonpayment. Alabama law sets the number of sanctioning days for nonpayment on a scale according to the amount owed. For fines and costs under $250, defendants can be sentenced to no more than ten days of jail or hard labor. Those owing between $250 and $500 can be sentenced to no more than twenty days. Debtors owing between $500 and $1,000 can be sentenced to up to thirty days, and for every additional $100 owed, debtors can be sentenced an additional four days.[61]

Most states (74 percent) allow for the amount of monetary sanctions to be converted to community service (table 2.1). When allowed under state statute, judges can sentence defendants to perform a set number of hours of community service in lieu of their financial obligations. Community service provisions give defendants a financial "credit" toward their monetary sanctions, usually calculated at the local minimum wage rate per hour of community service performed. Some state statutes allow judges to determine the rate, as in Ohio.[62] Under this type of system, judges specify a fiscal amount that will be credited toward legal debtors' outstanding balance for each hour of community service they perform. Each hour of service performed reduces the amount sentenced.

Community service provisions are problematic, however, given that many defendants are poor, precariously employed, unhoused, or have children. Similar to their inability to find the money to make financial payments, they also have difficulty finding time to meet hundreds of hours of service obligations. Further, many lack transportation to their assigned community service organization—a particularly acute problem for people who live in rural counties. In the violation hearings I observed, many individuals who were struggling to complete their community service sentence were sentenced to incarceration for their inability to do so; several of the courts I observed were also unable to assist people in finding a community service placement in the first place. Considering that many agencies not only bar people convicted of particular crimes from working in their organization but also cannot be counted on to keep track of the number of hours completed, it is clear that converting legal debt to community service hours often sets up further barriers to sentence completion and community reintegration.

Summary

Monetary sanctions involve a vast array of criminal justice–related fines, fees, interest charges, and surcharges. People caught up in the criminal justice system are frequently charged for their use of a state-appointed public defender, court services, a trial by a jury, and their own incarceration, supervision, and treatment, in addition to court-ordered restitution and non–criminal justice services such as judicial retirement programs and clean elections.

The consequences of incomplete payment or nonpayment are severe. When LFOs go unpaid, debtors can be regularly monitored and sanctioned with jail time. People without the means to immediately pay their sanctions are assessed additional penalties and can be charged usurious interest rates that compound their debt. Moreover, they can be denied the right to vote, to serve on juries, and to have their criminal record sealed or expunged. Some offenders carry court-imposed debt for life.

How exactly LFOs work, and with what consequence, can be better understood through a careful examination of the courts where they are levied, the clerks who enforce them, and the people who experience them. It is to those institutions and actors that I now turn.

═ Chapter 3 ═

Defendant Experiences with Monetary Sanctions in Washington State

Anyone who has ever struggled with poverty knows how extremely expensive it is to be poor.

—James Baldwin, *Nobody Knows My Name* (1961)

A s James Baldwin wrote over fifty-five years ago, it is costly to be poor in America. Compared to those who have access to wealth, people with limited means pay more, as a percentage of their income, for interest on car and home loans, to use credit or service debt, and in taxes. Poverty also exacts extra costs for people involved in the American criminal justice system. On paper, a legal financial obligation is a sentence stipulating how much a criminal defendant owes the state as a result of his or her involvement in the criminal justice system. Yet, in practice, an LFO is a form of punishment that levies an extra burden on poor defendants or people otherwise unable to pay it. People already saddled with chemical addiction, health limitations, and housing instability may be further burdened by the imposition of LFOs. Such obstacles can make it exceptionally difficult to make a successful transition from conviction back to one's community.

Monetary sanctions jeopardize former defendants' ability to meet basic needs. Legal debt forces them to make hard choices about which bills to pay and which to let go unpaid. People returning from criminal conviction experience blocked opportunities and suffer emotional strain. Debt also has a negative impact on their relationships with friends and family as their financial liabilities become part of a larger collective problem that looms large in low-income communities. Legal debtors' prospects for escaping their debt can be bleak, and many of them expe-

52

rience overwhelming fear, anger, and despair. Even among those la-beled "non-willful" debtors—those whose inability to make payments has been validated by the court—legal debt carries additional hardship as they are regularly summoned to court or arrested for outstanding warrants because of nonpayment.

Consequently, poor people's experience of criminal justice contact is not limited to the criminal justice system, or even the resulting collateral consequences, but is transformed into long-term, if not permanent, punishment by legal debts. LFOs create prisoners of debt. The consequences of LFOs are most acute for defendants who are impoverished or have limited financial means. Some are poor when they enter the criminal justice system, but others experience poverty for the first time after their conviction. Meanwhile, as the poor become ever more trapped in a cycle of poverty and debt fueled by the LFOs imposed by the criminal justice system, people with financial means are able to escape the burden of legal debt and at least begin to plot a path to successful reintegration and community reentry. The consequences of criminal justice contact are vastly different for them than for those who will carry legal debt for many years—or even the rest of their lives.

In 2007 my colleagues and I began interviewing people sentenced to LFOs in Washington State. We interviewed a total of fifty people that year, and I interviewed five more individuals in 2010. In the course of my research, I met Kathie, whose life illustrates how legal debt limits opportunities and forces people to structure their lives in a way that normalizes living with legal debt, criminal justice supervision, and the threat of incarceration and makes a life without these specters unimaginable. At the time of our interview, Kathie was a forty-nine-year-old white woman with four children, three of whom she supported financially. She was divorced but living with her ex-husband and his father, along with three of her children, in a three-bedroom apartment. She attributed her criminal history to living in poverty and having a drug addiction. Her initial LFOs were approximately $11,000. But after years of state-imposed interest at 12 percent, annual collection surcharges, and private collection fees, at the time of our interview Kathie's LFO debt totaled just over $20,000. She was employed at a community college–based reentry program that helped convicted felons obtain their GEDs and associate's degrees. Her job enabled her to make regular minimum monthly payments on her LFOs, but those payments were only enough to keep private collection agencies at bay; they hardly put a dent in the total she owed.

I also met Reuben, whose life illustrates how monetary sanctions teach people to accept as normal a lifetime of debt and the ongoing management of precarious fiscal circumstances. At the time of our interview, Reuben was twenty-four years old. Of Pacific Islander descent, he had been living in six different Washington, Colorado, and Minnesota correctional facilities since he was twelve. When he was sixteen, the juvenile court in Langston County, Washington, "declined" jurisdiction over him, and he was subsequently prosecuted and sentenced in the adult criminal justice system for assault, robbery, and possession of stolen property. When I first met Reuben, he was in a work release program—working at a local community college and attending the same school as a student during the day. Still living behind bars at night, he was anxious about the almost $6,000 in legal debt he would be solely responsible for paying once released.[1]

I met Nick through a community-based reentry organization that was trying to help him turn his life around. His life history reveals how people with legal debt become inextricably tied to the criminal justice system. Nick was thirty-eight years old at the time of our interview. An African American, he had been struggling with drug addiction and mental health problems since he was a teenager. When we met, he had seven felony convictions in James County, Washington, involving theft, robbery, and drug possession—crimes typical of someone battling a chemical dependency problem. As a result of three different convictions in 1991, 1992, and 1996, Nick had been sentenced to fifty-six months at the state prison, and he had also been in county jail several times. Many of his jail stays were for nonpayment of his monetary sanctions. By the time of our interview, he had accumulated a total of $3,178.06 in legal debt. Nick was not making regular payments on his legal debt. In fact, the reentry organization he was working with had made a recent payment for him, which included a $100 payment to the court clerk for collection costs. That payment had allowed him to be released from jail and reenter his community college program, which the organization had paid for as well.

I had known Lisa for a couple of years through our mutual involvement in community events before I interviewed her for this research. I was unaware that she had LFOs and knew few details about her life before our interview. Her story illustrates how the criminal justice system and legal debt block individuals' access to new opportunities and career advancement even when they are attempting to turn their lives around. Lisa was forty years old, African American, married, and the mother of three young adults, ages twenty-four, twenty, and eighteen. She was a grandmother of a five-year-old. Lisa had battled drug addiction since she was eighteen, and she had four felony convictions in Alexander County, Washington. Her convictions included two drug violations, theft, and an assault. She had numerous municipal citations and associated fines and fees for prostitution. As a result of her LFOs and the state-mandated interest charged on her outstanding balances, Lisa owed over $60,000 in LFOs, including fines, fees, restitution, and interest. Lisa's work at a reentry organization required her to undergo regular criminal background checks. Because of her debt, her legal record showed several active court files. This created challenges and obstacles for her in her work. She was frequently denied entry to jails and prisons to work with her organization's clients. Lisa said she was making regular monthly payments on her LFOs even though her debt continued to increase each month as a result of the interest and collection fees.

Vilma was the last person I interviewed for this book. Of all of my interviews, hers was the hardest. Any woman might easily find herself in Vilma's position—both a victim and a defendant in a domestic violence case. At the time of our interview, Vilma was a thirty-four-year-old Latina mother of three who had spent eight years in the Washington prison system for shooting the father of her son. She had been sentenced for assault and assessed $33,000 in LFOs, including restitution. Vilma was working in a two-year construction apprenticeship program and making regular minimum monthly payments toward her legal debt, but thirteen years after her conviction, the interest accruing on her outstanding debt had brought the total she owed to $72,000. Her story provides insight into the impact of legal debt even beyond its negative effects on financial security, housing stability, and employment opportunities. Specifically, Vilma's debt had affected her relationship with her current partner. In her story we see how LFOs affect family relationships as well as transitions through the traditional life-course stages of adulthood, such as completing formal schooling, getting married, and supporting children. These life transitions are vital to reintegration into social life and are associated with criminal desistance.[2]

Experiences of Legal Debt

In this chapter, I examine how carrying legal debt feels to debtors and how it affects them and their families on a daily basis. When asked to separate the effect of having a felony conviction from the effect of having legal debt, respondents commonly would not, or could not, do so. A large body of research has examined the impact of felony convictions—particularly drug offenses—and incarceration on individuals' ability to successfully reenter or reintegrate into society after conviction or incarceration.[3] Criminal justice contact certainly affects housing stability, educational attainment, employment, and family formation. But as I show here, the legal debt incurred in the process affects individuals above and beyond the stigma of criminal conviction and incarceration.

The Growth of Legal Debt

The most salient element of monetary sanctions is the debt it generates for those who receive this sentence. Our interviewees frequently described their frustration with the financial hardship resulting from LFOs and discussed their inability to make regular or substantial payments toward them. The average LFO debt among the respondents, including restitution, was $9,204. Those who said that they made regular payments toward their debt on average paid $31.25 per month. Because Washington charges 12 percent interest and an annual $100 collection fee, legal debt typically accumulates even when debtors make regular payments. Most of the regular monthly payers among our respondents saw their legal debt remain the same from month to month as the principal LFO decreased and the amount owed in interest increased. Some debtors' monthly payments were not even enough to pay down the amount of accumulating interest, however, and thus many watched their debt increase steadily with each billing statement.

For people of limited economic means, LFOs represent a significant financial burden. Using the average LFO amount sentenced in Washington—$1,347, not including restitution—figure 3.1 illustrates how LFOs grow under different payment plans. After five years of making a minimum payment of $5, the debt would increase by $477, to a total of $1,824. If the debtor made the average payment of $31.25, he or she would still owe $256 at the end of five years. A debtor would have to make regular consecutive monthly payments of $100 to pay off the average fine and fee assessed—and that would take over a full year of payments (see table A3.1).

Figure 3.2 illustrates how the total debt changes over time based on different monthly payments for the average debt of $9,204 among those we interviewed. This figure is much higher than the average amount of monetary sanctions in Washington because many of our respondents had multiple felony convictions and thus a great deal more outstanding debt. After five years, someone who had been sentenced to an LFO of $9,204 and was making the average regular payment of $31.25 would owe $10,667 as a result of the accumulated interest and surcharges—an increase of $1,463 over the initial debt. Even if this person made consistent monthly payments of $100—which would have been unrealistic for those we interviewed—he or she would still owe over $7,000 after five years (see table A3.2).

The Experience of Fairness

The significance of legal debt in the lives of debtors goes far beyond its financial consequences. Legal debt affects individuals' perceptions of

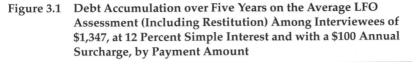

Figure 3.1   Debt Accumulation over Five Years on the Average LFO Assessment (Including Restitution) Among Interviewees of $1,347, at 12 Percent Simple Interest and with a $100 Annual Surcharge, by Payment Amount

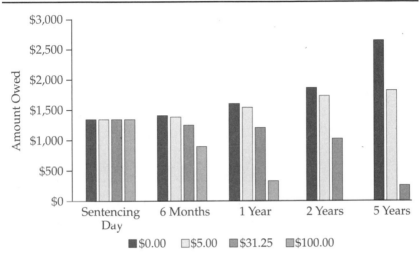

Source: Author's calculations.
Notes: Interviewees who said that they were making a regular monthly payment paid $31.25 on average. Monthly simple interest is calculated only on the principal, not on any surcharge.

the criminal justice system and their images of themselves and their futures. Many defendants felt that it was important to make financial payments to their victims and the broader "community" as reimbursement for the harm associated with their offenses. Some respondents, having internalized the concept of retribution, even viewed monetary sanctions as a fair sentence. These interviewees stated their belief that they should "pay for their mistakes."

At the same time, respondents expressed frustration with LFOs that were ballooning because of interest and the annual $100 collection charge added to their bill by the clerks. The vast majority of them were discouraged and angry about the court fees and costs imposed on them that seemed unrelated to the victims. Wondering why they had to pay fees for the court system, for paperwork, for their defense attorneys, and for their housing in jail and prison, many found it difficult to reconcile having "done their time" in prison with still being charged for these related costs. They recounted times when they were denied employment or housing because of their felony convictions, and they questioned why the state would impose additional financial

Figure 3.2   Debt Accumulation over Five Years on the Average Total LFO Debt (Including Restitution) Among Interviewees of $9,204, at 12 Percent Simple Interest and with a $100 Annual Surcharge, by Payment Amount

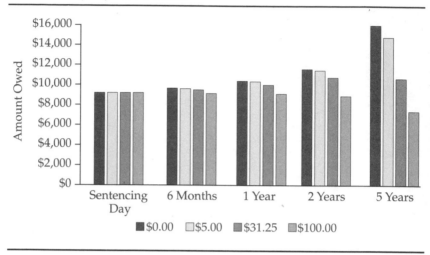

Source: Author's calculations.
Notes: Interviewees who said that they were making a regular monthly payment paid $31.25 on average. Monthly simple interest is calculated only on the principal, not on any surcharge.

hurdles when their finances were already limited and officials knew that.

Patrick expressed a concern common among our interviewees that the additional interest and surcharges had created a barrier that would never allow him to fully pay off his debt:

> [The LFO] was a part of the judgment and sentence, and I have no qualms about [paying] it. I'm willing to pay it, every single dime. Unfortunately, you know, uh, they took the opportunity, that opportunity, and made it a capital opportunity for themselves. They knew my situation. You know, I was broke, that's the reason I did what I did [the offense], and I was still broke in the prison system, so uh, they basically took advantage of the situation and said, "If you can't pay, we're going to put interest on it."

Many of the people I interviewed voiced a concern that interest and collection fees for unpaid balances were an additional burden imposed only on those who could not afford to pay the debt in full. It was not lost on the respondents that those who were unable to pay their balances in full were the ones forced to let interest and collection costs accrue. For them, it truly was expensive to be poor.

Many of our respondents described their LFOs as a moving target, one that they would never be able to hit. Left frustrated, angry, and increasingly cynical, several respondents described their relationship with the state as antagonistic. They felt that the criminal justice system was designed to make them fail and remain under criminal justice surveillance. Many, like Mike, suggested that the system—especially the design of LFOs—was set up to encourage the same behavior and lifestyles that had led to their criminal justice contact in the first place. In our interview, Mike said:

> I understand you have to pay your way, and the court has to pay its way, and they got to collect off somebody. But it seems to me like the way our criminal justice system works, you know, there's too many people making money out of corrections, and the corrections isn't correcting anything. It's more creating people who are unable to get jobs, who are unable to deal in society in ways that are, um, conforming, conform to the normal standards. So they work outside the block, and those kinds of things that they do, which are illegal, it just kind of compounds it. So they get into a system that, really, imprisons them in such a way that when they come out, they're still on the same drag.

Most of my respondents reported that fines and fees to reimburse victims' funds were appropriate; others questioned why they were charged victims' fees when their crimes had been "victimless," such as drug or property crimes. Steve expressed this idea best:

> I feel like, my crime was like, you know, selling, I was selling crack. So, I didn't really, I wasn't stealing money. So I still don't understand how that fit together [the victim penalty fee]. So, and then I think sometimes—and for myself it wasn't really a high amount, but I've seen amounts that are just like ridiculous, and where a person, they'll probably never pay it off, and I just don't think that's fair, to hold it over a person's head for the rest of their life, you know?

Others were similarly frustrated at being charged for their public defender. Garry noted the contradiction of being charged for a public defender during an interview: "They say you get a free lawyer, and then they charge you $750." John expressed similar frustration with what he viewed as a contradiction in the imposition of attorneys' fees: "It's like they tell you that, 'Hey, you're poor, you can't afford an attorney, so we're going to give you one,' so they give you legal financial obligations for it. It's really not too fair, no, it's not."

Many respondents felt certain that the criminal justice system, by imposing LFOs, was setting them up for failure. Patricia summed up this sentiment with her characterization of the "auto-jail" system in James County:

> What I don't think is fair is that here I am, I'm sitting in county jail, for a crime they say, so pay, meanwhile . . . here she [the clerk] is, sitting with those papers from DOC [the Department of Corrections], . . . saying, "Okay, you can't pay $25, you have no income at all." "That's right, I have no income whatsoever, don't have any income." And yet I'm not going to be released until I sign that paper and set myself up for a violation [by] saying I'll pay $25 a month. "I can't" . . . "Well, there's no way you can get" . . . Yeah, okay, if I whore myself on the corner, I can get it, oh, okay . . . you know? But you're not getting released until you sign it. So, so really, how fair is that? Why don't I just sign another violation paper? Cuz I don't have $25 a month, you know?"

Patricia had not been making regular monthly LFO payments and conceded that she did have options that would enable her to make those payments: she knew she could raise money to pay her financial penalties if she went back to the sex industry and prostituted herself. From her perspective, however, as well as that of the criminal justice system, turning to commercial sex work was not an acceptable way to resolve her legal debt.

It was not unusual for defendants to find themselves having to choose between jail, legal debt, and reincarceration. Such hard choices, presenting seemingly irreconcilable alternatives, had profound implications for their concept of justice and their relationships with their supervising judge, public defender, and probation officer (now known as a "community corrections officer," or CCO).

Attempting to Move Forward

In addition to its effects on debtors' finances and emotional well-being, legal debt exacerbated their existing troubles. Many of the people I interviewed described challenges in managing drug or alcohol addiction. Nick was addicted to crack cocaine and had mental health problems. These often co-occurring problems are common among people involved in the criminal justice system.[4] Nick described several attempts he had made to remain sober and regularly take medication that would help him stay mentally clear. Without such clarity, making the regular

LFO payments was financially difficult for him, and more generally he lacked the life management skills to keep on top of regular payments. At the time of our interview, he said he was enrolled in a community college and trying to make himself more employable. But he was also unstably housed: after a month or so of sleeping on couches in the homes of family and friends, he would relapse and end up living on the streets. Nick cycled between attending school, relapsing into drugs, experiencing bipolar depression, and being arrested and reincarcerated. Most of his stints in jail resulted from outstanding warrants for nonpayment of LFOs in James County, Washington. His legal debt and related contact with the criminal justice system for nonpayment only exacerbated his other problems and made it even harder for him to make a successful transition after incarceration.

Nick's experiences were emblematic of the lives and struggles of many of the legal debtors I talked with and observed, all of whom faced similar challenges. Pam, a public defender assigned to indigent defendants, discussed with me how hard it was for her clients to manage their lives. Acknowledging that her clients had done something wrong— and that some of them had committed, in her words, "horrible offenses"—she said that the broader society needed to realize how disorganized their lives were. I had just observed Pam's response to a judge demanding an explanation for why one of her clients had not been making payments toward his LFO. She had outlined for the judge her client's monthly income and expenditures: he was receiving disability payments from the state and had to put most of that $300 check toward his room and board at a halfway house. Acknowledging the defendant's indigence, the judge had reduced the mandatory monthly payment from $50 to $25. Nevertheless, as Pam would tell me, $25 a month was still too much for her client to regularly pay.

Pam explained to me that many of her clients had no regular income and that the source of income for those who did was usually a disability or social security check from the state or federal government. Moreover, most of her clients did not know how to manage money, at least partly because they had less than a high school education. Pam suggested that her clients committed illegal offenses and got caught up in the criminal justice system in the first place because of their irregular income and inability to manage money, as well as for other reasons. She painted a picture of a lifestyle and orientation toward even the most basic life management skills that was very different among her clients than among those who worked in and operated the criminal justice system. Making regular monthly payments might come easily to people like her or me, she said, but it was a difficult and sometimes insurmountable task for many of her clients. According to Pam, making regular monthly payments was unrealistic for her clients with uncertain or limited income, unstable housing, and poor physical and mental health. Having to find the resources to meet their monthly LFO bills and managing the criminal justice consequences for nonpayment simply exacerbated their preexisting troubles.

Like Nick, many of those I interviewed and observed in court hearings had little formal education and lacked what sociologists and economists call "social capital" and "human capital." They lacked the interpersonal skills to obtain employment or to maintain a job if they were able to find one. They were also deficient in the social skills needed to manage their day-to-day lives. With little work experience, they had even less experience in formal-sector jobs. Although monetary sanctions were at times the least of their worries, their frequent contact with the criminal justice system, their debt, and the associated court summonses, warrants, and stints of incarceration combined to create an ongoing nightmare.

The complex challenges of paying their LFOs was a recurring theme among my interviewees. David described the prospect of making regular payments toward his LFOs as "unrealistic" given his life circumstances:

> Well, basically, if I could pay for it, I wouldn't have been in the situation that I was at to begin with. . . . Knowing the status that I am, being unemployed or being homeless living on the streets, being able to make payments like that is unrealistic. . . . They can put any amount. If they were realistic, maybe I would try to pay it, but being $10,000 or $5,000, that's ridiculous, you know, to even think that I'm going to be able to pay something like that, it's unrealistic. And if they really stopped and thought about the situation that I'm coming into or going out of, they know themselves that it's not going to be paid, and to put interest on something that's not going to be paid, it's just getting worse, you know?

David's account of his inability to service his debt is supported by the math. He had several criminal convictions for which he had served time in prison. At the time of the interview, he was homeless, unemployed, and facing several thousand dollars of LFO debt. Even making the average payment of $31.25 a month toward the average LFO sentence for one offense, $1,347, debtors still owe money after five years of regular payments (see figure 3.1). It may be no surprise then that David and others in his position talked about the criminal justice system as an institution that did not care about rehabilitation, equity, or fairness, but as one that used LFOs as part of a larger system of control from which they felt they would never escape. Under constant pressure to make payments and related criminal justice surveillance, David felt that it was virtually impossible for him to move forward with his life and become more productive.

Obstruction of Major Life Transitions Some of my interviewees described their criminal offending as a "mistake." They were reflective about their criminal justice involvement and had resolved to "move forward," commonly stating that they planned to obtain further education or secure stable employment. But even those with the best of intentions viewed legal debt as an impediment to moving forward and regaining "normal" or "traditional" lives. These respondents were making regular LFO payments but were still under criminal justice surveillance and unable to move on with their lives. Kathie said that her debt, which had recently been transferred to a Langston County private collection agency, kept her from feeling like an adult. She had been forced to live with her estranged ex-husband, his father, and her three children for seven years, she said, because of her poor financial credit and inability to secure a housing lease under her own name.

> I have a very chaotic living situation. There is six of us in a three-bedroom apartment . . . [I'm] living in the same area with my husband that I'm separated from, and it's uncomfortable. There's some things that I need to make adjustment for my children. Just because of the situation. And Grandpa's eighty-something years old, and I'm sure he'd like to be rid of us. I mean, it's impacted a lot.

Kathie has a car payment, she said, but "I had to have my father-in-law be the primary person on the loan because they absolutely wouldn't look at me without having a cosigner."

Kathie's legal debt had limited her access to credit, making it impossible for her to buy a car or secure a home on her own, but more generally, Kathie's legal debt constrained her opportunities and made her feel powerless and lacking in control over her life. Kathie described her despair and fear that she would never be able to get out from under her legal debt and be able to lead an independent life.

> Kathie: It seems like one of those challenges that are insurmountable. It's like a paraplegic trying to climb Mount Everest. I mean, it just seems *that* impossible. It's like an insurmountable barrier, that seems like, I'm gonna die with this debt hanging over my head. And I'm never gonna be able to have my own little piece of property, my own little something. And it's not even about buying a house. I can't even rent a place. So, I, just personally—I mean, I

have men who'd like to marry me and all that, want to take care of me. I don't want to have that as an option. You know? I'm a very independent female, always have been, and it just seems like this is, not only taking a part of me financially, but it's taken a piece of me spiritually, you know. It's taken a part of my soul. I'm like, how am I going to rectify the situation without, you know, going crazy, or you know? [*laughs*]

Author: Robbing a bank?

Kathie: Exactly, that's exactly what I was thinking. Doing something in the criminal element, and that's where I got started in this place anyway.

Kathie's experience was echoed in other interviews with legal debtors who described how LFOs and related legal debt had affected their ability to fulfill the common adult responsibilities of providing for themselves and their families, finishing their education, getting a job, and establishing an independent residence. Respondents described feeling ashamed and embarrassed by the dependency induced by legal debt.

Strain on Family and Friendship Networks   Respondents commonly attributed their strained or severed relationships with family and friends to their legal debt. Vilma's experiences were emblematic of what happens when abused women attempt to fight back against abusive partners. After spending eight years in prison for assaulting her husband, Vilma was released from prison with over $72,000 in legal debt. She was particularly frustrated that most of her monetary sanctions were restitution for her victim's hospital bills, which she knew had been paid through her ex-husband's health insurance.

Not only did the legal debt limit Vilma's resources for herself and her children, but it stigmatized her and limited the types of relationships and bonds of trust she could build with others. In our interview, Vilma explained that after she got out of prison she met and fell in love with a man who helped support her and her children financially and emotionally, and they had a child of their own together. However, they decided not to get married because her LFOs had made Vilma a financial liability: her partner was scared of the financial implications of Vilma's LFOs for him if they married. Her LFOs not only prevented Vilma from being able to marry but also made it close to impossible to buy a home for her family. Her partner's brothers had offered him and Vilma financing for the purchase of their rental home—but then they found out about her legal debt and rescinded the offer, thus shattering her hope of owning a home and creating a stable living environment. Vilma told me about her relationship with "the family."

> Vilma: The family, the Lees. I'm with Jorge [Lee], one of the brothers asked us if we were interested in them purchasing a house so that they could help us own one. But one of the brothers found out that I owed some money, owed these LFOs, and he was like, "Oh, those are never going to go away, how are they ever going to own a house?" So they changed their mind. So more personally, that kind of hurt. I was like, "Wow, because I'll always have this debt." I didn't know what to say to that, like, what do I say in my defense? I don't know if it's ever going to go away.
>
> Author: Does your current partner now, he understands that you have this debt?
>
> Vilma: Yeah.
>
> Author: And what does he say about it?
>
> Vilma: Well, the only thing that we've been concerned about, we talked about it, like if we ever got married, because we become one, so my debt becomes his debt, right? So for legal reasons, we just don't want to do it.

LFOs limit people's ability to build attachments, make commitments, and establish traditional relationships, exactly the kinds of "bonds to conformity" that lead to criminal desistance. Unmarried poor couples tend to split up more frequently than married ones, contributing to what Sara McLanahan calls "fragile families."[5] The legal debt preventing Vilma from marrying her new partner, the father of her youngest child, could weaken the family bond they established, as well as the relationship between her partner and his brothers. Vilma's legal debt was a major obstacle and undermined her efforts to establish a stable family life and a secure future for herself and her children.

Criminal Justice Consequences

Poor legal debtors face a dramatically different type of justice than debtors with financial means. My interviewees talked about LFOs as a means for politicians and people working within the criminal justice system to keep them incarcerated or on court supervision, since monetary sanctions lead to the continual supervision of those who are unable to make sufficient or regular payments.

Deferred Prosecution

"Deferred prosecution" is a legal practice that is differentially applied to defendants with financial means and defendants with few financial resources. When deferred prosecution is offered to first-time offenders, typically they can complete their sentence within one year of sentencing, at which time their conviction is cleared from their criminal record. To qualify for a deferred sentence, defendants must meet all of the stipulations of their sentence—including their LFOs, such as paying for their drug assessments and drug treatment, fully completing the treatment, fulfilling their community service hours, and documenting all of these conditions. Furthermore, defendants are required to completely pay their LFOs, including restitution, within one year to qualify for a deferred sentence.

Deferred prosecution can lead to very different outcomes for defendants with financial means than for those without financial means. Someone who has a stable income or whose family members have wealth can afford to fulfill his or her legal and financial obligations within one year and qualify for a deferred prosecution. Being able to pay in full results in a clean legal record. Those who are unable to meet their legal financial obligations within one year cannot qualify for a deferred prosecution. Their conviction becomes part of the legal record, and they remain under court supervision until their debt—including the interest and collection charges added to their outstanding balance—is fully paid.

During my courtroom observations, I often saw defendants who had initially been granted a deferred prosecution but were unable to pay their LFOs in full and within a year. Although these defendants had met all other legal conditions, the judges converted their deferred prosecutions to criminal convictions subsequently included in their legal records. For instance, Jennifer had been convicted of possession of an uncontrolled substance in Alexander County and sentenced to twelve months of incarceration, two hundred hours of community service, $500 for the victim penalty assessment (VPA), and twelve months of Department of Corrections supervision.[6] She had received credit for two days served in jail and been offered a deferred prosecution, but when she could not pay her legal financial obligations within one year, her deferred sentence was converted to a conviction with a suspended sentence. The following is from my notes on her day in court:

> Prosecutor: "She failed to complete two hundred hours [of community service]. She's in a position where she does owe LFOs, and that puts her

in the position where unless she pays she can't request the deferred prosecution."

Defense attorney responds: "We request that you continue the case for one more week so she can pay her LFOs."

The judge asks, "Is she able to pay the $500 VPA?"

The prosecutor interjects, "$746.26 is the total amount."

Jennifer looks at the prosecutor, surprised by the increased amount. The prosecutor explains the increase in the amount is "because it collects interest."

Jennifer responds: "I work for a staffing agency. I don't have a permanent job. If it has to be paid by next Thursday, it has to be longer than that."

The defense attorney continues to try to make a case for her: "She did do the community service, and DOC dropped her and didn't explain how to transfer to Assisting Service."[7]

The judge responds: "I'll find that obligation has been met. I'll refer her to the clerk's office [for the payment plan for financial obligations]."

The defense attorney asks, "The [court's] jurisdiction will end on April 23—does the court dismiss or vacate? The sentence becomes a suspended sentence. The fine, if not paid within a certain time, it goes to collections."

The judge looks at Jennifer and explains, "You need to get on a payment plan."

The prosecutor asks for clarification: "If she can't pay by April 22?"

The judge responds, "The deferred sentence is converted to a suspended sentence."

Because Jennifer could not fully pay her LFOs, she could not get a deferred prosecution and her felony conviction remained on her criminal record, with her suspended sentence hanging over her head. If she failed to meet other conditions of her sentence, failed to make an LFO payment, or was arrested or charged with an additional offense, the suspended sentence would be imposed. At that point, she could be forced to serve the twelve months of sentenced jail time.

In my interviews with attorneys, the issue of the effect of lingering LFOs on poor defendants was a common theme. Lea, a defense attorney from Alexander County, questioned what happens to defendants when they have such long-term debt:

When it's such a high amount, I don't know that anyone realistically thinks that's going to happen. It just seems like we all just are like, "Right, this $70,000 is never getting paid back." And I don't know what happens. Does that eventually just get referred to a civil collection agency and then it just follows this person around until they die? Or is the greater effect just that you never can actually close their case because they haven't cleared all their obligations so now they can never petition to vote again? I don't know what the actual effect is fifteen years down the road when someone has some $70,000 restitution bill.

Lea's questions get to the heart of the issues regarding the permanency of legal debt and its effects. The extension of debt is relatively new in Washington. Legislation allowing debt to be carried for more than twenty years became effective on March 30, 2000. Before then, prosecutors could request that a judge impose a ten-year extension on debt; otherwise, it would be vacated, meaning that the defendant would no longer be obligated to pay. Since 2000, LFOs and associated legal debt have effectively become permanent financial obligations that defendants carry on their legal and financial records until they can pay them off.[8]

Other Burdens

Legal debtors face a wide array of accumulated financial consequences in addition to their sentenced monetary sanctions. Besides the LFOs imposed as part of their sentence, they are sentenced to other punishments that require payment. When legal debtors do not complete their court-mandated sentences, even if the reason is inability to pay their LFOs, they can be found in violation of court orders and become subject to incarceration. In our interview, Stew described how not paying his LFOs had affected him:

And if you're not paying [your LFOs], how can you pay to go to some, uh, outpatient treatment program, you don't have the money to pay for it, so then you don't have the money to pay for it, so then you're in noncompliance with the court order to be in this program, and then you're not compliant because you can't make the court payment, and you can't call them and say, "I can't pay anything this month." They don't want to hear that, they won't hear it.

In interview after interview, my respondents described a vicious cycle that linked their poverty to their criminal justice punishment. Defendants were obligated to pay money they did not have for electronic home monitoring, work release, community supervision, drug and alcohol assessment and treatment, and victim panel classes. Reuben said that he had to pay a daily fee to the DOC for his participation in a work release program, in which he worked about thirty hours a week and made $10.50 per hour. He was scheduled to be in the work release program for approximately four months, totaling about ninety workdays. We calculated that he would make about $5,600 during the work release program; at a rate of 21 percent of his gross wages, he would pay $1,200 in fees back to the DOC. Rueben felt extremely lucky to be in the program and to have the opportunity to get some employment experience. But for someone who had no savings and was about to be released from prison, these fees cut into his ability to set aside money to make the transition to free society, where his employment prospects were dim but he would still need money to cover food, shelter, and other basic living expenses.

Respondents struggled to make regular LFO payments and find money to pay for the drug addiction assessment and treatment ordered by their sentencing judge. My field notes include a court hearing for Mr. Peter, a man who was summoned for noncompliance for not completing his court-mandated drug assessment and treatment.

Judge: This is a violation. [I am] also concerned he pled over one year ago and finally goes in for assessment in May, which is a year and a half later.

Defense Attorney: He is trying to get an ADATSA (Alcohol and Drug Assistance Treatment and Support Act) to get funding help. They only go for inpatient. Not outpatient.

Mr. Peter: I have been working with a friend to get the money to get the treatment. I have the $220 that is necessary to get started, but there are $185 monthly payments for six months.

Judge: My concern is the evaluation wasn't until May 2. The plea in the case was one and a half years ago—it took you one and a half years . . . to get the evaluation.

Mr. Peter: Extreme mistake. No real excuse. I am working on the community service.

Judge: How many [hours] does he have now?

Mr. Peter: It was 240 hours, and I have 140 or 150 done.

Judge: Do you have any proof?

Mr. Peter: They should be documented.

Mr. Peter claimed that he could not fulfill his sentence because he did not have the financial resources to enroll in a treatment program. Washington's Alcoholism and Drug Addiction Treatment and Support Act program provides poor people with free or low-cost treatment services. Access to the program is limited, however, and defendants who cannot get approved for ADATSA incur significantly higher costs.

The cost of drug assessments and treatment, while well known within the courts, was rarely acknowledged in court hearings. Even judges seemed to be powerless to do anything about the expenses related to sentences. In our interview, Judge Jay said that he suspected many defendants did not appear in court when summoned for nonpayment or noncompliance on other sentences because they did not have the financial means to complete the sentence:

> And very often, like I said, [defendants] will not pay, or they won't show up, or something else, so it's in there, but it's part of something else, and it's hard to tell whether the root of the problem is financial, because very often, at least the excuse that's given for not doing the treatment or whatever is, "I couldn't pay the intake fee," or, "They kicked me out of the program because I couldn't pay," or . . .

Being obligated to pay for court-ordered sentences like drug treatment is another example of the barriers that indigent defendants encounter when trying to fulfill their criminal justice sentences; meanwhile, those with financial means can afford to fulfill all of the conditions of their sentences and end their punishment.

Emotional Despair

The emotional strain brought on by an inability to pay LFOs can lead to a profound sense of despair. Legal debt affects defendants' perceptions of fairness, their major life transitions, their relationships with friends and family members, and their entanglement with the criminal justice system. Interviewees commonly talked about just "trying to survive" under this heavy financial and emotional burden. They reported that their lives were "out of their control" and that they were "overwhelmed" and "frustrated." Many of my respondents were resigned to living a life of poverty and criminal justice surveillance. My conversations with them made it clear that their legal obligations and ongoing relationship with the criminal justice system deeply affected their sense of self and their identity.[9]

LFOs affect not only legal debtors but also court workers and defense attorneys. Several public defenders expressed frustration with the court system and its impact on their clients' lives and on the broader society. One defense attorney, Larry from Santos County, described his clients and his perception of how financial penalties affected them:

What's happening to them is that they're continuing to live at a very low functional economic and poverty level, and getting by. I think it certainly must contribute to a bad attitude, to be oppressively subjected to a set of costs that you know you're never going to have the ability to pay, and which are millstones around your neck, and for any effort that you might engage in to try to help yourself out, it just has to be a problem for people, and I think they tend to get desensitized to that issue, so that's how they survive.

Linda, a public defender from James County, discussed the types of defendants she represented and their offenses, which were related to their drug and alcohol addiction or mental illness. During our conversation, she pulled open her file cabinet drawer and read through some files to describe the types of offenses her clients were charged with. For them, "the LFOs are really bad," she said,

because these are people that, half of them, or most of them—I mean, come on—are people in prison or jail because they're either mentally ill, which then they shouldn't be there, but they're there. Or they have drug addiction problems. All the property crimes are because of drugs, all the drug crimes are because of drugs. And that's 80 percent of my caseload. Now, [*looking through files*] taking a motor vehicle—drugs. Possession of a controlled substance, forgery, ID theft—drugs. Burglary—drugs. Burglary—drugs. Unlawful possession of a controlled substance and a firearm—drugs. So okay, we've gone through the first ten [files]. Delivery of a controlled substance—drugs. This is all drugs. They're all drugs. Okay, third-degree assault, second-degree assault. Mental health, she [*referring to file in her hand*] just got released from the Sacred Heart Mental Health Institution for attempting suicide. She comes at a cop who's come on a welfare check because she's trying to gas herself in the garage. And she takes a screwdriver and says, "Shoot me, shoot me," to the cop. She's charged with third-degree assault and second-degree assault for having a screwdriver in her hand yelling, "Shoot me, shoot me."

The officer charged her with assault, Linda said, because he claimed to be "afraid of her." But Linda was certain that her client was just "trying to get herself killed. Come on. This thing should have been dismissed. This should never have been set up. But no, we're making money. It's giving me a job, and the prosecutor a job, and the clerks a job."

As can be seen from Linda's remarks, the frustration, anger, and resignation with the criminal justice system and the imposition of LFOs on people whose criminal involvement was intimately connected with their circumstances came not only from the debtors but also from their defense attorneys. Throughout my interviews and observations, the sense of despair over and submission to a dominating and oppressive system of social control was palpable among almost all of those involved in it.

Summary

A legal debtor's relationship with the criminal justice system is like the game of tetherball that children play on school playgrounds. Two children hit a ball about the size of a soccer ball—attached to the end of a long rope tied at the other end to the top of a six-foot metal pole—back and forth in opposite directions. The aim is to get the ball and rope completely wrapped around the pole. The ball, permanently attached to the pole, takes repeated blows from one child and then the other.

The people I interviewed described a feeling of being "tethered" to the criminal justice system. The "ball" was the debtor and the "rope" was their legal debt. Solely because of their impoverished status, these individuals were caught within the system of monetary sanctions and could never fully sever their connection to the criminal justice system. Instead, they were legally required to remain in regular communication with the court by reporting to status hearings and making regular payments toward their debt.

Legal debt generates this unique financial burden for criminal defendants who do not have the capacity to pay. Debtors face difficult choices, structural limitations, and emotional strain after they are convicted and after they serve their time in jail or prison. Even after they are released from incarceration or supervision, they continue to deal with legal debt. They are consumed by it, and it forces hard choices. Some respondents faced the choice of servicing LFOs or going to jail. For instance, the debt limited their ability to pay for housing, food, and medicine. For respondents with chemical addictions, finding clean and sober housing was especially difficult with limited financial resources and poor credit scores, and LFOs simply created an additional obstacle. Respondents told me that it was difficult for them to maintain regular medical regimes, even in the best-case scenario. One who was HIV-positive told me how difficult it was to afford his prescriptions; his treatment was repeatedly disrupted because he could not afford to pay for both the medication and his LFOs. Other respondents suffering from mental illness were unable to pay for prescription medications. A homeless respondent told me that he would use "extra" money he came across to take a public shower at a homeless facility in an attempt to stay clean or to prepare for a job interview. The shower cost $4.50.

The negative consequences of their felony convictions are compounded for poor defendants by monetary sanctions. Their legal debt cements their already precarious lives into a permanent state of financial insecurity. Impoverished debtors remain perpetual subjects of the criminal justice system who at any time can be called to answer for their nonpayment and may even be reincarcerated. Monetary sanctions attach poor defendants to the criminal justice system in unique and problematic ways—impeding major life-course transitions (debtors are unable to pay for schooling), discouraging marriage (partners do not want to marry legal debtors), and complicating the search for stable housing. Many legal debtors cannot envision a future that does not involve the criminal justice system.

Jobs, housing stability, stable unions, and a vision of a positive future self are the crucial "bonds to conformity" associated with criminal desistance.[10] Such bonds represent connections and attachments to conventional norms and values. Overwhelming financial debt, coupled with the other legal and social consequences of felony convictions, tether impoverished debtors to the criminal justice system, leaving them disappointed, frustrated, disillusioned, and with nothing left to give—the system of monetary sanctions having extracted the contemporary equivalent of a pound of flesh.

Given these bleak consequences of monetary sanctions for those sentenced to them, why have legislators designed this sanction, and how do judges apply and monitor compliance with it? The next chapter investigates the legal intent and outcomes of this sentencing practice.

= Chapter 4 =

The Legal Intent of Monetary Sanctions Versus Real Outcomes

The purpose of this act [regarding LFOs] is to create a system that: (1) *Assists the courts in sentencing* felony offenders regarding the offenders' legal financial obligations; (2) *holds offenders accountable* to victims, counties, cities, the state, municipalities, and society for the assessed costs associated with their crimes; and (3) *provides remedies* for an individual or other entities to *recoup* or at least defray a portion of the loss associated with the costs of felonious behavior.[1]

—Washington State monetary sanction statute, 1989

In 1989 Washington State legislators drafted a statute governing legal financial obligations. The explicit aim of the newly articulated system of monetary sanctions was to hold offenders accountable and provide a mechanism to recoup or collect the costs associated with the activities of the criminal justice system. Whatever the legislative intent, the experiences of defendants like Kathie, Reuben, Nick, Lisa, and Vilma reveal that financial sentences become unending punishments for people who lack the means to pay them.

Perhaps surprisingly, the indeterminate punishment system of LFOs was created at the same time that Washington, like other states, was reining in its sentencing guidelines for incarceration. Even as state legislatures were restructuring their sentencing guidelines and practices governing supervision in jails, prisons, and the community to limit judicial discretion, they were revising and expanding monetary sanctions and granting a wide range of judicial discretion in the application of these sanctions.

Indeterminate Versus Determinate Punishment

In the early twentieth century, U.S. penal policy was oriented toward rehabilitation. To encourage and reward desistance from criminal offending, courts usually imposed indeterminate sentences, which allowed for individualized assessments of criminal offenders, enabled judicial discretion in deciding the severity of punishment, and provided for periodic check-ins via parole hearings to assess inmates' progress toward rehabilitation. Since the 1960s, this rehabilitative penal philosophy has been under attack from both the right and the left. Conservative critics have argued that indeterminate sentencing schemes make it possible for "activist" judges to impose inappropriately lenient sentences, while progressive critics suggest that the broad judicial discretion associated with indeterminate sentencing policies is too often influenced by extralegal factors, especially defendants' racial and ethnic background. The shift toward determinate sentencing policies was a response to such critiques.

In the late 1970s, most state legislatures created state-level sentencing commissions, and twenty-two states, including Washington, and the federal system enacted sentencing guidelines to reduce the potential for racial and other disparities in sentencing.[2] Despite these sentencing reforms to curb judicial discretion, extralegal characteristics such as race, ethnicity, and gender have continued to affect sentencing outcomes, and the formal sentencing guidelines intended to limit judicial discretion have failed to stamp out discretion completely.[3]

Consistent with a broader move toward determinate sentencing, policymakers and practitioners in Washington designed a determinate sentencing scheme in the early 1980s through the Sentencing Reform Act (SRA) of 1981, implemented in 1984.[4] The stated aim of the SRA was to help make the criminal justice system more "accountable" to the public by developing a sentencing structure to guide the use of judicial discretion. The original act stipulated that the structured sentencing system would:

(1) Ensure that the punishment for a criminal offense is proportionate to the seriousness of the offense and the offender's criminal history; (2) Promote respect for the law by providing punishment which is just; (3) Ensure that the punishment imposed on any offender is commensurate with the punishment imposed on others committing similar offenses; (4) Protect the public; (5) Offer the offender an opportunity to improve him or herself; (6) Make frugal use of the state's and local governments'

resources; and (7) Reduce the risk of re-offending by offenders in the community.[5]

Among other major changes, the act established a determinate sentencing grid whereby judges use an offender score ranging from 0 to 9 (based on prior number and type of convictions) and an offense seriousness score (offenses ranked on severity) to determine the number of months to incarcerate an offender. The introduction of the sentencing grid did not completely limit judicial discretion, but the intent was to provide structure and guidance to judicial decisionmaking. Determinate sentencing criteria decreased some racial and ethnic disparity in sentencing.[6]

In addition to establishing a sentencing grid to guide judicially imposed sanctions, the act eliminated parole in Washington and shifted the responsibility for overseeing probation from the Department of Social and Health Services (DSHS) to the Department of Corrections (DOC). New terminology was introduced; for example, probation officers became "community corrections officers" (CCOs). After release from prison or jail, offenders were placed on "community supervision" or "under community custody."[7]

Around the same time Washington moved away from a formal system of parole, policymakers created a fiscal sentencing scheme that kept debtors who were unable to pay their legal financial obligations in a constant state of surveillance. The shift in sentencing ideology and practice highlights an interesting conundrum. Washington State law was revised to limit judicial discretion by requiring the use of a sentencing grid for the imposition of incarceration, yet the legislature provided no structure regarding monetary sanctions. A judge *shall* sentence a person convicted in Superior Court to a set amount of fines and fees and *may* impose a host of other fines, fees, restitution, and surcharges. At least sixteen formal fees that can be assessed are listed on the Washington judgment and sentence form. These do not include offense-specific fines, the cost of incarceration and supervision, mandated treatment fees and restitution, interest and collection fees, and surcharges. As a result, judges retain a great deal of discretion when determining the types and amounts of monetary sanctions to impose.[8]

Consistent with nationwide practices, Washington allows judges to assess people convicted of felonies a wide range of monetary sanctions. A number of costs associated with felony convictions are mandated by the state's criminal code. Table 4.1 details both the mandatory and optional fines and fees included in Washington's criminal statute. Judges are required to impose a victim penalty assessment of $500, regardless of the type of offense committed, and a $100 DNA collection fee. Fees

(Text continues on p. 81.)

Table 4.1   Allowable Monetary Sanctions and Other Financial Costs in Washington Superior Courts, 2015

Obligation Type	Amount Specified	Applicable Cases	Source	Example Amounts
Payments to victims				
Victim penalty assessment (VPA)	$500	Mandatory for all felony convictions	RCW 7.68.035	
Restitution	Up to twice the offender's gain or the victim's loss	Felony convictions involving injury to person or loss of property	RCW 9.94A.753	
Restitution interest	12 percent	Cannot be waived	RCW 10.82.090	
Fees or costs				
Bench warrant	$100	Bench warrant issued	RCW 10.01.160	
Filing fee or clerk's fee[a]	$200	All felony convictions	RCW 10.01.160: 10.01.07	
Department of Assigned Counsel (DAC) fee (court-appointed attorney fee)	Not specified	Defense attorney provided by state	RCW 9.94A.00	$400
Deferred prosecution[a]	$150	Prosecution deferred	RCW 10.01.10	
Crime lab analysis fee	$100	Lab work performed	RCW 43.43.690	
DNA identification system fee	$100	DNA entered into database	RCW 43.43.754	
Jury fee	$125 for six-person jury/$250 for twelve-person jury	Case adjudicated at jury trial	RCW 10.46.10	
Interlocal drug fund	Variable	Most felony drug convictions	RCW 69.50.41	$250

(Table continues on p. 78.)

Table 4.1 *Continued*

Obligation Type	Amount Specified	Applicable Cases	Source	Example Amounts
Incarceration costs	$50 per prison day / $100 per jail day	Convictions resulting in confinement sentence; cost of pretrial supervision	RCW 9.94A.760	
Emergency response	Actual costs	Vehicular assault and homicide	RCW 38.52.40	
Extradition costs	Actual costs	Extradition involved	RCW 9.95.210	
Extension of judgment fee	$200	Judgment extended after ten years	RCW 6.17.020	
Conviction or plea of guilty	$43	Any conviction	RCW 3.62.085	
Fines				
Violation of the Uniform Controlled Substances Act (VUCSA) fine	$1,000 to $2,000	Drug convictions	RCW 69.50.430	
Domestic violence penalty	Up to $100	Domestic violence convictions	RCW 10.99.00	
Other fines	Not specified	All	RCW 9.94A.50	
Collection costs				
County clerk	Up to $100 annually per case		RCW 36.18.016(29)	
Clerk convenience fee	$1 to $144 for payments of $1 to $6,000 (variable by county)		KCC 4A.630.120(B)(2)	A $1.90 fee on a $25.01 payment

Trust account service fee	$10 on each payment over $25 (variable by county)	KCC 4A.630.120(B)(2)
Interest	12 percent simple interest on fines and fees (not other collection costs); can be waived once principal is paid in full	RCW 19.52.020
Other costs associated with conditions of the court		
Domestic violence classes	Variable (up to $35 per hour of class)	"Court Ordered Classes," http://www.courtorderedclasses.com/DV.html
Drug or alcohol assessment	$125 to $250	Community Psychiatric Clinic, "Fremont," www.cpcwa.org/LocationsAndMaps/fremont.html
Drug or alcohol treatment[b]	Variable (based on assessment)	$1,450 for fifty-two hours $2,000 to $2,500 for one year of alcohol treatment

(Table continues on p. 80.)

Table 4.1 *Continued*

Obligation Type	Amount Specified	Applicable Cases	Source	Example Amounts
Electronic home confinement (EHC)	Variable fees (by city or county) for an average of sixty to ninety days		City of Renton, "Electronic Home Detention (EHD)," http://rentonwa.gov/living/default.aspx?id=240	$15 per EHC day + $25 application fee
DOC supervision fee	$10 to $50 per month		RCW 9.94A.780	
DOC supervision intake fee	$600 onetime fee (before October 1, 2011)/$475 per conviction (after October 1, 2011)		RCW 9.94A.780	
County work release	"Average daily per capita cost" of incarceration (variable board and room charges)		RCW 72.65.050	
Victim panel	$60	Persons ordered for DUIs	"King Count DUI Victims Panel," http://www.duivp.org/	

Source: Author-compiled review of revised code of Washington Statute and local jurisdictions within Washington that charge additional fees.
[a]Indicates that the fee may be imposed absent conviction (RCW 10.01.160). Incarceration costs and attorney fees cannot be imposed by the court without a conviction, although jails and offices of public defense may charge their own separate fees independent of conviction status.
[b]Author called agency on Warren County referral list for an estimation of costs.

may be ordered and sometimes must be paid even in the absence of a conviction.[9] Some optional costs include fees for a public defender ranging from $450 to actual costs; a fee for requesting a jury of $125 to $250, depending on the size of the jury; warrant costs of $100; court costs of $200; and an annual $100 collection surcharge. In Washington, LFOs accrue 12 percent simple interest compounded monthly from the time of sentencing until paid in full.[10] If a judge determines that a defendant is able to pay, he or she can be sentenced to pay $50 per day for incarceration in prison or the actual cost of incarceration in the county jail, up to $100 a day. A judge may waive the nonmandatory fines, fees, and interest during a sentencing hearing or in a hearing to modify the initial judgment and sentence.

The total amount of legal fines and fees sentenced by a judge must be included in defendants' judgment and sentence forms just like other sentencing requirements. Judges can set a minimum monthly payment amount, but they can also refer defendants to the county clerk's office to complete their financial declarations or have minimum amounts established that are later included in the official court paperwork. Judges can incarcerate legal debtors whose nonpayment they deem "willful."[11] Nonpayment can be considered a violation of court orders, and defendants can be sanctioned, as they can be for any other kind of sentence violation, with sixty jail days per finding of noncompliance for nonpayment of their minimum monthly LFO.

As a result of political mobilizing by the Washington State Association of County Clerks (WSACC), procedural rules governing the supervision and collection of monetary sanctions were significantly restructured in 2003. Until then, the DOC monitored the legal debt of criminal defendants across the state. WSACC organizers had argued that their organization could recover more money from defendants and suggested that the DOC was only interested in collecting DOC charges, not county or state penalties.[12] The 2003 legislation shifted the responsibility for collections in all nonstate supervised cases from community corrections officers to county clerks in order to "promote an increased and more efficient collection of legal financial obligations and, as a result, improve the likelihood that the affected agencies will increase the collections which will provide additional benefits to all parties and, in particular, crime victims whose restitution is dependent upon the collections."[13]

To meet their new responsibilities, county clerks' offices across Washington developed a wide variety of collection strategies and practices. Some offices simplify their collection procedures by contracting with private collection agencies; others wait for defendants to make payments; and others, through a combination of formal and informal policies, have created multilayered public collection units. Since the 2003 law passed, the legislature has added a $100 annual surcharge to cover the cost of collection services and the expansion of clerks' collection tools, which now include wage assignment and payroll deduction in addition to contracts with private collection agencies.[14] In line with the national trend toward expanding court-imposed user fees, in the past ten years Washington has also extended the length of time that a person can remain in debt, added collection surcharges, and expanded county clerks' discretion over the collection process.

The aim of expanding court user fees and increasing the amounts levied has been to "provide trial courts with additional resources to provide justice equally to the citizens of Washington." The fees imposed on defendants are meant to generate resources to fund criminal courts and establish "improvement" accounts, which cover a number of different expenses, from increasing judges' salaries and reimbursing juror costs to funding county law libraries. During legislative hearings, several court officials testified in favor of these policy changes, including municipal, district, and superior court judges.[15]

Policy Rhetoric

How did the political environment in which LFO legislation was passed develop in Washington? My analysis of the legislative debates on three bills and interviews with four state legislators revealed that sponsorship of a bill often does not indicate that a lawmaker has a strong opinion about its content. Rather, as explained to me by one legislator, many lawmakers sign on to a bill because of their "gut reactions towards issues" or because they view themselves as an "expert" on the particular topic. One legislator I interviewed labeled himself an expert on reentry issues and cited his expertise as the reason it made sense for him to be involved with voter restoration legislation. Other interviewees explained that they had cosponsored a bill because they were asked by a colleague to do so. "It was really based on professional relationships with the sponsor," as one legislator told me.

Among the legislative debates I analyzed was the debate over SB 6336 (1999–2000), which was aimed at "eliminating retroactive tolling provisions for restitution/legal financial obligations and allowing tolling for other forms of supervision." The bill allowed for the collection of LFO debt over the lifetime of a defendant, eliminating the previous ten-year collection and extension periods. The debate on this bill emphasized "the rights of the victim" and "the need for LFOs" as a tool for public safety. The bill describes offenders' responsibility to pay their

LFOs as a means of holding them "accountable" for their crimes and also indicates that holding offenders accountable for LFOs, even after they complete their supervision, is important for public safety. The debate showed that the committee had broad support for the bill. When the floor was opened for questions, there was no response, except for laughter, followed by a comment from the floor: "We all know how we feel about it." It was widely understood that extending LFO collections was a broadly popular idea.

Three key themes emerged from my analysis of interview data and the texts of debates surrounding the statute changes: "accountability," "victims' rights," and "indigence." Lawmakers speaking on behalf of LFO-related bills frequently invoked the notion of accountability to suggest that LFOs give defendants the opportunity to be "held accountable" for their crimes. In our interviews, one lawmaker told me that it was his understanding that policymakers never intended for offenders to pay back court-ordered restitution or court costs in full. Instead, he said, the goal was to establish a system that supervised offenders' attempts to make regular payments. From his perspective, making regular payments would give defendants the opportunity to demonstrate that they were becoming productive and rehabilitated citizens, and the payment process itself would show that they were being "held accountable and responsible for what they did." For this lawmaker, each payment represented a felon's move toward rehabilitation and retribution. During debate over SB 5168, which was a failed proposal to reduce the rate of interest on LFOs, one lawmaker argued that judges should have the authority to reduce interest on nonrestitution fines and fees because, "these [reductions in] interests encourage offenders to pay off their restitutions and fees." This lawmaker viewed LFOs as a mechanism for defendants to express remorse and demonstrate their sense of responsibility.

One lawmaker I interviewed described LFOs not as a punishment but as a responsibility that offenders owed to their victims and the broader society. "It's not punishment, it's a debt," he said:

> If you go to Nordstrom's and buy a dress, I assume you're going to pay for it. It's not like I get it free just because I feel like it. So these are costs that they've incurred through choices of their own. So it's not punishment so much, it's just, that's the cost of the decisions they've made. So we don't see legal financial obligations as a punishment at all. We do see it as a potential motivation to work their way out of bad decisions. So that's the reason we looked at trying to make it reachable. So that people could crawl their way out of it.

Policymakers viewed legal financial obligations as a system of accountability that provides the courts with an additional punishment and a means to supervise felony convictions. Among the lawmakers I talked with and observed in debates, LFOs enable offenders to demonstrate the extent of their remorse and their understanding of their accountability for offending. Making regular monthly payments symbolizes their effort to become rehabilitated and reintegrated into society by paying their debt.

Lawmakers also viewed LFOs, specifically restitution, as necessary to help victims recover from the physical or material losses they suffered. Lawmakers often acted as victim advocates, speaking in favor of legislation that would expand LFOs. They argued that expanded LFOs would not only provide money for victim advocate programs but also symbolically uphold "victims' rights." During our interview, one lawmaker linked victims' rights to the 2009 passage of a bill granting compliant debtors a provisional right to vote. This legislator had voted against the bill, and he explained to me that removing the right to vote until offenders paid their LFOs in full would encourage them to pay back their restitution and fees:

> Voting rights . . . voting is a privilege. And when you become a felon, you forfeit that privilege. And objectively, about how and when you restore it, is [an] important topic. If you get your freedom and rights restored, um, the incentive to pay restitutions declines, doesn't it? "I'm out of jail or prison, I've got my voting rights back, I've got my job. And so what if I owe a victim who I really stuck it to?" You let it go. So I've always favored this as good policy. You don't restore all of their rights until they have made things right with their victims in society. This is one of the principles I find very easy to support.

The concept of accountability and victims' rights were often discussed in tandem, with one used to justify the other: rhetoric about victims' rights and retribution often accompanied and was used to support statutes to expand LFOs and truncate the rights of offenders. This lawmaker believed that because a victim had been violated, and thus in a sense had lost his or her right to protection or safety, the offender had to similarly lose a right and, as part of the punishment process, be forced to "make things right" with the victim via monetary sanctions. This was how holding offenders accountable was often tied, in both the debates and my interviews, to their perceived obligations to victims and to the broader society.

While the poverty status of defendants was raised in legislative discussions, I found no evidence that legislators discussed specific guidelines or indicators for determining indigence. Instead, they seemed to assume that judges would apply some appropriate analysis to discern the poverty status of defendants. They implied in their policy discussions that judges would not impose fines and fees on defendants they determined to be poor. These policymakers characterized indigent offenders as repeat offenders and single parents on minimum wage. Both the legislative debates and my interviews with legislators reflected some recognition that many defendants could not pay fines and fees; these policymakers also seemed to think that many of those who could afford LFOs had probably been convicted of driving under the influence. In other words, even during legislative debates lawmakers recognized that LFOs could contribute to a two-tiered system of justice. One lawmaker I interviewed suggested that individuals of all income brackets are convicted of drunk driving and thus some would have the capacity to pay LFOs while others would not.

As I show in the remaining chapters, this assumption made by Washington lawmakers when they expanded LFOs in the first decade of the twenty-first century—that judges do not sentence poor defendants to LFOs if they determine that they are indigent or have no means or capacity to pay—was flawed. In my discussions with lawmakers and my review of the legislative debates on expanding and restructuring LFOs, lawmakers had strong ideas about who they thought offenders were and the importance of monetary sanctions as a symbolic representation of accountability, but they had little practical knowledge of how penalties were sentenced and monitored. This gaping disconnect between ideology and statute left judges and other court officials with considerable discretion in actually interpreting, applying, and enforcing policy and monetary sanctions.

Policy Outcomes

Two clear lines of reasoning arose in the language of LFO-related statutes and the political discourse to support the system of monetary sanctions. First, such a system was justified by the need to fiscally support the contemporary justice system. Legislators reasoned that defendants use costly resources within the courts and that they should pay for such services while incarcerated. This rhetoric implies that LFOs should generate sufficient revenue to at least partially pay for criminal processing and offset the costs associated with LFO-related assessment, monitoring, and sanctioning. And second, fiscal penalties should be assessed, it was argued, because they provide restitution for victims.

Table 4.2   Population Characteristics of Five Washington Counties, 2010

	Alexander	Langston	Santos	James	Warren
Population size	1,931,249	795,225	243,231	471,221	425,363
Nonwhite	35.2%	29.7%	52.3%	13.3%	18.2%
Latino	8.9	9.2	45.0	4.5	7.6
Black	6.2	6.8	1.0	1.7	2.0
Poverty rate	9.8	12.3	22.0	14.8	11.8
Voted Democratic in 2008 election	70.0	55.0	44.0	48.0	52.0

Source: U.S. Census Bureau, "USA Counties," http://censtats.census.gov/cgi-bin/usac/usatable.pl (accessed November 20, 2015).

The State and County Contexts

When I first began conducting research on monetary sanctions in Washington, I was surprised by how much LFOs and their consequences varied across the state. This impression of wide variation in how LFOs were sentenced and enforced across counties was confirmed when I interviewed community corrections officers. To evaluate this variation in practices, I selected five counties for in-depth observation—Alexander, Langston, Santos, James, and Warren—with an eye to achieving a mix of demographic characteristics that would reflect the broader population of the state.[16] I spent two years in these counties observing sentencing and sanctioning hearings and conducting interviews with judges, prosecutors, and clerks (whom I refer to collectively as "court officials"), as well as with defense attorneys, all of whom worked in the courts and were responsible for the imposition and enforcement of LFOs.

The counties I studied are illustrative of the variability across the state in population size and density, in urban versus rural populations, and in racial-ethnic and political contexts (see table 4.2). Alexander County is the largest county I studied: located in the western part of the state, it had just under two million people in 2010. It is urban, with an economy largely based on technology, the Internet, aerospace manufacturing, and defense businesses. Among the counties I studied, Alexander had the highest percentage of people voting Democratic (70 percent) in the 2008 presidential election. Langston County is somewhat smaller, with a population of almost 800,000 in 2010. Located just south of Alexander, it has the largest population of African Americans of the five counties in this study. The industrial base is a mix of manufacturing plants and industrial and distribution centers. James County is a midsize, largely urban county located in eastern Washington. It is predominantly white and has the lowest percentage of people of color among all the counties studied. It also has a relatively high poverty rate: 15 percent of its residents live below the poverty line. The local economy centers on military activities, higher education, and retail trade and finance. Warren County is also a midsize county, with just under 500,000 people, and is located in the southwest part of the state. Warren has few people of color. Its economy is diverse, with many jobs in the service sector, including health care, social assistance, retail trade, government employment, public education, leisure and hospitality, and a small amount of manufacturing. Santos County is located east of the Cascade Mountains, in the southeast part of the state. Santos is the smallest county of the five, with fewer than 250,000 people. The county is home to a relatively large percentage of Latinos and also includes a large Native American reservation.[17] Santos has a high poverty rate: 22 percent of its residents have incomes below the poverty line. Seasonal farming is the major industry in Santos County, which is a leading producer of apples, fruits, trees, nuts, and berries.

Criminal Justice Cost Recovery

"Collection Improvement" Programs

Court officials commonly claimed that LFOs were a source of revenue—collection programs across the United States and in Washington State do recoup a relatively large amount of money—and most of them said that obtaining money was in fact a primary goal of assessing LFOs. There is some truth to the idea that LFOs can be a significant source of state revenue. Across Washington, over 22,000 people receive felony convictions and sentences each year.[18] If each is charged the state-imposed mandatory minimum legal fee of $600, the state could recoup upward of $12 million annually. Four of the five counties studied regularly imposed additional fines and fees to help fund court services.

In my interviews with judges, prosecutors, and clerks, many said that forcing defendants to pay for court services justified collection sanctioning. The Washington Association of County Officials produces an annual report for the legislature that documents the revenue generated from LFOs. Much as companies compare month-to-month or year-to-year earnings in their annual reports, counties in Washington report year-to-year increases in LFO revenues. Counties that have collected the highest LFO amounts are frequently highlighted in these reports. Court officials viewed these year-to-year comparisons as an indication of efficiency or "success." In my interviews, many of them, as they described the ways in which they had attempted to improve their collection programs, expressed their frustration with defendants who did not pay their monetary sanctions. A judge in James County told me:

> The clerk has started a program, I'd say over the past three or four years, to try to collect all the delinquent LFOs. There are massive amounts of them, of noncollectable or uncollectable, or previously ignored LFOs, out there. And the clerk was tired of it, because we were constantly getting phone calls from people, "Where's my restitution?" "Where's this?" so he basically fired up the judges. And the prosecutors have really had to start the process of taking a look into these, bringing these people in, and settling these things, and getting them done.

As this judge revealed, court officials also raise money from defendants because they are sensitive to the distress of victims who are not receiving restitution payments. The local court officials I interviewed had been "fired up" when they realized that collection rates on LFOs were low; at least one of them was inspired to consider revising policies and practices to increase collections. Some had gone as far as imposing more punitive sanctions even on nonpaying debtors whose debt appeared to be uncollectable. Court officials commonly said that simply emphasizing collections more and developing more detailed procedures to track and sanction debtors would enable them to increase collections—and thus the amount of money available to support the work of the criminal justice system.

Warren County's public collection unit had an aggressive collection strategy. Judges regularly authorized prosecutors' requests to issue bench warrants for nonpaying debtors with outstanding LFOs who did not appear at their violation hearing and had not been excused. These bench warrants were issued so routinely that clerks sometimes prepared them even before the hearing. I was told that twenty-five to one hundred warrants were issued each week for failure to pay.

After issuing warrants, counties often assessed additional fees. Warren County officials made a deliberate attempt to cash in by changing the way most defendants responded to bench warrants. Previously, those who were picked up with a warrant for outstanding LFOs faced additional jail time unless they posted bail of $3,000, which they were unlikely to have. Thus, in order to get out of jail, they commonly relied on bail bondsmen who posted bail for them if they paid 10 percent, or $300, up front. Clerks told me that court officials realized that they could be collecting the equivalent themselves: the imposition of the $300 collection fee was a deliberate attempt to stop losing potential collections to bail bondsmen. After issuing bench warrants, Warren County clerks now call and send postcards to defendants to inform them of the warrant and let them know that if they pay $300 to the clerk's office the warrant will be canceled. Akin to posting bail in order to avoid pretrial detention, this practice enables defendants who can pay the $300 to avoid further judicial sanctioning, including incarceration for contempt.

I observed an interaction between the Warren County clerk and a debtor who had appeared for a "pre-docket" LFO monitoring meeting with the clerk. The clerk asked her if she would be willing to forfeit bail to the clerk's office, where it would be applied to her LFO debt: "Will you be giving your money over to me? Will you forfeit the money? You paid $300 bail." When the defendant agreed to do that, the clerk explained: "You have a $30-a-month payment. This is the first of twelve payment reviews. The bench warrant is cleared."

Warren County's decision to raise revenue from LFOs by attaching a cost to warrants was consistent with similar attempts across the country to develop collection programs. In the early 1990s, many U.S. jurisdictions began to explore ways to collect more money from LFOs, and some states authorized and implemented what are commonly termed "collection improvement" programs. These programs encompass a range of strategies that dedicate court staff to collecting LFOs, establish at the time of sentencing the expectation that LFOs are due, determine payment plans for those who cannot pay in full, and provide for strict monitoring of outstanding LFOs. Collection improvement programs outline best practices for addressing noncompliance, including telephone contact with debtors, wage garnishment or wage assignment, issuance of warrants, revocation of driver's licenses, and even incarceration. These programs update county- and state-level computing systems to facilitate record-keeping, contract with private collection agencies to assist with LFO collections, add state statutes to allow new methods and tools to assess debtors' finances, and impose penalties for nonpayment.

For example, after establishing the statewide Central Services Unit in 2010, Oregon introduced a centralized court accounting and collection system in 2012. At that point, the state held approximately $1.4 billion in outstanding legal debt. In an effort to recoup or collect some of that debt, Oregon imposed a tax intercept program that transferred outstanding legal debt to the Department of Revenue, which intercepted tax income payments and applied them to LFO debt. People with outstanding legal debt in Oregon can now have their state income tax refund garnished or reappropriated, and the state treasury can transfer money to the county where the LFO is owed. Thus, debtors anticipating a tax refund because they overpaid their state taxes are now likely to see their refund garnished and reallocated toward their legal debt by the state of Oregon. Oregon anticipates that the tax intercept program will combine with other collection programs to generate an additional $9 million in revenue per year.[19]

Jurisdictions report that these improvement programs have increased collection rates for outstanding legal debt. Between 2010 and 2011, Florida counties collected just over $900 million, which amounted to 69 percent of the state's outstanding assessments sentenced that same year. After starting an improvement effort in 2005, Texas now requires that cities with more than 100,000 people and counties with more than 50,000 implement a collection improvement program. The state claims that the programs have increased revenue from LFOs by $84 million.[20]

Collections in Washington State

What all of the rhetoric fails to consider, however, is whether new collection initiatives—and LFOs more generally—are cost-effective. How much money is being generated from LFOs? Given the average payment amounts, do monetary sanctions pay for the cost of the collection system itself? Data from the five counties in Washington show that a relatively small amount of outstanding debt is actually recovered compared with the total amount imposed on defendants. Since the total amount of outstanding legal debt is not publicly reported in Washington State, I have calculated the amount of debt collected in each of the five counties, including the number of outstanding LFO accounts and the average collected per open account (see table 4.3). In 2012 Washington State collected $29 million in fines, fees, restitution, interest, and surcharges.[21] Alexander County collected the largest amount of LFO dollars in 2012, at $4 million. Warren County recovered the next-largest amount, at $3.3 million, followed by James County ($2.4 million), Langston ($2 million), and Santos (just over $500,000).

Although a relatively large amount of money is recouped, the money is now generated from a great number of people sentenced to LFOs who are making very small payments each year. The average amount of annual payments is small in comparison to the average amounts sentenced.[22] Across Washington in 2012, legal debtors paid an average of less than $113 annually toward their outstanding monetary sanctions. Even with its own public collection unit that regularly monitors and sanctions legal debtors, Warren County collected $117 in payments on average each year per defendant. Annually, James County collected $68 per open account and Alexander County collected $36.39 per debtor; Langston and Santos Counties, which relied heavily on private collection companies, collected only $27 and $20 per account, respectively. In

Table 4.3 Revenue Collected in Five Washington Counties and in Washington State from Legal Fines, Fees, Restitution, Surcharges, and Interest, 2012

	Alexander County	Langston County	Santos County	James County	Warren County	Washington State
Average fine or fee sentenced in 2004	$600	$1,058	$1,823	$956	$2,530	$1,398
Outstanding LFO accounts in 2012	123,198	77,124	27,562	36,292	27,688	483,725
Average amount collected per account in 2012	$36.39	$27.09	$19.99	$67.98	$117.08	$112.27
Total amount collected in 2012	$4,000,934	$2,080,217	$640,631	$2,396,525	$3,362,903	$29,264,035

Source: Average fines or fees sentenced in 2004 (row 1) were calculated by the author from Washington Administrative Office of the Courts (AOC) data, 2004 (Harris, Evans, and Beckett 2010). The 2012 data (rows 2–4) are from Washington Association of County Officials (2012). The amount collected includes payments toward restitution, surcharges, and interest.

Table 4.4   Outstanding LFO Amounts and Cases in Alexander County, 2013–2014

Outstanding legal debt as of July 2014	$740,716,759
Amount recovered as of 2012	$4,000,934
Percentage of amount owed recovered	0.5%
Number of debtors in 2014	123,198
Average amount of yearly payment in 2012	$36.39

Source: Author's phone call with an Alexander County official, May 26, 2015.

contrast, the average amounts sentenced were $2,530 in Warren County, $956 in James County, $1,058 in Langston County, $1,823 in Santos County, and $600 in Alexander County. If the average amounts sentenced were relatively the same in 2004 as in 2012, each average annual payment was covering only 1 to 7 percent of the outstanding balance. The contrast between these average sentences and the average payment amount per year is bleak and suggests that unpaid LFOs go largely unpaid.

In addition to the large amount of outstanding LFOs in these five Washington counties, legal debt grows because of interest on accounts that are unpaid or not paid in full. Data from Alexander County indicate that 123,198 people owed LFOs in 2014 and that the total amount of outstanding debt—solely in this one county—was just under $750 million (table 4.4).[23] In addition, as figure 4.1 illustrates, between 2007 and 2012 Washington added an average of 18,830 new debt accounts each year to the outstanding LFO cases. The system of monetary sanctions continues to expand into the lives of people with criminal justice contact.

Three points are crucial. First, we lack publicly accessible data that would indicate the total amount of outstanding debt. Second, it appears that a very small percentage of what is sentenced in LFOs is actually paid. And third, the addition of new LFO accounts each year enlarges the need for a collection system and expands the number of people affected by it. Given the costs of collection, the regular reporting to court required of debtors, the repeated stints in jail for nonpayment or insufficient payment, and the costs of judges, defense attorneys, prosecutors, clerks, bailiffs, court reporters, and others who manage the debtors, it is hard to imagine that the system of LFOs is cost-effective or efficient by any standard.

The total amount of money collected for LFOs does not pay for both the initial costs of processing and convicting defendants and the additional costs of monitoring them for payment and sanctioning them for nonpayment. At best, the system may only be paying for itself. To il-

Figure 4.1   Five-Year Average (2007–2012) for Newly Added LFO Cases in Washington State and Five Counties

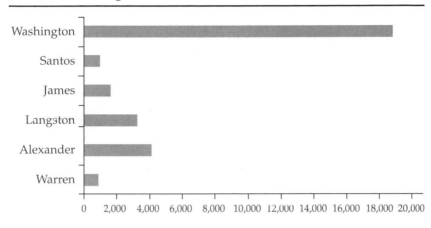

Source: Washington Association of County Officials (2012).
Note: Included are cases in which amounts are owed for restitution, surcharges, and interest.

lustrate how cost-ineffective the system is, I estimated the expenditures associated with the LFO monitoring and collection process in Warren County (for the full calculation, see the methodological appendix).[24] I conservatively estimate the cost of imposing and enforcing LFOs in Warren County to be $2.3 million annually. In 2012 Warren County collected $3.3 million in LFOs. Subtracting the estimated system costs of $2.3 million, that leaves $1 million recouped above and beyond what it took to impose the system on defendants. The 2013 county report shows that, in 2012, $1.1 million was transferred to victims for restitution, yet $1.8 million was recouped to the county. Viewed in this way, the enforcement of LFOs appears to cover the cost of the public collection unit and generate an additional $1 million. My estimate of the costs of running that unit does not include several unknowns, however, such as the number of hours that sheriffs spend locating debtors on their warrant pickups. Moreover, data are not publicly available to determine what amount of restitution goes unpaid each year, but it would be safe to assume that the money the county retained ($1.8 million) was diverted from repayment to victims in order to sustain the Warren County public collection unit. In sum, the Warren County system of monetary sanctions clearly does not generate enough money to assist with the prosecution, sentencing, and incarceration of debtors, nor does it generate large amounts of money in restitution for defendants.

Victims and Restitution

If the system of monetary sanctions serves little economic purpose—since the amount of money recouped is similar to the amount of money it costs to enforce the system—then what other purpose does it serve? In my interviews, court officials often justified the system of monetary sanctions as a mechanism to support victims. Judges commonly explained that defendants were required to pay court-ordered restitution to victims and the victim penalty assessment. Victims were reimbursed, for example, for wages lost as a result of their victimization or for the cost of their medical bills or lost property and insurance claims. Judges, clerks, and prosecutors told me that they issued calls, summonses, and warrants in response to calls from victims requesting restitution. An Alexander County prosecutor explained:

> I've had instances where victims have contacted our office saying, "Not a penny of my restitution has been paid, why hasn't there been a court hearing on this person?" I'll contact Laura [the clerk], Laura will say, "The court [the judge] doesn't want to set [a hearing] on that." I'll say, "Laura, you've got to override them and set it. It's restitution. It's not court costs, it's not the drug fund, it's not the DNA fund. These victims are calling us, we're supposed to be representing these victims and helping them in the process. They need at least a judge to tell them why they're not going to get any restitution." And the clerk's open to that.

Every court official I interviewed highlighted the importance of restitution to victims in the imposition and enforcement of LFOs. Even court officials in the least punitive counties said that reimbursing victims for their medical costs or loss of property was the primary function of LFOs. Defendant advocates and defendants themselves told me that restitution was important for victims and that it was also important for defendants as a way to demonstrate their rehabilitation and reintegration into society. This rationale underlies the Washington code that specifies how counties should allocate LFO payments once they are collected: "Restitution shall be paid [to victims] prior to any payments of other monetary obligations."[25]

Are Victims Really the Priority?

Despite court officials' victim-centered justifications for imposing monetary sanctions, evidence suggests that an interest in collecting revenue for general criminal justice practice competes with the commitment to

Figure 4.2   Distribution of LFO Collections in Washington State, 2003–2012

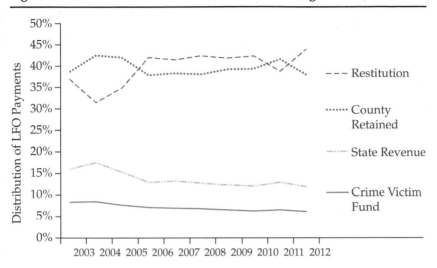

Source: Washington Association of County Officials (2012).

collecting money for victim restitution. Each county clerk's office maintains a database in which all sentenced amounts are broken down into three categories: fines and fees (combined), restitution, and accrued interest. So, for example, if I have been sentenced to pay $500 in restitution and $600 in fines and fees, I would make my payments to the clerk's office, and the clerk would then first write a check in the amount of my payment to my victim (as required by state statute) until that $500 has been repaid. I would then continue to make payments toward the $600 in fines and fees. Once my restitution and fines and fees have been paid, my payments would be applied to the interest that has accrued on both the restitution and the fines and fees. In addition to the fines and fees, restitution, and interest, I would also be responsible for paying the standard $100 annual collection charge added to my account.

One might assume that the primary source of reallocation of payments toward LFOs would be restitution, but in fact restitution does not represent the largest percentage of funds reallocated from payments. Figure 4.2 illustrates how payments to victims were retained by local counties and then transferred to the state and the crime victim fund. In every year since county clerks took charge of collecting LFOs, less than half of the revenue collected from defendants has gone to victims as

Figure 4.3   Distribution of LFO Payments in Five Washington Counties, by Percentage of Total LFOs Collected Within Each County, 2012

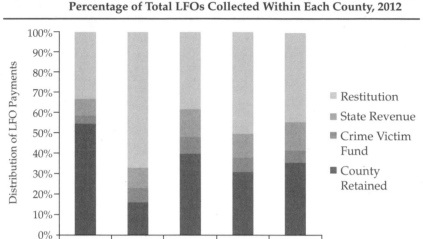

Source: Washington Association of County Officials (2012).

restitution.[26] Between 2003 and 2012, restitution represented 32 to 44 percent of all LFOs collected. In 2012, 44 percent of LFOs collected was paid as restitution directly to victims, and 38 percent was retained within the counties, ostensibly to cover operating expenses. Counties sent 12 percent of LFO collections to the state general fund, and 6 percent went into the state's crime victim fund. In effect, the law allows counties to pay for the cost of collection before paying victims. Thus, while restitution is the dominant explanation for the imposition and collection of LFOs—and the largest beneficiary ideologically—it does not get even half of the total collected.

Counties typically reallocated LFO collections to four types of funds: individual victim restitution accounts, the county expense fund, state revenue funds, and the state crime victim fund. Figure 4.3 illustrates the differences in how counties allocated LFO payments. Of LFO collections in 2012, Warren County retained 54 percent as revenue for the county, Langston County retained 40 percent, Santos County retained 35 percent, James County retained 31 percent, and Alexander County retained 16 percent. The amount redistributed to victims as restitution was in directly inverse proportion to the amount that counties retained for their local budgets. Alexander County allocated 67 percent of its

LFO collections to victims as restitution, James County allocated 51 percent, and Santos County allocated 45 percent. Warren County allocated only one-third of its LFO collections to restitution.[27]

The variation in the reallocation of monies could be due in part to the differences in the restitution amounts versus the fines and fees that are sentenced in each county. Nevertheless, the counties did indeed have different priorities in allocating the payments they received. In fact, even though Washington State statute mandates that all LFO payments be made to victims' restitution accounts before the VPA, DNA, and nonmandatory fees are paid, many clerk's offices process the $100 collection surcharge before paying victims. By treating the $100 assessment as a "service fee," not a legal fine or LFO, these county clerks can pay themselves first—or retain a larger fraction of LFO collections within county coffers—before passing money along to victims as restitution, to the state general revenue fund, or to the state crime victim fund. Labeling the fee an "annual assessment" for "collections supervision" thus places it in a separate category and gives the county greater discretion in how it is spent.[28] As annual assessments, LFO collections are not subject to the redistribution priority of making restitution payments to victims ahead of any other creditor. Annual assessments are also not subject to interest.

Under a system that prioritizes collection costs over payments to victims, payments toward collection surcharges can easily outpace the amount of money redistributed to victims. When the average annual payment per account ranges from $20 to $117 and the annual collection surcharge is $100, it is clear that little money is raised other than for the collection system itself. As such, some counties have prioritized their operating budgets over payments to victims.

My research revealed some stability over time in how counties redistributed LFOs. Figure 4.4 shows that Warren County consistently allocated the highest percentage of LFO collections toward county expenses and used a relatively small percentage to make restitution payments to victims. Alexander County consistently retained the lowest percentage of LFO collections and sent the highest percentage to victims as restitution.

Summary

The stated legal intent of monetary sanctions is to structure the sentencing process, hold offenders accountable, and recover the costs of the justice system, for the benefit of both the broader public and the victims. However, as this chapter illustrates, the system of LFOs, at least in

Figure 4.4   Funds Retained Within Five Washington Counties as a Percentage of Total LFOs Collected, 2003–2012

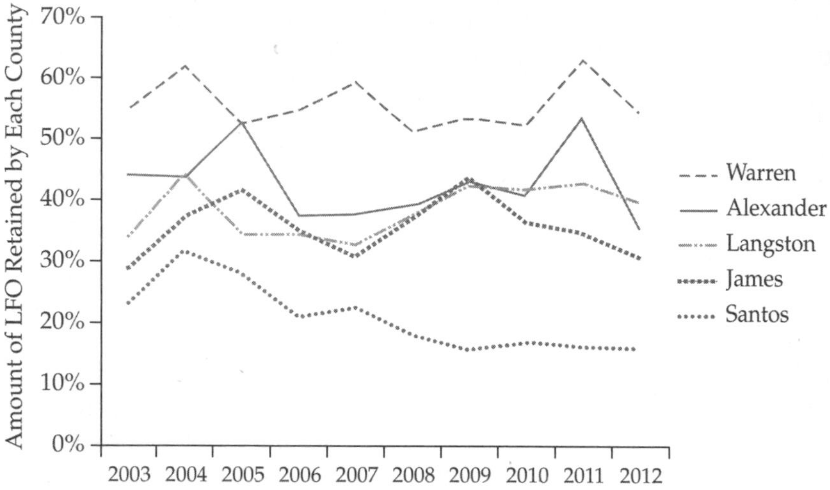

Source: Washington Association of County Officials (2012).

Washington State, does not recoup costs sufficient to sustain itself. Not only is the system financially inefficient, but meeting the needs of victims takes a backseat to filling county coffers. The system in Washington is organized in such a way that clerks usually—and legally—pay themselves first. If the monetary sanctions system is inefficient and victims of crime are not paid restitution, why then does the system persist? That is the question to which I now turn.

═══ Chapter 5 ═══

The Punishment Continuum

Mr. Nason had no income other than food stamps and had been unsuccessful in securing employment, despite attempts to try to find work. He was living in his car with his brother. It is unclear what he could have done to begin to make payments on his LFOs. Clearly, collecting aluminum cans, as the State suggested, is not a reasonable alternative and should not be the standard used by the court to determine whether the failure to pay was willful.

—Washington Defender Association and Center for Justice, amicus brief, February 8, 2010[1]

If monetary sanctions are not providing restitution for victims and do not cover the cost of the criminal justice system, what purpose do they serve? In this chapter, I examine the imposition and enforcement of LFOs as both a criminal justice punishment and a way to monitor criminal offenders. Ethnographic and qualitative interview data show that court officials develop and rely on formal and informal norms as they interpret and implement state statutes governing LFOs. I find evidence that LFOs are imposed and enforced in varying and uneven ways; the result is what I call a "punishment continuum." The amount of the monetary sanctions imposed by judges and the degree of monitoring and sanctioning for nonpayment performed by judges and clerks vary in severity along the punishment continuum.

On one end of the punishment continuum, James County regularly incarcerates people who cannot or do not pay assessed LFOs. In 2006 James Nason and his public defender decided to challenge this county's well-known policy of requiring defendants to report to jail when they fail to make payments, a policy commonly described by court officials and defendants in James County as "auto-jail." In fact, this term is so widely used that it appears in legal decisions throughout the state. In his challenge, Nason argued that he was unable to pay his LFO because he was poor, and he noted that the state allowed LFOs to be waived for indigent defendants. Thus, he argued, he should not have been forced to go to jail. It was common in James County for a county clerk to visit people who had been arrested and placed in jail for nonpayment and were awaiting a hearing by a judge; the clerk would encourage them to sign an affidavit stipulating that if they failed to make future payments, they would "automatically" report to jail for up to sixty days of confinement. Nason challenged this practice and had the support of many organizations, such as the Washington Defender Association and the Center for Justice, which filed an amicus brief on his behalf.

In 1999, at the age of eighteen, Mr. Nason had been sentenced to thirty days of confinement and $735 in monetary sanctions for a second-degree burglary conviction; he had "helped [a friend] take a couple of bags out of a storage shed." In 2006 he failed to make payments on his LFO and was summoned to court to explain why. At the time of his summons, Nason was unemployed, homeless, and sleeping in his car. His only source of income was $152 he received each month in food stamps. Despite his financial circumstances, the prosecutor argued that Nason was *willfully* violating the conditions of his sentence by not making payments. In fact, she claimed, "you can collect aluminum cans in order to pay your LFOs," and "we don't have any evidence that he did that."[2] The judge agreed and found Nason's lack of enterprise to be evidence of willful nonpayment and a violation of court orders. She sentenced him to sixty days in jail and ordered him to begin paying $25 a month toward his LFOs. In this county, other prosecutors and judges regularly made similar determinations of willful nonpayment.

Not all Washington counties, however, are as punitive as James County, nor do all of them interpret the legal concepts of "mandatory," "indigent," and "willful" in the same way. In Alexander County, for example, people are rarely incarcerated for nonpayment. A clerk explained to me that incarceration for nonpayment is reserved for cases where the court has identified a source of money that the defendant could use toward payments, such as a bank account or regular employment income.

These divergent interpretations of state law bear out the observation that each county's LFO process is shaped by the local "culture of punishment." At one end of the punishment continuum are the counties that impose large monetary sanctions to hold offenders accountable and that employ punitive and restrictive monitoring and sanctioning policies. At the other end of the continuum are the counties that impose smaller LFO assessments and are less punitive in how they sanction people with unpaid LFOs.

LFO Processes and Procedures

The Primary Decisionmakers

There are four key court officials involved in the imposition, monitoring, and sanctioning of LFOs.

1. *Judges* determine and sentence the amount of LFOs, decide whether interest will be imposed, and can establish the size of defendants' monthly payments. Judges also monitor legal debtors in court hearings.[3]

2. *County clerks* are pivotal in the LFO monitoring and sanctioning process. Each county has a head clerk who, in most counties, is elected and who hires and manages several other clerks to support the work of the office. Clerks manage court calendars, engage in policy advocacy, monitor LFO payments, and reallocate recouped money to appropriate local and state accounts. They have tremendous discretion in how they implement state policies on sanctioning people with legal debt.

3. Each county has an elected *prosecutor* who hires and manages deputy prosecutors. Prosecutors file charges according to state guidelines and make sentence recommendations to the court, including length of incarceration and types of community-based sentences, such as drug and alcohol assessment and treatment, community service, and electronic home monitoring (EHM). The prosecutor also recommends the types and amounts of monetary sanctions.

4. The role of the *defense attorney* is to represent the interests of his or her clients and to ensure that defendants receive equal protection and due process according to the law. Defendants with financial means commonly hire private criminal defense attorneys to represent them in court proceedings. Defendants who request public defenders must complete indigence screening forms to determine their eligibility. At the time they are assigned an attorney, those found to be "indigent and able to contribute" must sign a promissory note, which establishes a payment amount and the schedule on which they will pay toward their indigent defense.[4]

The Process

There are three stages in the system of monetary sanctions—sentencing, monitoring, and sanctioning for insufficient payment or nonpayment

Figure 5.1   The Institutional Processing of Felony Defendants: The Decisionmaking Stages and Related Outcomes

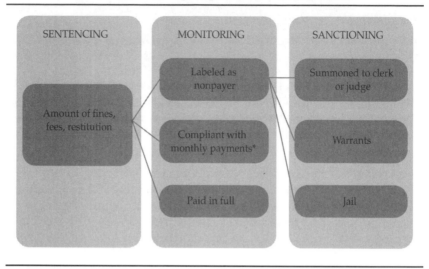

Source: Author's compilation.
*Remains under court jurisdiction until fully paid.

(see figure 5.1 for an overview). Counties vary considerably, however, in how they implement monetary sanctions and in how court officials interpret and apply the law.

Sentencing   Sometimes the sentencing hearing is held immediately after the trial or plea hearing, and sometimes it is scheduled for a week or two later. A sentencing hearing typically begins with the judge describing the types of offenses for which the defendant has been convicted and listing the statutorily mandated sentence ranges, including the number of days or months of possible incarceration. The prosecutor recommends a sentence. The defense attorney argues against the recommended sentences and may present mitigating circumstances for the judge to take into account. The defendant is given the opportunity to make a statement. Finally, the judge imposes the sentence.

My field notes include the following from a hearing in Langston County:

> The first person to be brought in from the holding cell is Kerry Frank, a middle-aged white woman. She had recently pled guilty to two charges of check forgery and is before the court to receive her sentence. The judge describes the allowable sentencing range for her offense and [her] offender

score[5]: "The standard sentencing range on count one is thirteen to seventeen months, on count two, it's four to twelve months. She agreed to a plea. Mr. Prosecutor?" The judge indicated that the prosecutor should describe the sentencing recommendation negotiated in the plea agreement. The prosecutor lists each sentence he recommends: "On count one, we recommend community custody for twelve months and Department of Corrections supervision. For LFOs, $200 court costs [CC], $500 VPA [victim penalty assessment], $100 DNA, $400 Department of Assigned Council [DAC]. On count two, the state recommends thirteen months, $100 DNA, $200 court costs, and $400 DAC." After an exchange between the judge and Ms. Frank about her participation in the offense and her children, the judge proceeds with the sentence: "Your offender score is three, thirteen months . . . $200 CC, $500 VPA, $400 DAC, $100 DNA. On count two, seven months, and they are concurrent. Thirteen months, credit time served seven days. Thirteen months concurrent custody . . . $200 CC, $500 VPA, $400 DAC. I won't impose a second DNA charge. Total is $2,300 on both counts."[6]

For two felony convictions of check forgery, Ms. Frank was sentenced to a total of thirteen months of incarceration and $2,300 in LFOs.

I also observed the sentencing hearing of a defendant named Fred Hampton in the same county and recorded the following in my field notes:

> Mr. Hampton accepted a plea deal. He is a middle-aged white man with a drug charge. He is out of custody. He was sentenced to 232 days of community service, drug evaluation, and treatment. He was assessed $200 in court costs, $500 for the VPA, $400 for his court-appointed attorney. There was no argument made by the defense attorney regarding his ability to pay or any inquiry from the judge about his financial circumstances. There was a brief exchange about where Fred could fulfill his community service hours.

For a felony drug offense, Fred Hampton was sentenced to 232 days of community service, drug and alcohol treatment, and $1,100 in LFOs. His sentencing hearing was short and routine.

Common to these two sentencing hearings and many others I observed was the imposition of sentences in addition to incarceration or community supervision time. Criminal defendants were assessed monetary sanctions, drug and alcohol assessment and treatment, electronic home monitoring, attendance at victims' impact panels, and community service hours. I regularly observed defendants receiving three or four sentence options. Fred Hampton was sentenced to community service, drug evaluation and treatment, and LFOs, and he was liable for the costs of his community-based drug evaluation and treatment. In his case, jail time was "stayed," or deferred. If the judge determined later that he had not adequately completed his sentence, he could be found in violation of court orders and sent to jail.

Restitution hearings for crimes involving physical harm or property damage to a victim are usually held several weeks to several months after the initial sentencing hearing; defendants frequently waive their right to be present at the restitution hearing. During the hearing, the prosecutor presents documentation of the cost of the crime to the victim, such as hospital bills, calculated amounts of lost wages, and insurance claims. The prosecutor requests that the defendant's sentences include the costs to the victim, to be paid directly to the victim, with interest, via the county clerk's office. When the judge sentences the defendant to restitution, the defendant is mailed a notice of the additional sentence. Because of the delay between the initial hearing and the restitution hearing, defendants may not immediately know the total amount of their LFO sentences.

After LFOs are assessed, defendants are required to make monthly payments to court clerks, who then send restitution payments directly to victims. In Washington, clerks are required to prioritize defendants' payments for restitution over other legal financial obligations. However, as chapter 4 illustrated, clerks use discretion in how they label different fines and fees and sometimes retain the first $100 or more that defendants pay before making restitution payments.[7]

Monitoring   Each county has its own collection strategy or way to monitor and collect outstanding financial obligations. Warren and James Counties have established "collection units" to manage defendants' fulfillment of their LFOs. Langston and Santos Counties transfer a defendant's LFOs to a private collection agency soon after he or she defaults on the payments. Alexander County employs a mix of strategies to monitor LFOs.

State law stipulates that after defendants are assessed financial penalties at their sentencing hearing, they must report to either the county clerk's office or the community corrections office. At that meeting, they must complete a financial declaration, similar to the form used to determine their eligibility for indigent defense services. Defendants are placed on payment plans that require minimum monthly payments for each outstanding account.[8] I never observed a judge set a monthly minimum payment for a defendant at the sentencing hearing. I also never observed a judge inquire about a defendant's ability to pay monetary sanctions prior to sentencing. Typically, it was the clerks who informally assessed defendants' ability to pay when they were establishing a payment plan. Most minimum monthly payments ranged from $10 to $50.

As noted, Santos and Langston Counties outsource LFO collections to private collection agencies. The counties that manage their own LFO cases employ a number of strategies to secure LFO payments. Clerks conduct regular in-person financial review meetings with defendants, and they regularly check state and national automated databases—like those of the Washington Employment Security Department and the Washington Department of Motor Vehicles—for financial status or employment updates.[9] When clerks find that a defendant is employed, receives government assistance, or has become the beneficiary of a legal settlement but is not keeping up with his or her monthly minimum payments, they file to have that person's paychecks or bank accounts garnished.

Sanctioning   Exactly whether and how defendants are sanctioned for delinquent or unpaid LFOs depends on where they are sentenced. People in Alexander County are summoned to SRA (Sentencing Reform Act) hearings. Defendants in James County have recoupment hearings, and defendants in Warren County are called for PV (probation violation) hearings. Although they are sometimes represented by defense attorneys, more frequently defendants have no legal representation during these court proceedings, which can have dramatically significant consequences for them. Failure to pay LFOs can result in the reinstatement of a defendant's initial sentence, for instance, or the defendant can be sent to jail for sixty days for noncompliance with the original sentence.

Payments are monitored within counties. Defendants with outstanding LFOs who miss a payment receive a summons to meet with either a clerk or a judge to explain the insufficient payment. Defendants can be required to refile their financial declaration if their circumstances have changed, and their monthly minimum payment amount may be reset. If they are under community supervision, they can be summoned to meet with their community corrections officer.

If defendants do not appear at their review hearing, a warrant is commonly issued for their arrest. Warrants are issued for failure to pay one's LFO or failure to appear at a court hearing. Defendants arrested on LFO-related warrants remain in jail until they are brought to attend a "first appearance," or violation hearing, before a judge. During my fieldwork in one county, a court clerk told me that sheriff's deputies routinely performed what she called "weekend warrant pickups." After identifying the warrants related to nonpayment, deputies would go to the last known address of those defendants to arrest them and take them to jail. Even defendants they found sleeping in a public park because they were homeless or unstably housed were brought into court on warrants related to nonpayment.

During the violation hearing, the judge determines whether the defendant is indigent; if such is the case, the judge can reset the payment amount or put the payment "on hold." These defendants are told to report to the clerk's office monthly to update their employment and income circumstances and make adjustments if necessary. However, if a judge determines that a defendant is willfully not paying, that person can be sentenced to jail time. Jail sentences for willful nonpayment range from five to sixty days.

Jail time is not imposed because of a new conviction, but *as a punishment for violating court orders*. In my fieldwork, I saw defendants effectively being held in contempt for nonpayment of LFOs or issues related to nonpayment.

Variability in LFO Practices

Across the five counties there was a great deal of variability in sentenced LFO amounts, in how legal debtors were monitored, and in how they were sanctioned for nonpayment. Table 5.1 illustrates the similarities and differences in practices across the five counties.

In 2004 the average LFO imposed for one felony conviction in Washington was $1,400, not including restitution. Judges in Warren County assessed LFOs that averaged $2,530. Next were Santos and Langston Counties, with average LFOs assessed of $1,823 and $1,058, respectively. Judges in James County assessed $956 per felony conviction, and judges in Alexander County assessed the average minimum of $600 mandated by state law.[10] Why do we see such variability within the same state in the amounts of LFOs sentenced? Do these differences persist after accounting for variation in the prevalence of difference types of crimes across the counties?

Factors That Increase LFO Amounts

Even in nearly identical cases, judges in Warren County assessed three times the LFOs assessed in Alexander, as illustrated by a few simple comparisons in table 5.2.

Lorin and Erin were charged with the same type of drug offense and had the same prior record, as indicated by the offender score of 8 for each man.[11] Lorin was sentenced in Langston County, where he was assessed $600 in LFOs, while Erin was assessed $3,860 in Santos County.

Chuck and David pleaded guilty to the same type of property offense and had similar criminal backgrounds, as measured by their offender score of 5. Chuck received an LFO assessment of $500 in James County, and David was sentenced to pay $1,970 in LFOs in Warren County. Finally, Tony and Darrin both pleaded guilty to violent offenses, and both had an offender score of 4, yet Tony was assessed LFOs totaling $500 in Alexander County and Darrin was sentenced to $1,410 in Santos County.[12]

The two key factors that should affect judicial sentencing of monetary sanctions are the offender score and the offense score. Offenders are assigned an offender score that is calculated at the time of conviction; ranging from 0 to 9, the offender score is based on the current type of conviction and the number of prior juvenile and adult felony convictions. The second factor, the offense score, ranges from 1 to 16 and represents the severity of all types of statutory offenses. Judges are required by law to apply the two scores to a sentencing grid to determine the length of a defendant's custodial sentence.

In my statistical analyses of the factors affecting LFO assessments, judges in each of the counties I studied applied the offense score in a statistically different way than judges in Alexander County (see tables A5.1 and A5.2). In four of the counties, the fines and fees that defendants were assessed increased with the seriousness of their offense. For example, in comparison to Alexander County, defendants sentenced in James County received 4 percent higher fines and fees for each one-point increase in their offense score. Defendants in Warren County received a 0.1 percent increase in their fines and fees with a one-point rise in their offense score. Offender characteristics also helped explain differential LFO assessments across counties. A one-point increase in a defendant's offender score increased the LFO assessment by 2 percent in James County and by 1 percent in Langston County, but seemed to have no effect in the other three counties. Defendants' race was a salient determinant of LFO amount in both Santos and Langston Counties, where whites were assessed lower amounts than similarly situated nonwhite defendants. Latinos in Santos County were sentenced to much higher fines and fees than non-Latinos sentenced in the same county.

The type of offense was related to the size of the LFOs assessed in three of the five counties. Defendants convicted of drug offenses in Warren, Santos, and James Counties were sentenced to significantly higher fines and fees than those convicted of drug offenses in Alexander and Langston Counties. Judges in Santos and James Counties sentenced offenders convicted of "other offenses," like property and nonviolent crimes, to lower fines and fees than judges in Alexander County did with the same type of offenders. Judges in Warren County imposed

Table 5.1 LFO Monitoring and Sanctioning Stages in Five Washington Counties

Stage	Action Taken	Alexander County	Langston County	James County	Santos County	Warren County
1	LFO is assessed (average)	$600	$1,058	$956	$1,823	$2,530
2	Clerk establishes payment plan	Yes	Yes	Yes	Yes	Yes
3	Failure to pay (FTP) is monitored	If payment is twelve months or more past due, or if restitution recipient contacts office	If payment is sixty days or more past due	Yes	If payment is sixty days or more past due	All cases are regularly monitored
4	LFO is sent to collection agency	No	Yes	No	Yes	No (has a dedicated LFO collection unit in the clerk's office)
5	Delinquency notice is sent to defendant	Yes	No	Yes	No	Yes (formerly through postcards but now through phone calls)
6	Attempt is made to schedule in-person financial review	Yes	No	Yes	No	Yes

#		County 1	County 2	County 3	County 4	County 5
7	Attempt is made to garnish wages or bank account	Yes	No	Yes	No	Yes
8	Failure to report (FTR) is monitored	Yes (if "substantial" amount of restitution is owed)	No	Yes	No	Yes (using automated system, clerk prepares FTP warrant)
9	Prosecutor's office sends notice of hearing to defendant	Yes	No	Yes	No	Yes (district attorney [DA] goes to the clerk's office once or twice a week to sign warrants and talk to judges)
10	Failure to appear (FTA) bench warrant is executed	Yes	No	Yes	No	DA prepares FTA or FTP warrants; clerk waits two weeks before issuing
11	Defendant is incarcerated for nonpayment	Yes (rarely)	No	Yes (auto-jail)	No	Yes (sheriff warrant pickups; "pay or stay" policy)

Source: Author's observations and interviews with county officials in the five counties.

Table 5.2   Examples of LFO Sentencing Variation in Washington Superior Court Cas
2004

Name	Charge	Offender Score	Sex	Race	Age	Adjudication Method	Fee and Fine	Count
Example 1								
Lorin	Drug	8	Male	White	40	Guilty plea	$600	Langsto⋅
Erin	Drug	8	Male	White	33	Guilty plea	$3,860	Santos
Example 2								
Chuck	Property	4	Male	Black	32	Guilty plea	$500	James
David	Property	4	Male	Black	31	Guilty plea	$1,970	Warren
Example 3								
Tony	Violent (Assault 2)	4	Male	White	21	Guilty plea	$500	Alexand
Darrin	Violent (Assault 2)	4	Male	White	21	Guilty plea	$1,410	Santos

Source: Author's analysis of Washington State Sentencing Guidelines Commission (SGC) and Admir trative Office of the Courts (AOC) (2004) data.

higher fines and fees on those convicted of "other offenses" than on those who had committed violent offenses. There was no such difference in Alexander County. Finally, judges in James and Langton Counties imposed much higher fines and fees on defendants who opted for a jury trial instead of plea-bargaining in Alexander County.

In sum, a variety of legal and defendant characteristics affected the size of LFO assessment in these five Washington counties. However, there was no consistent pattern in the factors that influenced sentencing amounts across the five counties. Rather, within each county, varying offense and offender characteristics had different impacts on the sentenced LFO.

The Punishment Continuum

Because county judges interpret and apply the state law guiding monetary sanctions in very different ways, counties can be understood in relation to their position on a punishment continuum that is determined in part by the average LFO imposed on criminal defendants. By this measure, Alexander County is the least punitive county in the study, while Warren County is the most punitive. Although this approach provides a useful account of penal policy, we still do not know the mechanisms that undergird differential assessments of defendants.

Monitoring   The type of collection method that counties use is another factor in their placement on the punishment continuum. Washington law allows counties to contract with private companies to collect public debt, and these private companies can assess additional "reasonable" fees for collecting the original transferred debt.[13] As a result, fees of up to 50 percent can be added to outstanding accounts that are transferred from the county to a private collection agency.

In my interviews, court officials in Langston and Santos Counties frequently examined the local constraints on their ability to monitor and sanction legal debtors or people with outstanding LFOs. Several officials explained that they lacked the resources to establish and maintain in-house collections for LFOs. After the Santos County clerk's office decided to contract with a private agency to collect delinquent or unpaid legal debts, those debts began to be automatically transferred to the private collection agency after thirty days.[14] The Santos County clerk I interviewed described how this agency helped them manage their caseload:

> We are so grateful for them [the collection agency]. . . . I can tell you what the situation before we hired our collector in 2004 was. Out of sight, out of mind. . . . If you're not being directly supervised by the state, the bill doesn't go out. They'd forget about it until a credit report comes up and shows the link. And since we've gone to collections the commercial collections agency has the skip trace ability and different tools that we can't afford in-house. And so that's not huge, but it's something.

Herbert, another Santos County clerk, bemoaned the expense of monitoring and sanctioning nonpayers:

> We just can't afford to [jail nonpayers]. When you're accruing additional expenses, somebody's not paying the bills, so you're putting them in, and they're going to be assessed the costs of their incarceration. Economically, it doesn't make sense. In my opinion, we're further ahead [than other counties] to have commercial collection. Get it out on their radar and have them turn over all the stones, rather than take up jail space. Our jail is an enterprise fund,[15] so they send a bill for local population to the general fund every year.

In Herbert's view, relying on a private collection agency is a much better route to go than the costlier alternative of trying to develop and maintain an in-house collection unit. For him, "it didn't make sense" economically to create a system that would monitor debtors and jail them if they were not regularly making payments.

In Langston County, court officials told me that LFOs provided financial resources that enabled them to maintain and increase their staff. One Langston judge said that their Office of Public Defense had insufficient resources and that in his view the cost of the criminal justice system needed to be transferred to defendants, although he did acknowledge that it might not be possible to recoup assessed LFOs: "I guess the point is maybe that the compensation is significant enough from [Alexander County's] Office of Public Defenders and wherever else they're funded that [Alexander] County defenders don't feel like they need it. But here, our public defenders are strapped. We don't recover a lot of that [fines and fees]. But we impose it."

Perceived financial constraints guide the monetary sanction process in some important ways. In Langston County, court officials were concerned about what they perceived as pressure from the county council, which looked to the sentencing process as a source for generating money. In our interview, Judge Morrison described how such pressure is applied:

> Judge Morrison: Okay, we want a twenty-third judge. Our job is to, which we're working on right now, is to create a budget for 2009. They're taking away money for 2008 and cutting budgets for 2009. But before we had these financial things, you know, they insinuate in their ways that, "Hey, you want this, we want that." We get the message.
>
> Author: More specifically, how do they send you that message?
>
> Judge Morrison: Well, there's lots of subtle ways to do it. "Well, judge, you guys have the worst collection rate on legal financial obligations, and you want a twenty-third judge! How are we going to pay for that?"
>
> Author: And how do you respond?
>
> Judge Morrison: [pause] How would we respond to that? Well, that's a good question. Diplomatically. In the same kind of veiled language.
>
> Author: What types of things do you think that they could do if they were upset with you?
>
> Judge Morrison: Well, they can. They control the money. There's three branches of government.

Judge Morrison knew that county elected officials were telling the judiciary that they needed to raise funds from defendants to support the costs of criminal justice processing. He reiterated his belief in the separation of powers to make the point that the county council treated the county judiciary as just "another department," versus another branch of government, and one with the potential to generate revenue. By contrast, I interviewed officials in another county who viewed monetary sanctions as too costly to impose on and collect from defendants whom they characterized as impoverished. In Langston County, such defendants were viewed as a potential source of county income.

Even though both Santos and Langston Counties used private collection agencies, their judges and clerks exhibited a great deal of discretion in how they managed legal debt. In both counties, once defendants completed all other parts of their sentences except full payment of their LFOs, their cases were transferred to a private collection agency, but court clerks had a great deal of leeway in determining when or if cases could be "pulled out of collections." One Langston County clerk explained:

> Clerk: We take the payments for LFOs here, we don't set up payment plans with them, and they just pay according to their CCO. Once they are released from [ordered community] supervision, which we are notified of, we see if they still have a balance on their case. We send them a notice, they have thirty days in which to respond to us and set up a payment plan, or they do go to collections. There's always going to be that gray area, though. I would venture to say probably 25 percent of the cases that we send notices out on don't set up payment plans with us, but they make payments. They're making payments, they continue to make payments with us, but they don't bother to call us and set up a payment plan. We obviously don't send those cases to collections.
>
> Author: You just keep them?
>
> Clerk: As long as they're making payments, we're not going to send them to collections. But we do give those particular cases a specific code. . . . And we do check those cases about every sixty days to make sure they're still making payments. And the first time they miss, they're gone [to collections].

In spite of Langston County's formal contract with a private collection agency, the clerk's office retained the discretion to maximize the county's collection amounts by developing informal procedures, which it applied on a case-by-case basis. Thus, even those who had not formally established a payment plan or made a fiscal declaration could avoid being turned over to the private collection agency by making regular payments.

Alexander, James, and Warren Counties had developed in-house public collection units and engaged in time-consuming and detailed monitoring of people with outstanding LFOs, though they varied in how they managed cases. Alexander County policies were nonpunitive; it ranked low on the punishment continuum. The seven clerks who worked solely on LFO collections regularly reviewed defendants' LFO payment status and made further inquiries into the cases of those who had not made payments. Both my interviews and observations of sanctioning hearings showed that in Alexander County defendants were rarely incarcerated for nonpayment.

"The Unit"   On the other end of the continuum, Warren County has a detailed and multilayered collection and sanctioning process.[16] LFOs are handled in an independent section of the clerk's office that is housed in a separate building two blocks away from the courthouse. It was often referred to as "The Unit" during my interviews with defendants and court officials. The Unit has eight full-time employees dedicated to monitoring the collections of approximately 35,000 legal debtors. After the sentencing hearing, when a defendant meets with a clerk to complete a financial declaration, the clerk's office assigns that defendant a "caseworker" from The Unit. Caseworkers make regular phone calls to defendants' homes or places of employment when payments are late. In our interview, one of the clerks from The Unit described the standard protocol:

> Right after court, if people have not made their payments and failed to appear, she will start calling everyone, and say, "You were supposed to be in court yesterday, or a couple of days [ago]. You haven't made a payment, the judge issued a warrant for your arrest, when can you get that payment in here so you don't have a warrant?" And that's helped immensely, and people are real thankful that we've called. Because some people just space and forget. And then if she can't get ahold of them, we usually will wait about two weeks to see if a payment was sent and it just hasn't gotten here. If that doesn't happen, the warrant is issued, and then a postcard is sent, and it says, "You have a warrant for your arrest, you have two weeks to respond. Failure to do so may [result] in an officer showing up and arresting you." And then there are some of the guys that I used to work with probation and parole who are officers who will go out and do warrant sweeps for me on occasion.

Court officials around the state frequently pointed to Warren County's LFO collection process as exceptional, though not everyone meant that in a positive way: some said that Warren sanctions nonpayers too severely. However, others looked to Warren County for ideas for their own collection processes; one referred to the county as "a model for how collection should and could be processed."

Decisions to Incarcerate

The use of incarceration for nonpayment is another factor contributing to the position of the five counties on the punishment continuum. Two legal routes can lead to the incarceration of nonpayers. First, counties commonly sanction nonpaying defendants by issuing a summons to appear before a judge or clerk to explain why they have not made payments on their debt. If a defendant does not appear in court, a warrant for contempt associated with incidental or deliberate nonpayment or with failing to make a court appearance is issued. Some attorneys explained that many defendants avoid attending their hearing because they believe that they will be sent to jail if they appear for a summons. It is failure to appear, however, that triggers further sanctions. When law enforcement makes contact with defendants with outstanding warrants for contempt related to LFOs, they are arrested and brought to jail, where they often remain before being brought before a judge within twenty-four to seventy-two hours. Considering that arrest and incarceration as a result of a warrant is punishment in itself, it is understandable why individuals would go to some lengths to avoid the police or report to court if they knew they had a warrant issued or suspected they were about to receive one.[17]

Receiving a court sanction for nonpayment is the second route to jail for some legal debtors. Judges and clerks have the power to send people with outstanding legal debt to jail by holding them in contempt and labeling them "willful" nonpayers. In Alexander County, jail stints were imposed for noncompliance. In both James and Warren Counties, specific local policies guided the incarceration of legal debtors, who could be jailed for five to sixty days (depending on whether they were in James or Warren County), and additional jail time could be imposed for each delinquent account. Jail time for nonpayment or failure to appear was technically not a new sentence but rather a consequence of violating court orders. Court officials explained that they jailed legal debtors to demonstrate to them that they had to fulfill their court obligations, including payment of their legal debts. In our interview, a prosecutor from Warren elaborated: "Well, incarceration . . . [is] intended to modify behavior. . . . Hopefully, it'll change their attitude. A guy with a bad attitude is going to maybe change his attitude. It may or may not work, but literally, that's pretty much what you're stuck with."

The well-established processes in James and Warren Counties that resulted in jail for nonpayment were commonly referred to as "auto-jail," "pay or stay," or "pay or sit" policies. These policies require defendants to either pay a certain amount toward their delinquent accounts or remain in jail for a set period of time to receive a daily credit toward their monetary sanctions. A James County defense attorney explained the county's auto-jail policy described at the beginning of this chapter:

> Defense Attorney: They would bring this form to jail. And they waive, right here [*showing me the line on the form*]. This is waiving.
>
> Author: Waive the right to an attorney?
>
> Defense Attorney: Waive the right to an attorney. And then it'll get presented by the clerk, presented by the prosecutor, but no [defense] attorney will be signing this.
>
> Author: And then they get released once they sign it?
>
> Defense Attorney: Well, it depends on what they've agreed to do. The clerks will go meet with them and say, "We want you to do thirty days," or, "We want you to do sixty or ninety days."
>
> Author: So someone's arrested for nonpayment. They go to jail, they don't see an attorney? They just see a clerk with this paperwork? And they'll agree to do twenty days and a $50-a-month payment, sign it, and they get out in twenty days?
>
> Defense Attorney: Right.
>
> Author: And they sign the paper because . . . ?
>
> Defense Attorney: Because the clerks tell them, "If you don't sign this, you're going to go to court and I'm going to ask for three times the amount of jail time."

Nason v. Washington established that the trial court must hold a hearing to determine a defendant's ability to pay before he or she can be jailed for nonpayment. Policies across the state, including James County's auto-jail policy, had failed to include this step and were thus violating defendants' right of due process. After *Nason v. Washington*, auto-jail was discontinued as a formal policy in James County, but in practice impoverished legal debtors are still routinely incarcerated after a brief hearing to assess indigence.

Warren County's "pay or stay" policy gives defendants with outstanding LFOs the option of either "admitting" or "denying" the state's allegation that they violated their sentence or failed to pay their LFOs. Defendants are told that they can either *pay* a certain amount of money, typically ranging from $50 to $100, or they can *stay* in jail for a sentence ranging from ten to sixty days, depending on how many prior violations they have. Defendants can get released if they promise to make a payment before the next review hearing, or they can remain in jail until someone makes a payment on their behalf.[18] Here are my field notes from such a hearing in Warren County, one of several that I observed:

> Defendant: Sir, I want to pay, but ask if it can be lowered a bit. I've started a new business window cleaning.
>
> Judge: Are you admitting the violation?
>
> Defendant: Yes, sir.
>
> Judge: How many days have you been in jail?
>
> Defendant: I came in yesterday in custody, I was picked up yesterday.
>
> Judge: It's hard to fathom if you have income you don't make regular payments. Ten days plus credit for one day. If someone pays $75, you can get out. When you get out, make the monthly payments. If you make monthly payments, you don't have to go to jail. It seems like this is a foolish way to do [to punish people]. We won't have to bring you in here.

During another arraignment hearing, I observed a thirty-year-old woman who had been arrested the previous day on an outstanding warrant for nonpayment. Her outstanding debt was the result of a conviction she received when she was twenty years old, ten years earlier. At the time of her hearing, she had paid $1,116.17 but still owed $3,155.09. The prosecutor recommended that she pay $100 as a monthly payment or serve fifteen days of jail time. I recorded the following in my notes:

> She admitted her violation and said: "I actually left [Warren County] to better myself. Just now came back to Warren. I actually have the money to pay to make $100 payments." The judge responded by asking, "You have $100 and you were just about to come and pay?" She responded, "Well, not just about." The judge asked, "Can someone come down and make a payment [for you]?" She replied, "No." The judge concluded the hearing by ordering ten days in jail with credit for one day, and stated, "If someone pays $100, you can get out the day they pay."

The day I observed the hearing for the debtor who had just started a window-cleaning business, the prosecutor told me that somewhere between eight and fifteen people had been brought in that day for nonpayment or failure to appear, representing 25 percent of the court's daily caseload. These defendants were told that they had to have some-one come to the courthouse to pay a set amount of money or they would have to stay in jail for a number of days. If these "pay or stay" candidates promised to make a payment once released but did not do so, they would receive a summons to attend a probation violation hearing. At that PV hearing, judges would admonish them for nonpayment or insufficient payments, but in some cases would modify the payment. In other cases, however, judges would sentence the defendant to jail for nonpayment.

One day I observed a PV hearing at which eight defendants were being tried for nonpayment of LFOs or failure to appear. None of them had a defense attorney present to represent them. At the outset of hearing each case, the judge would ask the defendant if he or she wanted an attorney present, stating, "You have a right to have a hearing about whether you willfully violated your court orders, and you have a right to have an attorney present if you cannot afford [one], at the public expense." One defendant responded to this query by stating, "Don't want an attorney. I don't want to pay more money." He explained that he was before the court that day for nonpayment of court fees and he did not want a public defender because he knew he would be charged for the attorney and could not afford it.

One man who had been arrested a month earlier on a warrant for nonpayment and put in jail was brought forward to see the judge at his PV hearing. I recorded his exchange with the judge, the prosecutor, and the clerk in my field notes:

Defendant: I paid some money, I didn't pay it all.

Prosecutor: The state is asking him to pay $75 or be taken into custody for ten days. The state feels the integrity of the defendant is weakened without paying the $100 [because he didn't pay the full amount he said he would]. In a 1998 case, he was assessed $1,997, it's thirteen years old, he has paid $1,383.

Defendant: I have a good payment history.

Clerk: He paid five collection fees, $1,000 drug fund. The balance is $646. His jurisdiction was extended and had a $200 fee.

Judge: What do you have for a payment history?

Clerk: Two payments in 2011, March 10, $12, and December 25, $15. On June 12, 2010, $25.

Defendant: I have a good history of paying.

Judge: That's an issue.

Defendant: I got a job, I will pay every Friday $25. I had a charge in Charlie County, I had to pay them off. Now I'm doing you guys. I work for Dollar Tree since May, and I can pay.

Clerk: He made one $25 payment [*indicating that the defendant paid his full payment minimum only one time*].

Defendant: I'll pay $25 tomorrow.

Judge: Do you promise to come back? [*indicates that he will release the defendant*]. I need to give you credit for doing that [partial payment]. That is the right thing to do. You made some of the payment.

Defendant: I do apologize. Guys, I'm sorry.

The prosecutor, with the support of the clerk, urged the judge to impose jail time in light of the defendant's poor payment history. The defendant begged for more time to make payments. The judge, ultimately siding with the defendant, cited his partial payments as evidence of his trustworthiness or his good intentions.

Even in just this one state, there is no way to track exactly how many people are sanctioned for nonpayment of LFOs. Nor can we tell exactly how many people are incarcerated for nonpayment-related reasons. One recent report estimates that 20 percent of the people incarcerated in the Benton County, Washington, jail were there for nonpayment-related reasons.[19] However, no automated court data exist that would allow the identification of people who are incarcerated solely for nonpayment of monetary sanctions. Jails often code prisoners as "awaiting trial," serving a "sentence," or being incarcerated for a "violation of a sentencing condition." Nonpayment-related sanctions are in the last category, but no further detail is systematically provided that would allow an identification of the exact percentage of those incarcerated solely for nonpayment.

All we do know for certain is that this scene of a brief, yet intense, assessment of a legal debtor plays out many times every day in this courthouse, as well as in others across the state. An obvious take-home point is that incarcerating debtors for nonpayment is counterproductive, since doing so inevitably incurs further costs for local and state criminal justice systems.

Summary

Judges and clerks have tremendous discretion in how they go about assessing, monitoring, and enforcing LFOs, even in just five counties in one state. There is great variation in how judges sentence defendants and in the severity of their sentences, and clerks have considerable decisionmaking power in the monitoring and punishment of legal debtors. Unlike the strict sentencing guidelines used for custodial sentences, court officials decide when, how, and how much to sentence and sanction legal debtors based on their interpretations of legal concepts such as "willful," "indigent," and "hardship." Neither case law, which aims to protect poor defendants from incarceration for their inability to pay legal debt, nor the Supreme Court, in establishing in *Bearden v. Georgia* (1983) that courts must find that a defendant is "willfully" not paying court-imposed monetary sanctions prior to incarcerating them for violation of court orders, has clearly defined "willful."

My courtroom observations and interviews with court officials and defendants show that court officials develop their own interpretation of "willfulness." People with legal debt are deemed willful nonpayers if they are either employed or receiving state-issued benefits like disability or unemployment but not making LFO payments. Court officials have encouraged debtors to seek illegal "under the table" day labor, ask family or friends for loans, or even beg for money by the side of the road in order to service their LFOs.

The legal concepts "indigent" and "hardship" are also subject to locally specific interpretations and meanings. For example, in some counties even homeless people are expected to find a source of income to make payments. As I observed, officials in one county did not view stage 4 cancer as a hardship and asked the dying defendant to secure a loan from his mother to make his LFO payments. The application and enforcement of monetary sanctions—specifically, the different ways in which legal concepts are interpreted and applied—vary according to the local culture of punishment. A county's punitive orientation does not directly map onto the size of the LFOs it assesses. Instead, how it assesses, monitors, and enforces LFOs more nearly describes its position on a punishment continuum. As David Garland notes in *Punishment and Modern Society*, "In a sense, each institutional site gives rise to a distinctive world of its own with its own characters and roles, statuses and rule-governed relationships—as anyone who moves from one setting (or jurisdiction) to the other will readily experience."[20]

This "distinctive world," or culture of punishment, is both embedded in and represented by court officials' interpretations and applications of the law. The explicit policies and well-honed norms within a county illustrate its punishment culture and ideology. It is within these local contexts that legal statutes and concepts are interpreted, legal categories are generated and applied, and decisions are made. Figure 5.2 illustrates the placement of each of the five counties along a punishment continuum and describes its distinct sentencing, monitoring, and sanctioning practices.

ure 5.2   The Location of Five Washington Counties Along a Punishment Continuum, by County Culture

Alexander County court officials . . .	Langston County court officials . . .	Santos County court officials . . .	James County court officials . . .	Warren County court officials . . .
ve a "realistic" orientation	Are aware of having few financial resources to administer LFOs	View defendants as gang members and link poverty and criminality	Have a "punitive" orientation and view LFOs as an additional penalty	Have an "accountability" orientation
ew defendants as impoverished	Use LFOs to recoup court costs	View county resources as limited ("We don't have resources")	Have the goal of "holding offenders accountable"	View LFO payments as an expression of remorse
ave the goal of making victims "whole"	Have low expectations about defendants' ability to pay	Have low expectations about defendants' ability to pay	Have an "auto-jail" policy	Have a "pay or stay" policy
se terms such as "anti–debtors' prison"	Consider LFOs an "impractical" sentence	Invoke "temporary indigency"	Regularly label defendants as "willful" nonpayers and incarcerate them	Assume that "everybody can pay something"
ely on public collection practices	Rely on private collection agencies	Rely on private collection agencies	Rely on public collection practices	Rely on public collection practices
ssess minimum amounts	Assess serious and persistent offenders and those opting for trial more; assess whites less	Assess serious offenders, drug offenders, and Latinos more	Assess serious and persistent offenders and those opting for trial more; assess those convicted of "other offenses" less	Assess serious offenders, drug offenders, and "other" offenders more; assess maximum amounts
verage LFO = $600	Average LFO = $1,058	Average LFO = $1,823	Average LFO = $956	Average LFO = $2,530

ource: Author's observations and interviews with county officials in the five counties.

At the least punitive end of the punishment continuum is Alexander County, where officials described defendants as impoverished and socially dislocated people who should be punished for their offenses, but in a realistic way. Court officials called for sentences that were practical and could be completed. Alexander County imposes the smallest fines and fees and prioritizes the monitoring and sanctioning of nonpaying debtors who owe restitution.

Court officials in Langston County spoke of defendants in much the same manner as court officials in Alexander County. At the same time, Langston officials talked of the financial imperative to collect LFOs; judges spoke of being pressured to impose legal fines and fees to generate revenue to cover court costs. One judge explained to me that the county council viewed the outsourcing of collections to private agencies as financially prudent policy. Judges in Langston County impose higher fines and fees on people with prior offenses, those convicted of serious offenses, and those who opt for a jury trial. Although Langston officials impose relatively high fines and fees on criminal defendants, they do not practice punitive monitoring and sanctioning of nonpaying debtors; nor are they aggressive in their attempts to collect LFOs from nonpayers. Langston County relies on monetary sanctions to recover some court processing expenses by imposing user fees on frequent users of the court system and those who require more elaborate services.

Santos County is in the middle of the continuum. The discourse here was similar to Alexander and Langston Counties: Santos officials also lamented their limited fiscal resources for LFO collections and their incarceration of nonpaying debtors. Santos contracts with a private collection agency to recover outstanding LFOs, but officials said that they wished they could adopt policies and practices similar to Warren County's to better collect outstanding debt. Judges in Santos County impose the second-highest average LFO amounts on defendants at sentencing. Serious offenders and those convicted of drug offenses receive relatively higher fines and fees. Santos County uses monetary sanctions to recover court costs and imposes them on those convicted of serious offenses.

James and Warren Counties are at the punitive end of the punishment continuum. Officials in both counties described the system of monetary sanctions as an additional way to punish offenders for their crimes and "hold offenders accountable" for their actions; they also felt that nonpayers were deserving of further incarceration. Although both counties use incarceration to sanction defendants with outstanding legal debt, there are important differences between them. James County judges impose relatively low fines and fees at sentencing, whereas Warren County judges impose relatively high LFOs. Judges in James County commonly impose optional fines and fees on defendants. The fact that defendants who are persistent offenders, defendants convicted of serious offenses or drug offenses, and defendants who opt for a trial by jury are sentenced to higher fines and fees suggests that LFOs are used in James County to punish offenders in a unique way.

Warren County judges show little restraint: they impose all legally allowable fines and fees and have the highest average LFO per felony conviction among the counties studied. Warren County judges are indiscriminate in their imposition of LFOs. All convicted defendants in the county are commonly assessed the maximum fines and fees. Moreover, the county has the most aggressive and punitive monitoring and sanctioning practices. People with outstanding LFOs are routinely incarcerated for contempt of court associated with nonpayment of LFOs or failure to appear in court for LFO-related summonses.

The distinctive punishment culture of each county is reflected in how its officials structure and implement monetary sanctions. The analysis in this chapter has shown that the nature and severity of punishment practices depend on local culture and that both the interpretation and enforcement of state law depend on where it is being applied, and to whom. Wherever the law and the authority of its enforcement are ambiguous, the door is left open to nearly unfettered discretion in its application. The result is unequal justice for offenders and victims alike.

Chapter 6

Law in Action:
Bureaucrats and Values

> Many poor persons have been taken and imprisoned a long time, for very small sums of money, to the utter ruin of their families, and without any real benefit to the creditors; and forasmuch as it will be a very great hardship and charge upon a poor prisoner, confined for a small debt . . .
>
> —Laws of the Commonwealth of Pennsylvania, 1729–1730, regarding the incarceration of poor debtors[1]

As far back as the early 1700s, Pennsylvania policymakers were suggesting that it is futile to place debtors behind bars. One hundred years later, in 1833, the U.S. government banned the federal use of debtors' prisons but left the power to states to determine when incarceration is appropriate for certain types of debtors.[2] Today, as chapter 2 illustrated, all states allow a system of punishment and incarceration of people who cannot pay legal financial obligations, although, as I have shown in the past two chapters, there is wide variability among them in how they assess, monitor, and sanction LFOs. This chapter builds on chapter 5 to more carefully examine alternative explanations for this variability in monetary sanctions across jurisdictions.

Street-Level Bureaucrats

People who work at the front lines of institutions, like the clerks at the glass window at the Department of Motor Vehicles, cashiers at the checkout counter at the grocery store, or airline representatives at the help desk at the airline gate, wield discretionary power. Frontline employees have the authority to provide information, to process a purchase or application in a timely manner, or to deny assistance. Employees who process files, applications, and complaints prioritize their work—and thus their response to clients and customers—in relation to a host of factors, including their assessments of character, status, respect, and the appropriateness or justification for requests for service. As Celeste Watkins-Hayes notes: "Discretion is not merely a product of random decision making, it is embedded in a certain interpretation of who clients are, what they should expect from institutions, and how agencies should in turn define 'help.'"[3] Even in large bureaucracies, people exhibit discretion in how they implement policies.

The daily processing of defendants through what I have called the "system of monetary sanctions" is shaped by their face-to-face interactions with judges and clerks—officials whom the sociologist Michael Lipsky calls "street-level bureaucrats."[4] All court officials working in the criminal justice system have some form of discretionary authority over the people and cases they process. Police, intake and probation officers, judges, attorneys, and clerks all possess some degree of discretion in their decisionmaking. To be sure, politicians, practitioners, and researchers have debated the appropriate amount of discretion for judges, and one outcome is that determinant sentences and mandatory minimum sentences now limit judicial discretion in criminal custodial sentencing. Relatively recent policy has also shifted toward attempts to limit the racial and ethnic disparities in outcomes that have resulted from judicial discretion by, for instance, giving prosecutors more discretion in how they craft offense charges. Yet it remains a standing principle of our justice system that judges have some discretionary power to fit a sentence to a defendant.[5] Unlike sentencing guidelines for jail or prison sentences, judges exercise a wide degree of discretion in sentencing and monitoring LFOs and sanctioning noncompliance.

A fundamental principle of the American criminal justice system is that judges have discretionary power to establish justice that fits the crime. Discretion is thus built into our criminal justice system to allow for individualized assessments of defendants. In one of my interviews, a judge from Alexander County described discretion as a fundamental feature of the contemporary criminal justice system:

> The cops, probation people, people who are relatively unaccountable to the general public, have a huge amount of discretion. There's a thing called community-policing function, cops catch people doing stuff and turn them loose all the time, and when they finally get tired of that, then they'll turn them over to the system. Then they get due process, and then it gets much higher up, the more power you have, the less ability you really have to use it [discretion]. So there's . . . a big hidden area where the rubber meets the road.

In institutions that process people every day—what Yeheskel Hasenfeld terms "people processing institutions"—individuals and their cases are transferred from gatekeeper to gatekeeper, with each official making characterizations, attaching labels, coming to decisions, and giving directions for the next stage of processing.[6] Teachers, police officers, social workers, judges, public lawyers, court officers, and health care workers are all gatekeepers and bureaucrats, and how they process people creates, informs, and constitutes policy. As Lipsky points out, bureaucrats "exercise wide discretion in decisions about citizens with whom they interact. Then, when taken in concert, their individual actions add up to agency behavior." Thus, street-level bureaucrats play two roles: they make decisions about clients, and they develop policy and procedures as they deem necessary. Lipsky argues that street-level bureaucrats are autonomous and have tremendous discretion.[7]

The autonomy of court officials (or street-level bureaucrats) in the system of monetary sanctions is made possible by the ambiguity of the state laws governing the imposition, monitoring, and enforcement of LFOs.[8] With no clear guidelines about how to interpret and implement the law, individual court officials are compelled to design local policies and practices, with the almost certain consequence that these policies and practices reflect local norms, resources, ideologies, and motivations.

I contend that how counties interpret and implement LFO law is affected by court officials' cognitive and emotional orientations toward punishment. Court officials have cognitive maps or schemas that contribute to and reflect the political and social context in which they work daily to process defendants and interpret the law. Court officials also have emotional orientations to punishment that reflect their sensibilities. Court officials make moral judgments about justice and defendants, and they have sentiments or feelings about victims. Taken together, these emotional sensibilities and cognitive orientations not only arise from the local orientation toward punishment but also produce it. Cognitive and emotional orientations to punishment, or what Garland terms "sensibilities and mentalities," are important factors that affect punishment practices and outcomes.[9] Such concepts can be analyzed from the discourse of court officials, whose sensibilities and mentalities are embedded in how they discuss and describe defendants in their courtrooms and how they perceive ideal practices of justice and punishment.

In the remainder of this chapter, I illustrate how local court officials' cognitive understandings and emotional reactions inform their interpretation and implementation of the state laws governing monetary sanctions.

The Discretion of Court Officials

In Washington State, only one of the court officials directly involved in the interpretation and implementation of the system of monetary sanctions is elected: the superior court judges who preside over felony-related hearings are elected to four-year terms. Nevertheless, all court officials, even the non-elected, appointed professional staff, exercise a great deal of discretion and decisionmaking power in the processing of debtors, with very little public oversight or accountability.

The Judges: "We All Kind of Deal with Our Own Deck"

A principle of the American criminal justice system is that judges are granted discretion to individually adjudicate cases and determine appropriate sentences for each defendant. As the following prosecutor made clear in our interview, judges believe that they need discretion to adequately perform their judicial responsibilities, and they abhor suggestions that their decisionmaking power should be limited.

> I would argue that there needs to be more discipline and uniformity in them [LFO procedures]. Now, for folks in Alexander County that might mean it [the LFO amounts imposed] goes up a little bit. Because I think we trend on the lower side. But in other counties, it might mean that it goes down. The problem with that is judicial discretion. I have found that getting any legislative reform through that would suggest restricting judicial discretion is a nonstarter, because the judges are very powerful and they don't like it. And the judges in Alexander County who don't impose [LFOs] won't like it, and the judges in other counties who impose ungodly LFOs won't like it. They like their discretion, and their discretion's been chipped away before, so they bristle at it. No matter what form it comes in, they do not care for restriction of judicial discretion.

As the elected representatives of the court, judges have the ultimate decisionmaking power in the courtroom. They adjudicate defendants, determine whether due process procedure has been followed, and apply sentencing statutes to each case. Sentencing judges have discretion to determine the amount of defendants' fines and fees, to decide whether they are indigent, and to have the last word on whether they are in willful violation of their sentence. Judges also determine whether to impose sanctions on nonpaying debtors, and in what amounts.

Across the board in my conversations, judges mentioned the importance of discretion. A James County judge explained the importance of discretion in allowing for individualized assessments of defendants:

> Author: Has your county developed any guidelines across the bench, to make the [LFO] assessment?
>
> Judge: You're looking at assessment by judges and is there any guideline that we have that provides some continuity from department to department?
>
> Author: Exactly.
>
> Judge: Uh-huh. No.
>
> Clerk: That's true, because different judges—
>
> Judge: And frankly, I'd be looking at my own guideline if I didn't like it anyway. [*All laugh*]
>
> Author: [*laughing*] You're a judge and you have the discretion to do that?
>
> Judge: It's the nature, it's the nature. Because I would think that would be almost contradictory to taking a look at each individual case on the merits if you're already locked in.

As in my conversations with other judges, this judge talked of discretion as a means to assess defendants' cases individually. He noted that even if the judges in his county decided to structure the system of monetary sanctions differently—for example, by developing guidelines or rules to guide decisions—he would use his own guidelines.

Judges have flexibility in whether and how to monitor defendants' payments. They also have the authority to convert original sentences to punishments they deem more appropriate or realistic for defendants to complete. In my courtroom observations, I saw judges convert LFOs into hours of community service and service hours into LFOs. A judge from Langston County described how she considered the possibility of converting a sentence:

> Sometimes I'll have a defendant that has done more time [in jail awaiting adjudication] than we may be asking on a sentencing recommendation. And then we have again those standard fines and costs that we impose. I haven't had it lately, but when I was doing domestic violence, oftentimes defense attorneys would ask the court to allow the excess time that the defendant had served to account for some of their LFOs. So they do have a calculation of like $18 a day in jail. So we've had opportunities where,

"Okay, you've been in longer than you would have been in on this particular crime. We'll allow your excess time to count towards some of your monetary court costs and fines."

The extent to which sentences are negotiable depends on the judge assessing the case. During sanctioning hearings, I observed defense attorneys, prosecuting attorneys, and judges openly discuss whether a defendant was in or out of compliance with his or her original sentence. If a defendant was in compliance, they would discuss whether the defendant should be labeled as having fulfilled the sentence, and if so, they would move to terminate court jurisdiction. If a defendant was out of compliance, they would sometimes negotiate a revised sentence. In either type of case, defendants were the subject of a negotiation in which judges would use their discretion in their individualized assessment of sufficient rehabilitation.

The Prosecutors: "The Prosecutor You Get Makes All the Difference"

Prosecutors have tremendous discretion in how they craft their recommendations to the court. Prosecutors can advocate for higher or lower fines and fees, argue that someone is a willful nonpayer, or even request jail time for nonpayment. In our interview, one defense attorney from James County described the importance of prosecutors' discretionary power, particularly in relation to LFO hearings.

Defense Attorney: It's interesting. Depending on the prosecutor you get makes all the difference. That's in all of the units. I would say the biggest factor determining how your case is going to go forward and what your penalty or punishment is going to be is who the prosecutor is. . . .

Author: So then, what's driving the amount of LFOs for the prosecutors? Why are they [imposing monetary sanctions]?

Defense Attorney: It's their own personal belief systems.

Author: In terms of their payoffs as a career? Does it help them?

Defense Attorney: This is probably one of the least, one of the least [helpful for careers], this [LFO] is not a career docket.

In this defense attorney's opinion, being assigned to work as a prosecutor on LFO-related hearings—or the "LFO docket"—does not help build a legal career. There is no status to be gained by the amounts that prosecutors sentence or the number of defendants they label as willful nonpayers. Instead, this attorney suggested, what determines how prosecutors interact with defendants is their own belief system.

In our interviews I gained the impression that many court officials, particularly defense attorneys, believe that prosecutors control the system of monetary sanctions. Prosecutors represent victims and the state during all hearings, and thus their arguments and recommendations to the court are viewed by all court actors as having disproportionate influence on judicial decisionmaking and outcomes. For instance, a prosecutor from Warren County described how he "brokers deals" with defendants. He would recommend that a defendant be sentenced to work release if the defendant agreed to pay a higher percentage of his or her income toward outstanding LFOs.

> Prosecutor: I do work release screening, which is individuals being released from the institution. And there's another way we get money. . . . [With] an individual who wants to come to work release, we have a statutory amount that we can collect. In other words, there's a certain amount collected from them. You can broker a deal and say, "Look, this individual wants to come, if he's wanting to come to work release and he's going to make money, he should have to pay, because he owes so much in the way of financial obligations, he should have to pay more of the money that he's making towards legal financial obligations. How about another 10 percent?"

> Author: In a monthly payment?

> Prosecutor: Well, another 10 percent of his income. And of course he's going to want to get himself established and to come down and find a job. And so he goes out, he finds a job, he gets a benefit out of it. He gets to go to work release. And this is an individual from an institution that we are collecting financial obligations for victims. We're very conscious of that. . . . And there's a number of individuals that pay. They don't have a problem with paying an extra 10 percent to come to work release, and all of that is collectable to send to your victim. Because the money goes to the victims first.

Claiming to represent victims when he negotiated with defendants, this prosecutor said that he would use the threat of jail time to encourage defendants to pay outstanding LFOs.

> Prosecutor: Individuals that get stubborn and say, "There's no way I'm going to pay," sometimes they get me involved in those.

Author: What can you do?

Prosecutor: Bring them into court.

Author: Warrant?

Prosecutor: Yeah.

Prosecutors exercise discretion in their assessments of defendants' behavior and character. One prosecutor explained that he had the authority to forward the case of any defendant he viewed as "unruly" to the judge for further punishment.

The Clerks: "I'm Just Enforcing the Judge's Orders"

The imposition of monetary sanctions has expanded the breadth of the discretion of court clerks. Serving as the face of the court in their daily interactions with defendants, clerks play multiple roles in the system of monetary sanctions. From both their perspective and that of other court officials, one of their responsibilities is to carry out judges' orders. County clerks, in the words of a Warren County prosecutor, are "basically an extension of the judge, doing what the judge has ordered." As a Santos County clerk put it: "We're the stewards of the paperwork."

In addition to managing paperwork, court clerks formalize informal procedures. In effect, they are the primary decisionmakers in the LFO process: they establish monthly payment amounts; they monitor payments; they collect and reallocate payments to victims, the state, or county coffers; and they communicate with prosecutors and judges when they believe that a debtor should be sanctioned for nonpayment, late payment, or insufficient payment. As gatekeepers who have the power to declare legal debtors to be in or out of compliance with court-ordered sentences, clerks drive and control the experiences and outcomes of people with LFOs. In most counties, a head county clerk is elected, but in a few they are appointed by the county council. However, within the courts where I observed and interviewed court officials, it was not the elected clerk establishing and implementing local policies and managing the day-to-day process of the system of monetary sanctions, but rather the non-elected bureaucrats.

There are many types of clerks within a courthouse: those assigned to a judge who manage the courtroom calendar, those who manage and file paperwork, those who attend violation hearings and appraise judges about outstanding debt, those who accept payments, those who act as "case workers" to monitor debtors, and those who manage the clerk staff. Clerks also play a pivotal role in political advocacy. The Washington State Association of County Clerks (WSACC) has appeared before the Washington State Legislature to advocate for maintaining current state budgets that allow them to monitor and collect LFOs. In addition, they frequently advocate for the expansion of the types and amounts of fees and surcharges that can be added to defendants' sentences and for additional collection tools, such as access to confidential databases. They also advocate against revisions to the statute that would reduce interest and eliminate collection costs.[10] The expansion of LFOs has correlated with the expansion of clerks' powers and ability to operate independently. Clerks' associations also hold conferences and annual meetings to discuss court-related business, including processing and monitoring monetary sanctions. In Washington, clerks' active testimony in legislative public hearings against the proposed decrease in allowable fines and fees—for example, their support for increasing collection fees to up to $100 per case per year and for extending legal debt for the duration of debtors' lives—has led to tension between various courtroom actors in many counties. An Alexander County defense attorney explained her frustration with clerks' engagement in policy:

> My whole problem, even last year in the legislative process, I see the clerks' job as collecting LFOs, not to act as advocates for either side. The crime can be as crazy as is possible. It could be anything. And that's not their job to worry about it. Their job is not to worry about victims, their job is not to worry about whether or not somebody is a good person or not. That's not their job. Their job is to collect LFOs. And under the statute, yes, they do have the ability to review people's payment schedules and set them in some circumstances, initially set them. But I have a problem when they are advocating against legislation because they feel that victims are [not being taken into account].

This defense attorney was not the only court official with concerns. I was told repeatedly during interviews with judges and prosecutors—and saw for myself in courtroom hearings and legislative debates—that court clerks wield enormous amounts of day-to-day discretion and policy authority in Washington.[11]

When I said during a conversation with a Santos County clerk that I had not realized the importance to the court of the clerk's role, the clerk responded: "Put it this way: when the clerks are on the hill, the legislature runs. So we apparently have an intimidating factor with them. Or not so much intimidating I would say as, we don't back down. We're here, we don't work for the judges, we're the executive officer of the court, and we're here to preserve the public's record and the public's business." This conversation certainly made it clear that clerks recognize the power they have within the criminal justice system and among legislators who design the state law governing it.

Assessments of the Law and of Moral Character

As I argued in chapter 5, counties develop policies and practices that reveal their own county-level punishment "culture," but even within counties I observed variability in approaches to monetary sanctions. This happens to some extent because court officials use discretion at two levels: in their interpretation of the law and in their assessment of defendants. For instance, a defense attorney from James County described one judge with a different opinion about the use of "auto-jail":

> [He] refused to apply the auto-jail provision. Even though the Court of Appeals said it was constitutional, he was like, "You know, I don't like this, I'm not going to do it." Because he knew it was unconstitutional. And wasn't fair. And the whole idea is, before you put somebody in jail, they have a right to be heard by a judge. Not a clerk. A judge. So yeah, he refused to. . . . Now it's unconstitutional. The state could still request it, and with another court it was considered constitutional, because that's what the Court of Appeals said. So, he just had his own philosophy, "This is unconstitutional, and I'm not going to allow it." But another judge could allow it. So when the Supreme Court came back and said, "Nope, it's unconstitutional, it violates due process, they have to have a hearing before you can put them in jail," he was—all of us were basically— vindicated.

This judge's ideological opposition to the sanction of incarceration for nonpayment of LFOs ran counter to the local practice of other judges. Other court officials also made individualized decisions about how to interpret law and assess the character of defendants. The same James County defense attorney described how two prosecutors in James County approached the "auto-jail" issue:

Defense Attorney: [The first prosecutor] is a wonderful, wonderful man.

Author: And what does he do?

Defense Attorney: He understands it. He gets it. He knows these people are poor, he doesn't try to slam them. He's got compassion, he's understood. And he's not trying to squeeze a turnip.

Author: And he'll give . . . [*pause*]

Defense Attorney: And he'll be as generous as he can. The other [prosecutor] . . . [*pause*] I had a case where the person was in the hospital, in a motorcycle accident. The person had been paying on their fines religiously for years. The person started missing payments because [he's] in the hospital. I mean, [he's] in the hospital for months. And so they send [him] a summons, "You have to come to court." [His] doctor had written a letter to the clerk's office, saying, "This person is in the hospital, [he] can't pay [his] fines, we don't know when he's going to be out." That basically wasn't good enough. The church was trying to pay this family's mortgage, to do everything for this family, because he's in the hospital. And we went round and round with [the other prosecutor]. Finally, we had another doctor send a letter and all this kind of stuff, but it took so much energy and expense. I think we probably have five continuances on that case. So the energy, the time waste, the expense, on a ridiculous issue like that. That drove me over the edge.

I, too, observed in court hearings that even people in the same position, like the two prosecutors this defense attorney described, had different orientations toward defendants, made different assessments, and recommended different treatments. I repeatedly observed differential application of the law that could only be explained by differences in individual values and beliefs about justice. In other words, monetary sanctions are assessed, monitored, and sanctioned at the discretion of court officials who do not necessarily have formal legal training and whose ranks include many who have no public accountability.

Besides their values and beliefs, their assessments of legal debtors' moral character also influence how court officials interpret and implement LFO law. Prior research on courtroom decisionmakers has illuminated the effect of such assessments on courtroom dynamics and adjudication.[12] In my interviews, some court officials described defendants as "poor," "marginalized," "minorities," "high school dropouts," "unemployed," "drug-addicted," "trying to game the system," "criminally minded," "lazy," and "not being accountable for their offending." They seemed to have little sympathy for most defendants and would refer to their "negative" lifestyles and "poor character."

Others who talked about defendants in more sympathetic ways pointed out the structural problems some people faced, such as living in a poor neighborhood, and the influence of their social and employment conditions on their lives and opportunities. When asked to explain why Alexander County assessed relatively low fines and fees, one prosecuting attorney responded:

> I think the judges in Alexander County are more progressive. I think they're more in tune to [the defendants'] socioeconomic status. And they have a more progressive mentality towards not wanting to look and feel like a debtors' prison. And I think judges elsewhere, particularly in more suburban or rural counties, are more conservative. So they look less at someone's economic status and more at being tough on crime.

A judge in Santos County said that many of her defendants were involved with gangs and violence. I asked her why she thought that was the case:

> Judge: I think it's a question of poverty, I think that's a big part of it. You've got a lot of kids who are bored and don't see any future, and they get involved in the gang culture. . . . I've been involved in the criminal justice system for over thirty years, and the lack of any . . . you've got a sixteen-year-old kid who thinks nothing of shooting somebody. It's bizarre. It's just bizarre. Taking somebody's life is no more important to them than "What am I going to have for dinner?"
>
> Author: And you think that comes from . . . ?
>
> Judge: I think it's a poverty thing, I think a big chunk of it is poverty, and lack of opportunities. It's a problem. It's a real problem. Lots of drive-by shootings, lots of lead flying around.

Some officials described defendants as coming from very complicated environments. One public defender was representing a man who was appearing before the court for failing to make recent payments toward his LFOs. His outstanding debt was $914.45, and he had also failed to obtain a court-ordered drug assessment and enter a treatment program. When the public defender told the judge that his client was unemployed and thus unable to pay for the drug assessment and treatment program, the following interaction ensued:

> Judge: How are you living?
>
> Defendant: Barely.
>
> Judge: Any financial assistance?
>
> Defendant: Food stamps.

Judge: No unemployment [insurance]?

Defendant: No.

Judge: What are you going to do?

Defendant: I'm trying to find employment, but it is difficult.

Judge: [*to defense attorney*] Are you aware of where he can get an evaluation without a cost?

Defense attorney: There was an agency, but they are sending out letters saying they are no longer offering low-cost assistance at this time.

Judge: We suspended this for one year. There are 285 days still out there. We are seven and a half months up to the year. Part of the agreement you had with the state was you get the assessment. I really need to see that be done here. So you need to be more aggressive in looking for possible options. Go to the state and see if they have anything.

Defendant: Would the counter where they give food stamps be the place to go?

Judge: I don't know. It wouldn't hurt to ask. How much time, defense? We should set it over this time? As long as he is pursuing it and he has evidence of that, I don't mind. As long as you don't get into trouble, that's good.

At another time in our interview the same judge expressed his frustration with the lack of drug treatment facilities available to poor people. The judge's focus on these kinds of structural limitations rather than on the individual character or failings of the defendant informed his decision to not incarcerate or further reprimand him.

Court officials in Warren County spent a lot of time explaining to me the motivations for defendants' illegal behavior. Several of my interviewees told me that criminality is a character trait. A Warren County prosecutor described types of defendants:

And an individual who is choosing to spend [their money] on drugs or choosing to spend it on tattoos or choosing to spend it on fingernails or alcohol or drugs, that individual's got money, it's just that their priority is to spend it somewhere other than someplace that they should be spending it, which is establishing a household, trying to. And I'm not saying that works for all people, but it works for some of them. And it's trying to ferret out which people are employed and which ones are not employed.

And the ones that are not employed, are they because they don't want to be employed or because they can't find work?

This prosecutor believed that some defendants choose to live a criminal lifestyle and that part of his job was to sift through his caseload and try to determine which defendants were trying to change their lives in a direction that he thought was most appropriate and which were not.

Notably, Warren County court officials did not discuss defendants' structural environments or the resources available to them. Instead, they stressed the importance of defendants' moral character, which they often suggested, perhaps not surprisingly, was "deficient." Their view of their defendants helped define for these decisionmakers who was deserving of fines and fees, who was indigent, and who was a willful nonpayer. Thus, a complex interplay between their punishment ideology, their orientation towards the law, and their assessments of and assumptions about defendants shaped how they applied and enforced monetary sanctions.

American Values and Beliefs

County court officials were oriented in varying degrees toward what are commonly seen as the uniquely American values of personal responsibility, meritocracy, and paternalism. The degree to which court officials believed in these values was a factor in their use of discretion in sentencing, monitoring, and sanctioning defendants.

Personal Responsibility Many court officials expressed a commitment to the idea that all defendants are personally responsible for their past and future behavior. Many also believed that defendants are responsible for the costs associated with their crimes, including the state-imposed user fees. Underlying these beliefs was an ideology about personal responsibility. Officials frequently characterized defendants' ability to make payments as dependent on their willingness to make a "good faith effort" at redeeming themselves. This ideological orientation was fully consistent with the intent of the state's LFO legislation, which in fact explicitly states: "Payment of legal financial obligations is an important part of taking personal responsibility for one's actions. The legislature therefore supports the efforts of county clerks in taking collection action against those who do not make a good faith effort to pay."[13] Even people who were unstably housed or homeless were not exempt from these court officials' expectation that they were responsible for meeting their LFOs. A judge from Warren County described different interpretations and applications of the monetary sanction statute to defendants who were homeless:

> Well, we tried to make the standard, tried to alert judges to the possibility that we need to be more proactive in, if a person comes in and it's obvious they can't make any payment, to release them to try to . . . figure out so that they don't keep coming back into our system, because they're indigent. That's kind of a struggle for that. I think there are probably some judges who think that we should require them to show up more often and provide proof that they're actually looking for work and that sort of thing. And some people who I think are more, well, if they've been living homeless for two years on the street, then it doesn't make a lot of sense to keep having them come back and say, "I'm homeless and on the street."

Thus, judges had discretion to decide which legal debtors would be monitored for nonpayment and to what degree they would be monitored and sanctioned. I observed some judges attempting to differentiate between homeless people who were unable to make payments and homeless people who potentially could make payments. Other judges who believed that everyone, even defendants who were unstably housed or homeless, had the potential to pay something toward their LFOs and "just needed to work harder" to find resources would explicitly assess whether defendants were trying hard enough to secure employment and would see their character reflected in their efforts. Other judges saw homelessness and unemployment as conditions of a temporary indigent status and thus required defendants to regularly report to court to prove their poverty. One judge did acknowledge a particular situation in which a defendant's indigent status would not be temporary: someone sentenced to life without parole. Nevertheless, he noted, "the Department of Corrections takes money from those people, off the dollar an hour, whatever it is they earn." He elaborated on why he would not impose further sanctions on such a defendant:

> Judge: I just felt that it's just, life without parole was quite enough. Even though they committed terrible, terrible crimes, and I thought life without parole was appropriate, not that I have any discretion in those cases, one of them was a capital case who the jury didn't find, chose not to impose the death penalty, so the only other sentence is life without parole.
>
> Author: You could cite that case and just say, "We don't have to impose the victim penalty assessment"?

Judge: Yes, but generally we do impose it. How do I know the next day the guy's not going to hit the lotto? I don't know that.

Author: The lifer?

Judge: Not him. I'm talking about anybody, because I always impose it except under those couple of circumstances [like the lifer just described]. And I'm comfortable doing it, because I know our clerk's office is not going to do anything to people, or even ask us to do anything to people, unless there is clearly a willful failure to pay.

Most of the court officials I talked with, however, told me that they believed all defendants, regardless of their indigence, could make financial payments. One prosecutor would not have made the judge's exception for a lifer:

> The other thing in [this county] is that [the judge] always makes a finding that a person is financially able to pay. Courts consider the total amount owing, his past, present, and future ability to pay legal financial obligations, and financial resources and the likelihood his status will change. But here's something that's interesting. An individual who is in the institution [jail or prison], doesn't mean they can't pay, even if they're doing, I've got an individual doing life. We're collecting money. If an individual who is doing life without parole can make payments . . .

Many court officials told me that they found it reasonable to impose fines and fees on almost any defendant regardless of their current ability to pay. One judge recognized the unlikelihood of some people ever paying significant LFOs, but she continued to impose them on every defendant, reasoning that even those who lived in poverty or were unstably housed might someday be able to make LFO payments. Another judge described cases in which defendants won a legal settlement or inherited money that enabled them to pay. Such a possibility, they told me, was why they believed that LFOs should always be imposed. This belief was buttressed by judges' trust in their clerk's offices to manage LFOs appropriately. The judge from Alexander County, for instance, felt certain that the county clerk's office would not recommend sanctions for nonpaying defendants unless it had established that their nonpayment was willful.

Other judges did not require monthly check-ins to establish indigence. A judge from Alexander County told me that he would regularly tell the clerks to collect outstanding nonrestitution penalties for fines, fees, surcharges, and interest through the civil system, not the criminal system. He said: "When I do this calendar here . . . and the LFO is not restitution, I tell the clerk's office, 'Collect it civilly.' I don't want to hear about it again."

Informal procedures for collections were also guided by ideas about personal responsibility—for example, in clerks' use of their authority to transfer LFO payments collected by a private collection agency back to the clerk's office to be managed. A clerk from Santos County explained that clerks, based on their judgment of the defendant's efforts to make LFO payments, can decide not only to hand a defendant's legal debt over to a private agency for collection but to have it returned to the clerk's office for collection. The latter case could arise when third-party inquiries are made about the defendant's outstanding loans. "Let's say they're trying to buy a house—that happens a lot here. Well, it did. And the mortgage company will want to know how much they owe so they can include it in the loan. So if there's an option like that, then definitely I'll pull it out." In just such a case, the clerk noted, he transferred the defendant's outstanding LFOs out of the private collection agency, because the clerk believed the man's effort to get a mortgage indicated that he "would be willing to pay [his LFOs] off."

The implication here is that defendants who are able to move on in their lives are privileged over those whose economic resources do not improve. Because this debtor applying for a mortgage had the ability to fully pay his LFOs, the clerk was willing to transfer the fines and fees back to county collections, thereby eliminating the private firm's additional collection costs. The clerk characterized this debtor as working hard to purchase a house and as "willing to pay" the LFOs. After he paid off his principal and half of his interest, the remainder of the interest was waived. In contrast, because of their inability to fully pay their LFOs, poor people's debt remains in the hands of private collection agencies. As their collection fees and interest continue to accrue, they feel the full force of James Baldwin's observation that "it is expensive to be poor."

Another clerk described how she decides to pull a case out of private collection:

Author: Once the thing goes into collections, can it ever be pulled out?

Clerk: Yes.

Author: Under what circumstances does that happen?

Clerk: We have to make sure that [the collection agency] hasn't started any kind of legal action, like garnishment. If they haven't, then I go into this screen that I just showed you, and I look at their notes to see if this person has talked to [them] about making a payment to them recently, and now as a last resort they're just coming down here to see if they can swing a deal with me or the guys over there. And if everything looks okay, all we have to do is call [the collection agency] and pull the case out.

Before doing so, the clerk added, she would "ask a few other questions" and assess whether the person was "being cordial, if they're treating you like you want to be treated, like you treat people, that's my motto." Assured on these points, she would then pull the debtor's LFO file out of private collection. Notably, this clerk based her decisions on whether to remove files from the private collection agency on her assessments of defendants' manners: Did they make mean or inappropriate statements to collection agency representatives? Were they "cordial" to clerk's office staff? In general, she assessed the merits of a case in terms of the degree of deference a debtor showed to collection staff.

Court officials knew that transferring cases to private collection agencies introduced additional burdens on defendants. Thus, many described their decision to transfer or remove a case as either a "favor" they would confer on certain defendants or an additional penalty or sanction they would impose on others. This situation reveals the intersections between court officials' assessments of defendants' character and their cultural beliefs about whether defendants are working hard and taking responsibility for shedding their negative past. Although court officials varied a great deal in how they interpreted personal responsibility, the concept was ever-present in their assessments of individuals' willingness to pay their LFOs.

Meritocracy   Going hand in hand with a belief in personal responsibility was a belief in meritocracy: the idea that everyone has the resources or capacity to work hard to raise money. Court officials frequently characterized defendants as either "working hard toward paying off their debt" or not. A corollary of the belief in personal responsibility, court officials' belief in meritocracy was based on the premise that all defendants have the opportunity to work hard and make regular monthly payments—and thus to demonstrate their remorse, their accountability, and, ultimately, their worth to society.

Court officials told me that defendants' payments, manners, and "good" behavior should demonstrate their effort to be good citizens. Hard work would lead to redemption. Their assumption, sometimes explicitly stated, was that all defendants have equal economic, physical, intellectual, and emotional opportunities to generate the fiscal resources to make regular payments—which thus represent symbolically their value to society.

I asked a prosecutor about a homeless person I had observed in court. Arrested the previous day for nonpayment, he had spent the night in jail and then been brought before a judge. Not knowing the outcome of the case, I asked whether the judge had released him from jail:

> Prosecutor: Yes. If they're truly indigent and can't pay, the court often will turn them loose. But individuals, even a person who's homeless, has got the ability to go and apply for a job. And that's one of the things I was suggesting to the court on that one guy. I said, "Have him go and show that he's making an effort to find employment." We also have people that stand alongside the freeway entrance and exits.

> Author: With cardboard signs?

> Prosecutor: Yeah, with cardboard signs that say, Will work for food. You know how much those people make sometimes? Some of those people make $100 a day.

> Author: Wow.

> Prosecutor: Not all of them make that much, but there's good money to be made in standing along the street corner and asking.

Another prosecutor echoed this idea that defendants should make every possible effort to demonstrate remorse by paying their LFOs:

> We told [defendants], "You can pick up cans alongside the road. If you get aluminum cans, you can get money for the aluminum." Even if [they] can't work and [they] don't have a job, they're making money somehow. Individuals have to eat, and we have individuals that are homeless that, they're truly homeless because they can't do anything else for themselves, but you also have those ones that are elective and don't want to work. And they collect their food stamps and they collect their other stuff and I don't know what all. If in fact an individual's been on drugs or they come in under the influence, whether it's under drugs or alcohol, that stuff costs money, it's not free. So they're getting money to spend it somewhere. I'd often indicate that sometimes it's the priorities of life that determine, and it makes a difference I think. Does that make sense?

These prosecutors' beliefs about hard work and accountability and their moral judgments about people engaged in drug use guided their assessment and enforcement of LFOs. Even if local policy demanded only small monthly minimum payments, they saw those payments as essential to defendants' willingness to demonstrate accountability and remorse.

The belief that in a meritocracy everyone has the ability and opportunity to work hard and raise money also informed court officials' interactions with defendants. A clerk from Langston County described how he determined when to negotiate with defendants over reducing their interest payments.

> We definitely work deals with individuals if the cases are here still [rather than in private collection] and they've made a good effort to make monthly payments. Do we give them that information up front? No. But if someone comes to the counter and they have, let's say they have $50 [left to pay] on their principal and the interest for the last six years has accrued to the point—I've seen it in the thousands [of dollars], depending on how big the original case was. [And the defendant says,] "Is there anything we can do to this interest?" And I'll say, "Yeah, there is. We can get half of it waived." I've set up that deal with our judges. And for most of the cases, my theory when I talked to [one of the judges] about it is, why not get half of it now versus $10 or $20 payments for the next thirty years? And he agreed with me. So we do waive up to half [of the interest]. And we have a merged document on Word that we just fill in the blanks, case number, defendant name, the wording is there, and we send them upstairs to [the judge], and he signs them.

Thus, deals were brokered not only when court officials assessed defendants as compliant with their court orders and as making a "good effort," but also when they saw that making a deal would be advantageous to the clerk's office—for example, when a defendant would pay several thousands of dollars immediately toward his or her LFOs directly to the clerk's office.

A Langston County clerk assisted defendants in petitioning the court to have the interest on their LFOs waived. Before doing so, he required that defendants both demonstrate "good faith" efforts to make payments on their LFOs and pay the principal LFO sentenced and half of the accrued interest. For example, if the interest was $500, he explained, "they have to give us $250 before we send that order up [to the judge]."

In contrast to the Langston County clerk practices, when defendants in Warren County have paid their principal balance in full, the clerks will assist them in filing paperwork to request that a judge waive the remaining interest. Thus, Langston clerks were not the only clerks I observed who used discretion in their collection efforts based on their personal beliefs about defendants' ability to generate resources to make their minimum monthly payments. Langston County differed from Warren County, however, in that Langston also prioritized recouping as much money as possible from defendants, including monies from interest; Warren court officials focused instead on payment of restitution, fines, and fees. In their view, once a defendant had demonstrated his or her accountability by paying the principal debt, they were happy to assist that person with the waiving of interest.

In my observations, court officials across the state of Washington frequently assessed defendants' moral character and their subsequent processing of defendants' cases would be informed by these assessments.

Paternalism   Bureaucrats' use of discretion is also shaped by paternalism. Donald VanDeVerr describes paternalism as a system whereby those in power control their subjects in the name of protection and thus create a tension between the controlling body, which presumes it knows what is best for the majority of society, and the rights of individuals.[14] People who are processed within an institution have their rights limited for their own protection or betterment. For instance, a paternalistic criminal justice system tells female employees who work with probationers that if they get pregnant, they will be reassigned once their pregnancy begins to show and not allowed to work with clients. By the same token, schoolchildren can be required to wear uniforms to equalize class differences and, in certain contexts, protect them from gangs.

Paternalism is expressed in the system of monetary sanctions via the assessment of fines and fees, the monitoring of payments, and the sanctioning of nonpayers. Politicians and court officials told me that without monetary sanctions, defendants would not work toward rehabilitation or accountability. Some court officials told me that the heavy oversight and monitoring of debtors' monthly payments helps debtors by keeping them under surveillance and accountable to the criminal justice system. Paying their LFOs constrains debtors, while at the same time giving them an opportunity to demonstrate remorse by "righting" the wrongs they had done to society, work toward regaining certain legal rights (like voting rights), and express their sense of accountability. However, legal debt limits the rights and freedoms of debtors with limited economic capacity.

The LFO monitoring procedures that the five Washington counties employed reflected the paternalism embedded in the system of monetary sanctions. Official payment documents were issued to enable debtors to avoid LFO-related arrests. But debtors were also left to the mercy of court officials by the formalized monitoring requirements that they stay in constant communication regarding their housing and employment and by the strict due dates for payments.

"The Unit" in Warren County used what it called "payment review" to monitor both first-time legal debtors and those who chronically missed payments. The payment review established a regular series of court appearances—every month on a specific Thursday—to monitor debtors and hold them, as many court officials termed it, "accountable" to their debt. They were told to report to the court every two months after making four consecutive payments, every three months after six consecutive payments, every four months after eight consecutive payments, and every six months after ten consecutive payments. After debtors had successfully made twelve consecutive payments—or regular monthly payments for one year—they were taken off payment review. They were expected to continue to make regular minimum payments or risk being placed back on payment review. Missing just one payment would return them to the first step of payment review (monthly reporting to the court). The non-elected clerk who established and monitored this system told me that "debtors needed a system to encourage their payments." She said, "Without such a system, they would not make regular payments."

Since many legal debtors in Warren County had failed to make consecutive payments, the payment review caseload was large. In December 2011, there were 682 defendants on payment review in Warren County, with 1,024 outstanding LFO accounts. If each of them met with a judge for just ten minutes, it would take over 113 hours of court time—or nearly two-thirds of a month—to address all defendants' situations. Because it would be time-prohibitive to hold separate hearings for all of the people on the review calendar, defendants were excused if they made a payment before or on the hearing date. If they made a payment on the hearing date, they received what was called a "Thursday Letter" from the clerk. If they made a payment the day of the hearing between 9:00 AM and 12:00 PM, the letter was given to them as their official "excuse" from appearing before the court. The letter specified the date for their next court hearing or payment date.

I sat with the collection clerks on one of their once-a-month Thursday court days and recorded my observations of two payment interactions:

A young Asian American man came up to the window and told the clerk that he wanted to use his debit card to make a payment for his friend. The friend was apparently on the young man's mobile phone during this interaction. The man made a $100 payment and paid the extra $2.59 for the service fee.[15] The clerk gave him a receipt and said that "Johnnie"

[was] "excused from court today. His next payment review date is January 26. He owes $50 a month. If he pays, then he doesn't have to go to court."

A man came to the window with a receipt. He had made a payment at the court clerk's office. [There were two payment locations—one in the courthouse and one at The Unit, separate from the courthouse.] He was making a payment for his wife, who he said [was] permanently disabled. The receipt indicated payment "unknown." It seemed there was a mistake. The case worker called the front desk, where the man made the payment a bit earlier. The front desk indicated he did make a $200 payment, but the total payment due was $300. He said he could pay the other $100 on December 26 when he got his bonus from work. The case worker said the payment amount would be fine and that [his wife didn't] need to come to court. The man asked, "They're not going to come knocking on my door [to arrest her]?" The case worker replied, "The warrant is still issued, but pay $100 on December 26 and we'll make a note."

The procedures at Warren County's "Unit" illustrate how courts oversee debtors and reinforce the state's paternalism as normative for debtors and their friends and family. People with LFOs understood that not making payments or attending court when required could lead to their arrest and incarceration. Thus, once a month, Thursday mornings were busy at The Unit, with lines of people at the payment window making payments and receiving letters excusing them from court. I also observed phones ringing nearly constantly on the day of the LFO hearing. The most common questions from callers, clerks told me, were: "Have I made my required recent payment?" "Do I need to come in person to the hearing?" and "Are there any warrants issued for my arrest?"

Each clerk in The Unit had a specific role to play: preparing for the 1:00 PM court hearing, accepting payments, processing paperwork for potential warrants to be issued, and answering phone calls. From what I could hear coming from the cubicles in the open room, case workers were friendly and very familiar with the debtors. They called them by their first names, asked them how they were doing, asked if they were able to get an anticipated job, and frequently ended phone calls with, "Have a nice day."

The clerks took a lunch break at noon and around 12:45 began to prepare materials for the next part of the day. I accompanied them once as they brought a rolling file cart down the street to the courthouse and initiated the pre-docket meeting. We walked into an empty courtroom (the judge was not present), and the clerks set up three stations on the sides of the judge's seat. As defendants walked into the courtroom, they formed a single line. Some came in and sat down in the galley, but then soon realized that they could bring their receipt to the clerks. The tension in the room was palpable. Some had their hands in their pockets, and some were looking at each other, trying to figure out what they were supposed to do. Others appeared to have been to these hearings before; they would go straight to a line to wait to talk with a clerk. As they waited to pay or be heard, some defendants were visibly frustrated and talked with each other in line, complaining that they did not have money or that they were tired of having to keep coming to court.

The clerks did nothing, as far as I could tell, to limit public exposure of personal LFO information. They talked with defendants in regular conversational tones and specific criminal and financial details could be overheard in various parts of the room. All private information seemed potentially on public display. Some defendants' voices would quiver when they talked to clerks or the prosecutor, who was also present accepting receipts. And some defendants were visibly upset, appearing to be on the verge of an outburst of either anger or tears.[16]

The interactions were brief. After asking defendants for their names or case numbers, clerks would ask them about their LFO payments or lack thereof. Each clerk had a laptop computer for looking up the initial LFO amount and the amounts and dates of any payments that had been made. If a defendant had made a payment earlier in the month, or on that day but did not have a Thursday Letter, the clerk made a note of the payment in the computer file and gave the defendant a paper called a "memo of disposition," which included the next review date and the next payment due date. If defendants had made the minimum payment or paid what they told the judge on the day of their arraignment that they would pay in order to be released from jail, they were told they would not have to appear before the judge.

Interactions between debtors and clerks were consistent across clerks. Here is an account of one interaction:

A middle-aged African American man handed the clerk a receipt for $50. The clerk asked:

Clerk: You are supposed to make a $100 payment. Do you have $50 more, or should I move you over [to appear before the judge]?

Defendant: I haven't been able to work. I had surgery on my back.

Clerk: Wait to see the judge.

Defendants who did not have receipts for payment or who had made insufficient payments were told to sit in the gallery and wait for the judge. The day I observed the pre-docket meeting, there were 581 people listed on the court calendar. One of the clerks told me that it was a "relatively light calendar" that day; for the next probation violation hearing, they expected to see upward of 800 people on a single day.

Even counties with a less punitive cultural orientation toward punishment strictly monitored defendants' LFO payments and jailed defendants for unpaid monetary sanctions, using similar ideological justifications. I talked with one judge in Alexander County about a defendant he had originally sentenced four years earlier. Framing the case as an example of an "indigent person who the clerks keep going after," the judge said that the defendant had been cycling through the LFO process and that he had "pulled him off" because he wanted to review the case personally. He remembered that he had been the sentencing judge and wanted to review why the defendant had been arrested repeatedly when he himself had found the man indigent and unable to make his LFO payments at an earlier hearing.

The judge read me a summary of the court records. The defendant, Mr. Frank, was sentenced in October 2007 when he pled guilty to possession of a stolen vehicle. In December, he was sentenced to the mandatory minimum LFO of $600 in Alexander County. In June 2008, restitution was set at $1,410.13. That, combined with the $600 he owed, amounted to $2,010.13. A series of violation notices were issued. Mr. Frank never made his minimum monthly payment of $25 and never responded to his mailed summonses to appear in court. As a result, the first bench warrant related to his case was issued in June 2009. The clerk's office indicated that the victim in the case had been "very persistent" in calling the clerks and requesting restitution payments. Mr. Frank was arrested in September 2009 for failure to appear at a violation hearing and spent seven days in jail awaiting a hearing. The sentencing judge imposed credit for the time he served and ordered his "immediate release." As a result of accumulating interest and the clerk's annual $100 collection surcharge, Mr. Frank's LFO obligation was now $2,547.02. In December 2010, another notice was sent to Mr. Frank for failure to pay. In January 2011, Mr. Frank attended a violation hearing with a defense attorney and the judge determined that he should pay $50 a month. Mr. Frank failed to follow court orders and a bench warrant was issued for his arrest in March 2011. He was arrested that month and spent eight days in jail before being released and told to complete a new financial declaration with the clerk's office.

This judge expressed a great deal of frustration with the LFO collection process: the clerk's office's prioritization of the victim and emphasis on payment were in direct conflict with his attempt at leniency for this defendant. He told me that he did not understand why clerks repeatedly issued bench warrants when the defendant was unable to make payments. Clerks acknowledged in Mr. Frank's file that they could not locate employment or assets information on him. They could not find any source of income, like wages, to garnish. The file included a note that "all administrative collection efforts have been exhausted." At the same time, notes showed that the victim "had contacted their office repeatedly for assistance." Nevertheless, clerks were persistently pursuing LFO collection in this case, apparently in response to the victim's inquiries about payment. A remarkable amount of judicial and clerical time was being spent on trying to extract $25 a month from Mr. Frank. In addition, he had spent a total of fifteen days in jail as punishment for his failure to appear in court to explain why he was not making payments. As another judge in this county described it, this process was like trying to "squeeze blood from a turnip."

With court officials' mentalities and sensibilities conflicting within the same courthouse, the result is confusion and inconsistent processing of individual cases, both within counties and across the state. Paternalistic practices across jurisdictions remain in place, however, ensuring that defendants will experience strict scrutiny and surveillance from court officials, repeated bench warrants, arrests, and incarceration for nonpayment, and ongoing admonishment for not complying with court orders, whatever their financial circumstances.

Summary

The linchpin concept linking the American values of personal responsibility, meritocracy, and paternalism to the system of monetary sanctions is accountability. Court officials want to ensure that defendants are "being held accountable" for their offenses, and they do so in part by making them financially responsible for the costs of processing their own case and their use of the criminal justice system. Indeed, both defendants and court officials understand criminal justice practices and policies in terms of accountability, in particular financial accountability.

The court officials interviewed for this study regularly invoked the concept of accountability, but with varying meanings. For instance, some court officials talked about accountability as a means to ensure that every defendant is assessed all allowable fines and fees. These officials suggested that defendants need to understand that a certain dollar amount for their LFOs symbolizes their remorse and allows them to demonstrate their accountability for their actions. For defendants they viewed as compliant and complicit with court orders, clerks would commonly be willing to negotiate debt amounts. In contrast, they gave no "extra" assistance—such as supporting a petition to the court to waive interest or pulling a file from a private collection agency—to defendants they deemed uncooperative, unremorseful, or unaccountable.

This discretionary application of LFOs was consistent with the intent of the state's LFO legislation. Court officials' overlapping and mutually reinforcing beliefs about the character of offenders and the expression of their accountability generated the layers of procedural scaffolding from which they interpreted and applied the law. The punishment practices that resulted were specific and localized expressions of both an institutional and an individual punishment culture. I observed a defendant who was suffering from stage 4 cancer, another who was homeless, and too many to count who had significant physical and mental limitations. But court officials viewed as paramount the efforts of even these defendants to be accountable by trying to make payments, even if that meant begging for money by the side of the road.

Previous research has made a distinction between offender accountability and system accountability. "Offender accountability" refers to the expectation that an offender must take ownership or responsibility for his or her prior offending actions and future actions while on supervision. Such accountability is premised on the assumption that the criminal justice system provides supervision to hold people accountable by monitoring their behavior and assessing their progress toward desistence and rehabilitation. "System accountability" focuses on how criminal justice procedures and resources support or further punish individuals involved in the criminal justice system. Leslie Paik writes: "Accountability-based penal policies have the potential to further exclude the socially marginalized populations and exacerbate existing racial inequalities while ignoring how the state has failed in fulfilling its responsibilities to its citizens."[17]

Monetary sanctions shift accountability from the criminal justice system to offenders. The imposition of legal financial obligations allows for the differential punishment of people who are unable to regularly or completely pay their legal debt. Court officials commonly claim that they are monitoring offenders to give them the opportunity to demonstrate their accountability, but the fact is that most poor defendants can never fully pay their LFOs and court officials have become deaf to their indigence. Within a court, however, it is unclear who is responsible for recognizing that many defendants cannot pay their monetary sanctions, and thus the implications of the indigence of some defendants remain unaddressed.

In the concluding chapter, I summarize my findings, outline my final arguments, and suggest next steps for research and policy.

Chapter 7

The Permanent Punishment

The futility of severe punishment and cruel treatment may be proven a thousand times, but so long as society is unable to solve its social problems, repression, the easy way out, will always be accepted. It provides the illusion of security by covering the systems of social disease with a system of legal and moral value judgments.

—Georg Rusche and Otto Kirchheimer, *Punishment and Social Structure* (1939)[1]

The system of monetary sanctions is a system of "legal and moral value judgments" that disproportionately affects poor people who enter the courtrooms, jails, prisons, and supervision of the criminal justice system. Court officials rely on financial sentences as an economic resource to pay their bills and as a symbolic tool to measure defendants' remorse and rehabilitation. In a system where payments toward legal debt equal accountability and rehabilitation, poor defendants or people without the capacity to pay can never succeed in being accountable or being rehabilitated. Thus, the system of monetary sanctions disproportionately punishes the poor in contrast to those with financial means. Indeed, LFOs enable the state to permanently punish the poor as their legal debt grows over time with the addition of penalties and accrual of interest. The result is unending frustration, social and financial strain, and emotional burdens for people with legal debts that they cannot pay.

What We Now Know About Monetary Sanctions

Despite twenty years of declines in crime rates, forty years of criminal justice expansion and budget shortfalls have led to increasingly tight criminal justice budgets. Jurisdictions across the nation now regularly impose criminal processing user fees on defendants to balance "the budget on the backs of the poorest people in society."[2] Because the disadvantaged and poor, people of color, and those with low levels of formal education and limited employment prospects are disproportionately involved in criminal justice systems, LFOs constitute a unique sanction that affects defendants' lives above and beyond the other consequences of criminal conviction and incarceration. Further studies must be done across the country to determine the local policies, procedures, and practices used to govern monetary sanctions. Although much of my evidence comes from a single state, there are good reasons to believe that LFOs are imposed in similar ways, with similar consequences, around the country. In California, people are charged a $300 fine if they are unable to pay their LFOs in full. Alabama imposes a 30 percent collection fee on people who are unable to pay their LFOs in full. Florida allows private collection agencies to charge an additional 40 percent surcharge on the principal LFO.[3] Under the "pay or appear" practice in Illinois, a mentally ill man was ordered to pay $100 a month from his disability benefits of $690 a month and to appear monthly in court hearings for a three-year period.[4] In Rhode Island in 2007, on average eighteen people were incarcerated each day for nonpayment of court debt. The average amount owed was $876.[5] A study of defendants in fifteen states found that monetary sanctions result in long-term cycles of debt, that nonpayment regularly results in reincarceration, and that legal debt negatively affects debtors' chances for successfully reintegrating into society.[6]

As sentencing courts across the United States continue to loosely interpret what it means to be a "willful" nonpayer, LFOs are now being challenged in the courts as inadequate grounds for incarcerating people with arrears. In *Illinois v. Davis* (1991), for example, the appellate court found that the state's presentation of the defendant's unemployment status was not sufficient evidence of willfulness and that the resulting court decision to incarcerate the defendant was inappropriate.[7]

Monetary sanctions have been identified as a critical factor in the recent unrest in Ferguson, Missouri. During the writing of this book, an unarmed black teenager named Michael Brown was killed by police. Protests ensued, and people from across the United States descended on the city to express outrage at the killing and raise issues of racial injustice more broadly. Research conducted by a local public defender organization found evidence of racially disproportionate policing and criminal justice processing. In just the city of Ferguson, over $2.2 million had been raised in municipal "fines and public safety" in 2012. That equals a payment of $272 per household in one year. Further, the city had issued over 24,500 warrants in one year, averaging 1.6 warrants per adult resident.[8] A subsequent report by the U.S. Department of Justice drew attention to disproportionality in the imposition of monetary sanctions, specifically in Ferguson. After the investigation, U.S. Attorney General Eric Holder summarized the Justice Department's findings: "Our investigation has found overwhelming evidence of minor municipal code violations resulting in multiple arrests, jail time, and payments that exceed the cost of the original ticket many times over."[9] Similar investigations of police practices were recently launched in Baltimore, Maryland, after the civil unrest that resulted from the 2015 death in police custody of Freddie Gray. Investigations of monetary sanctions across the United States have revealed a nationwide practice of imposing financial penalties on people who are involved with our systems of justice and many jurisdictions relying on the fines and fees to generate needed resources to fund local governments.

Decoupling Justice from Punishment

The system of monetary sanctions is part of a larger system of criminal justice. Despite this connection, it has little coherence within or communication with other domains of the criminal justice system. The decentralized bureaucracy made possible by an ambiguous statute offers significant discretion to "street-level bureaucrats"—judges, clerks, prosecutors, and defense attorneys—without much supervision or accountability.

In every jurisdiction I studied, judges did not know how LFOs were implemented by other judges in their own courthouse—much less by other judges in the state—or how they were monitored and enforced by clerks. When I asked them how the collection process worked, judges directed me to talk with the clerks. Judges' general lack of knowledge about LFO implementation, monitoring, and sanctioning processes highlights the decoupling of LFOs from the imposition of justice. Only rarely did a judge take full account of a defendant's situation, and court officials were rarely aware of the total amount of time and resources their clerk's offices were devoting to imposing virtually unrecoverable LFOs; consequently, they gave little consideration to what was involved in the continual monitoring and sanctioning of LFOs. Fewer still outside of the criminal justice system are aware of how much time county clerks and judges spend imposing and monitoring LFOs. And even legally savvy defendants and attorneys do not fully understand how LFOs undermine legal rights to due process and the equal application of justice.

Monetary sanctions empower clerks to enforce highly individualized policies. In enforcing sentencing orders, they devise means for overseeing and sanctioning unresponsive or insolvent defendants. As a consequence of the ambiguity in the statutes, clerks wield a great deal of power in how they judge defendants, and few safeguards are in place to protect defendants against uneven or unjust sanctioning or abuse of power. The exercise of power is a central feature of the system of monetary sanctions. Judges, clerks, and prosecutors use LFOs to control people with legal debt. After punishment has been dispensed within a courtroom, within the confines of a jail or prison, or through the imposition of labor in a community service program or work crew, debtors continue to face perpetual punishment simply because of their inability to pay.

Punishment through monetary sanctions is imposed on and experienced by a wide range of people. During a probation violation hearing, I observed a young man, Scott, waiting in line; he was called up to the clerk's station in front of me. As Scott handed over $35, the older man who accompanied him told the clerk that he was not his father but his employer. The clerk began by saying:

> Clerk: You were supposed to pay $100. You were in for sentencing. You were released from the jail and told to pay $100. Do you have $65 more?
>
> Scott: No.
>
> Clerk: You will have to wait for the judge.
>
> Employer: What happens if he doesn't pay the $65?
>
> Clerk: He could go to jail. Do you have a credit card with $65?
>
> Scott: No, it's all I got. [*He walks away.*]
>
> Employer: Will the judge give me time to scrounge around for more money?
>
> Clerk: No.
>
> Employer: So I have to go to the ATM right now?
>
> Clerk: Yes.

Both the employer and Scott leave and later return with a payment receipt. While the employer is paying, I hear him give the clerk a mailing address that includes "care of."

Clerk: Are you related?

Employer: No, I have a vested interest. *As of today I own him.*[10] He is one of my mechanics.

Just like social control systems of the past—slavery, indentured servitude, and convict leasing—the system of monetary sanctions generates perverse, indeterminate, and punitive relationships both within and outside of the criminal justice system.

Even when debtors provided documentation that they had no means to make payments, clerks and judges scoured them for resources. They inquired about conspicuous spending habits, looked at fingernails for recent manicures, and asked about tattooing and smoking. Regular summonses to court were mailed, wages were garnished to tap into defendants' financial assets, bench warrants were issued, and sentences that had initially been stayed, deferred, and diverted were revoked. When people failed to appear in court, they were arrested and incarcerated.

Many court officials and defendants alike recognized that whatever the costs of not appearing at an LFO hearing, there were also costs associated with showing up. Defendants were fearful of being incarcerated, and many were frustrated by their inability to pay; some did not even know they had been served because they had no stable place to live where they could receive mail. In more punitive counties, defendants with legal debt were regularly incarcerated for nonpayment. But even in less punitive counties, jail time was used to punish nonpaying offenders, particularly those who owed restitution. The variation in experiences of justice and punishment led to arbitrary justice and impeded a sense of fairness.

Maintaining Class Inequality

Monetary sanctions reinforce existing class inequalities by sentencing a population that is often undereducated, unemployed, homeless, and physically or mentally disabled to pay relatively large amounts of money. The criminal justice system manages the poorest of our society. Surveys of county jails across the nation have highlighted the impoverished circumstances from which inmates are pulled. Nearly half (44 percent) of inmates in local jails have less than a high school diploma or GED. Overwhelmingly, felony defendants come from poverty-stricken neighborhoods with high rates of under- and unemployment and failed school systems. Monetary sanctions reinforce existing inequalities and exacerbate poverty in these areas by overburdening already marginalized people with debt they can never pay off.[11] It is no exaggeration to say that imposing financial penalties on such defendants directly sustains poverty.

Perpetuating Racial and Ethnic Inequality

Existing racial and ethnic disparities in criminal justice contact and its consequences are exacerbated by the imposition of monetary sanctions. African Americans, Native Americans, and Latinos are disproportionately convicted and incarcerated, and the burden of monetary sanctions is disproportionately borne by people of color. While one in one hundred American adults eighteen years of age or older live behind bars, there are dramatic differences by race: one in eighty-seven white men, one in thirty-six Latino men, and one in twelve black men are incarcerated in the United States. Among recent generations, people who drop out of high school have much higher odds of being incarcerated than those with a GED or diploma. Of black men born between 1965 and 1969, 30 percent of those without a college education and 60 percent of those without a high school diploma had gone to prison by age thirty-five. The risk of incarceration has only increased for more recent generations: of men born between 1975 and 1979 who dropped out of high school, an estimated 28 percent of white men, just over 19 percent of Latino men, and 68 percent of black men have experienced prison. Becky Pettit and Bruce Western have concluded that "prison time has become a normal life event for African American men who have dropped out of high school."[12] Monetary sanctions, solely because racialized communities are the disproportionate focus of the criminal justice system, are imposed in a disparate way on people of color and thus are implicated in perpetuating racial and ethnic inequality.

The Place of Monetary Sanctions in the Legacy of U.S. Social Control

Criminalization and Debt

The United States has a long history of both informal and formal practices linking the punishment of its marginalized populations to processes of debt. Debtors' prisons were transported from Europe, where they were common, and used in the United States up until the early 1830s as a way to punish impoverished people who were unable to pay their private debts. Today monetary sanctions incarcerate people who are free but poor.

U.S. history provides several other examples of systems of social control that link criminalization and servitude. One of the earliest systems was the institution of slavery. From the seventeenth century until the mid-nineteenth century, the American economy was based on plantation farming and relied on fiscally inexpensive laborers—enslaved Africans. From the 1830s through the 1850s, as the economy began to industrialize, enslaved people were "leased out" by their "owners" to work on railroad construction and in coal mines.[13] Termed "slave leasing," the practice lasted until the legal abolishment of slavery in the 1860s.

"Convict leasing" is another example of a U.S. social control practice linked to debt. Similar to slave leasing, convict leasing began in Alabama in 1846 and lasted through 1928. For a fixed rate, state prison systems would lease their inmates to private individuals and companies engaged in plantation farming, railroad construction, and coal mining. Some historians suggest that the practice of convict leasing replaced the use of slave labor. In fact, previous owners of enslaved people were able to lease convicts to work the same land that enslaved people had previously worked.[14] As a system, convict leasing enabled states to manage their costly prison systems, control their unemployed African American population, and generate state income. When the violent and deadly treatment of prisoners by private entrepreneurs came to light, states began to abolish their systems of convict leasing throughout the early 1900s, with North Carolina being the last state to end the practice in 1933.

During the late nineteenth century and the early twentieth century, a new form of social control emerged, particularly in the South: African Americans were disproportionately arrested, convicted, and incarcerated in comparison to their white counterparts as authorities enforced the "Black Codes" that had been developed to monitor the behavior of the formerly enslaved.[15] These laws codified certain everyday behaviors of African Americans: standing in one area of town became "loitering," and walking at night was now "breaking curfew." Also listed under the Black Codes were "crimes" such as "free negro alone" and "insulting gestures." African Americans in the South convicted under the Black Codes were incarcerated and made to labor. As a result of the Black Codes, the percentage of African Americans in prison grew exponentially.[16]

Around the same time, an extensive prison system was developed in the South in the interest of maintaining the racial and economic relationship of slavery; this revised system of social control imposed forced prison labor.[17] It is commonly believed that the Thirteenth Amendment to the U.S. Constitution, ratified in December 1865, outlawed the use of slavery for everyone. Yet the actual language allows for the involuntary servitude of people convicted of crimes.[18] Slavery is legal for convicted offenders, and hard labor can be viewed as an expression of offenders' debt to society for their crimes. As the historian Douglass Blackmon explains: "Every southern state except Arkansas and Tennessee had passed laws by the end of 1865 outlawing vagrancy and so vaguely defining it that virtually any freed slave not under the protection of a white man could be arrested for the crime."[19]

At the very same time in U.S. history when African Americans were freed from slavery—with no wealth, income, or formal education and while living in impoverished states—a system of conviction and punishment was developed by local leaders that allowed for their legal reenslavement.[20] Moreover, the system permitted the imposition of forced labor as punishment.

Even today, state administrators still view the use of convicts for labor as a profitable and productive enterprise. One example of the type of plantation farm where prisoners are forced to work is Louisiana's Angola Prison. In 1880 the former Confederate major Samuel James purchased the 8,000-acre plantation that is known today as Angola— originally named for the region in Africa where the plantation's workers were from—with the goal of using convict labor as field hands. The James family ran the plantation using convict labor until it was purchased by the state of Louisiana in 1901 and converted into a prison. Slave quarters were transformed into prison cell units.[21] Louisiana continues to rely on prison and jail inmates as inexpensive farm and textile laborers. In 2015 convicts in Louisiana put to work as farm laborers generated $2 million in agricultural profits for the Department of Corrections. Prisoners also work in other industries, such as the manufacture of office furniture, clothing, custom trash receptacles, and horse pens. In total, prison labor generated just over $11 million for the state of Louisiana in 2011.[22]

Throughout American history, state officials have forced some people to labor as slaves or as those deemed to be criminals or moral affronts in order to generate fiscal resources for both private and public industry. Systems such as debtors' prisons, slavery, slave leasing, convict leasing, and forced labor camps have been used by state and local governments as well as by private business owners to extract labor, to punish the impoverished, and to remove citizenship rights from those labeled as criminal offenders.

Social Control and Power

Monetary sanctions are used both to punish inappropriate behavior and to invade the lives of those deemed criminal. The criminal justice system has extended its reach beyond the walls of jails and prisons to control the actions and statements of felons in the name of "accountability." Within the past twenty years, the criminal justice system has developed specialized drug, alcohol, family, and community courts and day reporting centers where people are forced to regularly act remorseful, urinate in cups, notify probation officers of all their activities, and report their behavior and thoughts to judges. All of their actions are subject to court officials' interpretations of the degree to which they are remorseful or contrite about their original offenses. Further, social control mechanisms criminalize public spaces for certain people, and probation serves as a way to scrutinize their every movement. In an accountability-centered era of social control, the imposition of monetary sanctions serves as an important tool that keeps people under the legal supervision of the criminal justice system. Defendants cannot be deemed to have been held fully accountable for their crimes until they pay their financial penalties.

The use of monetary sanctions as a form of punishment of criminal offenders serves in much the same way as prior mechanisms to control and further marginalize citizens deemed unworthy of redemption. The national use of monetary sanctions across state courts is consistent with past and current legal methods of controlling the bodies of people by incarcerating them, labeling them as distinctly different, and allowing legal discrimination against them and the extraction of their labor or other financial resources. The current mechanisms control marginalized populations in the same way that has prevailed throughout U.S. history: by imposing physical incarceration and economic sanctions on them. The story of monetary sanctions is about the management of poverty, the maintenance of inequality, and the punishment of the poor in the United States.

Why We Should Care

The imposition of LFOs further marginalizes offenders—politically, socially, and economically. Because of the lack of court data, we do not know the extent of total debt owed by legal debtors in the United States, nor is there much information about the total amounts collected by state and local jurisdictions. There is also no consistency in how courts and jails keep track of defendants incarcerated purely for nonpayment. We do not know how many people are being jailed or how much money is being spent to incarcerate people for nonpayment. Future research should examine the total criminal justice resources consumed in managing legal debtors, collecting outstanding debt, and sanctioning those who have not made payments. An economic analysis would shed light on the financial efficiency of the system of monetary sanctions. We also lack data that would help us analyze the relationships between the imposition of debt, the amount of LFOs, and subsequent arrest, probation violation, conviction, and incarceration. Another question remains unaddressed: how might the practice of monetary sanctions, and the related consequences for those who are unable to pay, enforce or undermine public safety?

In sum, monetary sanctions prevent many defendants from successfully reentering their communities after their conviction, developing positive social and emotional identities that would promote their desistance, becoming financially independent, and living stable lives. Policies should be developed to ensure that only defendants with the ability to pay at the time of their conviction are sentenced to nonrestitution sanctions. Clear criteria should be incorporated into state monetary sanction statutes that define "indigent" and "current ability to pay." Judges should be required to apply each criterion to arrive at individualized assessments of defendants' current financial status. Only those with financial resources and incomes—from sources other than state or federal benefits—should be deemed eligible for monetary sanctions. Furthermore, collection costs and interest should not be applied to outstanding debt; by imposing additional punishment on those unable to make payments in full, these charges amount to a penalty for living in poverty or precarious financial circumstances.

Reformed practices such as these would ensure that victims are truly the priority in the punishment process and that indigent defendants would avoid being saddled with legal debt that they will owe forever and instead receive a realistic punishment that they have the means of fulfilling.

Conclusion

In Greek mythology, Sisyphus was sentenced to the punishment of pushing a giant boulder up a hill over and over again. Once he reached the top, it would roll back down the hill, where it waited for him to push it back up. The key difference between today's legal debtors and Sisyphus is that at least Sisyphus had a brief break as he walked down the hill before restarting his endless task. For legal debtors shouldering the burden of increasing legal debt, the hill just keeps getting higher and higher. When, if ever, will legal debtors be deemed as having demonstrated their remorse and accountability for their offenses? How can they remove the stain of their criminal records legally and socially? How can policymakers and practitioners expect poor people to pay when they have nothing to give?

The present-day system of monetary sanctions is neither as physically egregious nor as publicly known as the systems of convict leasing and forced labor camps, but it has eerily similar practices, and the consequences are the same for those with criminal convictions—political, social, and economic marginalization for life. Thus, the linkage between criminal justice and social control institutions that overselect for the poor and for people of color remains embedded in U.S. criminal justice practices. One exceptional and prominent iteration of the U.S. system of social control of the poor and socially marginalized is the monetary sanction system.

Consistent throughout the history of the United States has been an inextricable and insidious link between social control, class, race, and economic burden, be it labor or debt. By interrogating this particular punishment tool of today's criminal justice system, *A Pound of Flesh* has presented evidence about the durable bond between mechanisms of social control and inequality in the United States. The system of monetary sanctions is eerily reflected in literature's classic stories of systems of control and justice, from the surreal and hopeless situations in which debtors find themselves as they face bureaucratic absurdity and experience alienation and persecution in the writings of Franz Kafka to similar depictions of debtors' prisons in the works of Charles Dickens.[23] In the reality of so many individuals' lives, monetary sanctions generate and perpetuate poverty. The criminal justice system has become a stratifying institution that labels its subjects and further decreases their status in society. The imposition of legal debt compounds the stratifying power and consequences of the justice system. Because people of color and the poor disproportionately make contact with the criminal justice system and are more likely to be convicted and incarcerated, legal debt is particularly oppressive for members of these already disadvantaged groups. People are sentenced to marginalized status, condemned to poor credit ratings, kept under the continual surveillance of the criminal justice system, and regularly incarcerated.

The U.S. legal system promises evenhanded imposition of justice and due process, but that promise is not kept by the system of monetary sanctions, which permanently punishes the poor. This system is at odds with a social and economic system premised on equality of opportunity, if not outcome. Monetary sanctions harken back to the times of debtors' prisons, slavery, and the Black Codes, social control institutions that prized one's property, ability to labor, and skin color above all else. People who make contact with the criminal justice system experience hyperpoliced neighborhoods, underfunded and poor-quality schools, a lack of decent housing, and a shortage of living-wage jobs. They are then saddled with felony convictions and related collateral consequences. There is no question that after the sentencing of LFOs the only collateral that defendants have left is a pound of their flesh. In naming and uncovering this social control practice, describing the system and related outcomes, and analyzing the rhetoric used to justify its existence, we can clearly see that the system of monetary sanctions is a "natural" extension of prior systems of social control in the United States.

Methodological Appendix

Chapter 1

As very little scholarly attention has been paid to monetary sanctions, I attempted to gather all and any types of data available in order to illustrate the national and state-level system of monetary sanctions. The initial phase of my study relied heavily on descriptive and statistical analyses. After highlighting the practice and consequences of monetary sanctions in contemporary U.S. punishment systems, I decided that I needed to explore monetary sanctions practices on the ground level. As such, my analysis is a "kitchen sink" illumination of contemporary sentencing practices regarding fines and fees. In my mixed-method approach, I combine a variety of data sources (interviews with court personnel, defendants, and policymakers, observations of court sentencing and violation hearings, national and state legal statutes and case law, county-level fiscal and account information, and Washington Administrative Office of the Courts [AOC] sentencing data) with several analytic strategies (open and closed coding of interview and observation transcripts, hand-diagraming of relationships between concepts and issues coded, closed coding of legal statutes and case law, descriptive statistical analysis of county fiscal data and court data, and OLS regression of court data) (see table A1.1). I use the data to present both a broad description of the reliance on monetary sanctions nationally and a narrow analysis of how legal debtors are sentenced, monitored, and punished for insufficient payment or nonpayment in Washington. I sought and received the University of Washington's Institutional Review Board approval to conduct every aspect of the study.

Chapter 2

A number of graduate and undergraduate research assistants helped me assemble the review of the national monetary sanction statutes. During a sociology senior research practicum that I taught in the spring

Table A1.1   Description of Data Collected for Study of Monetary Sanctions Practices and Policies in Five Washington Counties

	Number/Data or Document Type	Year
Observations	135 total	
Sentencing hearings	85	2010
Violation hearings	50	2010, 2011
Interviews	102 total	
Felony defendants[a]	50	2007
Case studies	5	2011
Judges	15	2008–2011
Attorneys	14	2011
Clerks	8	2011
State legislators	4	2011
Community corrections officers	6	2007
Statistical data		
Census data	State and county level	2000, 2010
Washington courts[b]	3,300 cases	2004
Legal documents	Varied	
National and state criminal statutes		
State, appellate, and supreme court cases		
Online legislative session hearings		

Source: Author's summary of data used in book.
[a]The author's collaborators interviewed forty-one of the felony defendants and collected their surveys.
[b]Washington State Sentencing Guidelines Commission (SGC) and Administrative Office of the Courts (AOC) (2004).

of 2011, a law librarian and I trained twenty-five students in searching both the Internet and the law library for relevant state statutes. I assigned each student two states for which they were to conduct a close coding of each state's statute references to fines, fees, surcharges, and interest for felony convictions. Their research provided the initial template for tables 2.4 and A2.2. Two graduate research assistants, Jorge Martinez and Heather Evans, and an undergraduate research assistant, Peter Keckemet, reviewed every citation and state statute for accuracy (and filled in incomplete or missing states), and Heather constructed table A2.2, which lists all references. The undergraduate seminar students were: Asma Abdulrahman, Nahom Beyene, Arnel Custic, Trupti Gadgil, Stacey Giffen, Daniel Ha, Gordon Hayes Jr., Roxana Johnson, Hai Xin Lu, Sean Millsap, Fahima Mohamed, Meagen Morrice, Rachel

Table A2.1   National Characteristics of U.S. State Monetary Sanctions Procedures, 2014

	Yes	No	Provisional	Unknown
Impose fines and fees on felons	100%	0%	0%	0%
Charge additional financing fees	63%	25%	0%	12%
Charge for public attorney	69%	29%	0%	2%
Incarcerate legal debtors for nonpayment	90%	4%	0%	6%
Sentence to community service	68%	20%	4%	8%
Allow debtors to vote	41%	33%	26%	0%

Source: Author's review of national state statutes.

Nusser, Kainon Pierce, Joseph Pugh, Matthew Rabon, Iain Redding, Taylor Richman, Leah Rust, Anna Shwab, Holly Tracy, Seerat Virk, and Thuong Vo. I am grateful for their work on what I now refer to as "the monster table."

Chapter 3

Interviews with People Who Had Felony Convictions

Respondents with felony convictions were recruited through approximately fifty flyers posted over a period of two months in a variety of clerk, court, social service, and DOC offices, as well as by word of mouth. Two colleagues from a previous study and I interviewed and surveyed fifty people who had at least one felony conviction from one or more of the five Washington counties. The sample obtained is a convenience sample. The aim of the data collection was to talk with people who owed legal debt to understand their perspectives on the criminal justice system and how their financial sentences had affected their lives.

We paid participants $20 for their time. Each interview began with a survey questionnaire to ensure that the following key background questions were consistently asked of all respondents: the year of the respondent's last felony conviction; the number of felony convictions; estimated amount of legal debt; monthly income; demographic characteristics; housing situation; marital status; and number of children.[1] After the surveys were administered, interviewers posed more open-ended questions to assess how legal debt had affected our respondents. How had they acquired information about their LFO? How was their monthly minimum payment determined? Did they make regular pay-

(Text continues on p. 178.)

Table A2.2   Legal Citations for Federal and State Review of Monetary Sanctions Statutes and Related Consequences, 2014

State	Example of LFO (Fine or Fee) Statute	Example of Fees and Surcharges for Felony Convictions	Charge for Public Defense?
Alabama	Alabama (ALA) Code, Title 13A, Criminal Code—Section 13A-5-11	ALA Code, Section 12-17-225.4	ALA Code, Section 15-12-25(a)
Alaska	Alaska Statutes (AS), Title 12, Section 12.55.035	AS, Title 12, Section 12.55.051	
Arizona	Arizona Revised Statutes (ARS), Title 13, Chapter 8, Section 13-801	ARS (annotated), Sections 12-116.01(A)-(C) and 12-116.03	ARS, Section 11-584(C)-(E)
Arkansas	Arkansas (AR) Code, Title 5, Section 5-4-201	AR Code, Section 16-98-304 (2012)	AR Code, Section 16-87-213
California	California Penal Code (CPC), Section 1170	CPC, Sections 1464 and 1214.1(a)	CPC, Section 987.5
Colorado	Colorado Revised Statutes (CRS), Sections 18-1.3-401 and 16-11-101.6	CRS, Section 16-11-101.6	CRS, Section 21-1-103(3)
Connecticut	Connecticut General Statutes (CGS), Title 53a, Chapter 952, Section 53a-41	CGS, Sections 54-143 (2012) and (54-56i)	CGS, Section 51-298 (2012)
Delaware	Delaware (DE) Code, Title 11, Chapter 41, Section 4101	DE Code, Title 11, Chapter 41, Section 4104	DE Code, Title 29, Chapter 46, Section 4607
District of Columbia	District of Columbia (DC) Code, Section 4-516	DC Code, Title 4, Chapter 5, Sections 4-516 and 15-709	
Florida	Florida Statutes (FS), Sections 775.082 and 775.083	FS, Section 938.03(1, 4)	FS, Section 938.29(1)(a)

Penalty for Incomplete Payment or Nonpayment	Community Service Provision?	Incarceration for "Willful" Nonpayment?	Can Debtors Vote?
ALA Code, Section 12-17-225.4	ALA Code, Section 12-23-18	ALA Code, Section 15-18-62	ALA Code, Section 15-22-36.1(a)(3)
AS, Title 12, Section 12.55.051	AS, Section 12.55.055	AS, Title 12, Section 12.55.051	AS, Section 15.05.030
ARS (annotated), Sections 12-116(a) and 13-810		ARS (annotated), Section 13-810	ARS (annotated), Section 13-912(A)(2)
AR Code, Sections 5-4-205 and 16-92-118			Brennan Center for Justice
CPC, Section 1214.1(a)	Nieto (2006)	CPC, Section 1205(b)	California Secretary of State's Office, "Voter's Guide"
CRS, Section 16-11-101.6	CRS, Section 18-1.3-104	CRS, Section 18-1.3-702	Colorado Constitution, Article 7, Section 10
CGS, Section 54-147 (2012)		CGS, Section 54-92b (2012)	CGS, Sections 3 and 9-46a
	DE Code, Title 11, Chapter 41, Section 4332A	DE Code, Title 11, Chapter 41, Sections 4105(d) and 4334	
		DC Code, Title 16, Chapter 7, Section 16-706	Bannon et al. (2010)
Bannon et al. (2010)	Florida Statutes Annotated (FSA), Section 938.30(2)	Bannon et al. (2010), 22	FS, Section 775.089

(Table continues on p. 168.)

Table A2.2 *Continued*

State	Example of LFO (Fine or Fee) Statute	Example of Fees and Surcharges for Felony Convictions	Charge for Public Defense?
Georgia	Official Code of Georgia Annotated (OCGA), Title 17, Section 17-10-8	OCGA, Sections 15-21-92 and 15-21-93	OCGA, Sections 15-21A-6(c) and 17-12-51
Hawaii	Hawaii Revised Statutes (HRS), Title 37, Chapter 706, Section 706-640	HRS, Sections 706-648 and 706-648	HRS, Section 802-7
Idaho	Idaho Statutes (IS), Title 18, Section 18-112; Title 19, Chapter 47, Section 19-4708(4)	IS, Sections 19-2516, 31-3201H, and 31-3201(3)–(5)	
Illinois	730 Illinois Compiled Statutes (ILCS), Section 5/5-4.5-50(b)	Bannon et al. (2010), 10	725 ILCS, Section 5/113-3.1
Indiana	Indiana Code (IC), Section 35-50-2-4	IC, Section 33-37-4-1(a)	IC, Section 33-37-2-3d(3)e
Iowa	Iowa Code (IC), Section IC 909.2	IC, Section 911.1	IC, Sections 910.9, 815.9, and 815.14
Kansas	Kansas Statutes Annotated (KSA), Section 21-6611	KSA, Section 28-172.b	KSA, Section 22-4529
Kentucky	Kentucky Revised Statutes (KRS) (annotated), Section 534.030	KRS, Sections 24A.175 and 346	KRS, Section 31.211
Louisiana	Louisiana Revised Statutes (LRS), Title 15; Louisiana Code of Criminal Procedure (CCRP), Sections 890.2, 884, and 885.1	CCRP (annotated), Article 887(F)(2)	LRS, Sections 15:175(A)(1)(f) and 15:176

Penalty for Incomplete Payment or Nonpayment	Community Service Provision?	Incarceration for "Willful" Nonpayment?	Can Debtors Vote?
OCGA, Section 17-14-14(d)	OCGA, Section 17-10-1(d)	Bannon et al. (2010), 6	Georgia Constitution, Article II, Section 1(3)
	HRS, Section 706-644(4)	HRS, Section 706-644	Bannon et al. (2010)
IS, Section 19-4708(1)	Canyon County, Idaho, "Sheriff's Inmate Labor Detail Program"	IS, Title 18, Section 18-303; Idaho Criminal Rules (ICR), S33(f)(1)	Bannon et al. (2010)
Bannon et al. (2010), 17	Bannon et al. (2010), 15; for drug offenses (e.g., possession of cannabis): 720 ILCS, Section 550/10.3(e)	730 ILCS 5/5-8-6(d) explicitly bans incarceration	Bannon et al. (2010)
IC, Section 33-37-5-22(4)c		IC, Section 33-37-2-3d(2)	Bannon et al. (2010)
IC, Section 909.3	IC, Section 909.3A		Bannon et al. (2010)
KSA, Section 16-204	KSA, Sections 21-4728 and 21-6604	KSA, Section 22-3425	KSA, Section 21-6613
	KRS, Section 534.070	KRS, Sections 534.060 and 534.070	Bannon et al. (2010)
Bannon et al. (2010), 6	CCRP, Article 895(D)	ACLU (2010), note 8	Bannon et al. (2010), 20

(Table continues on p. 170.)

Table A2.2 *Continued*

State	Example of LFO (Fine or Fee) Statute	Example of Fees and Surcharges for Felony Convictions	Charge for Public Defense?
Maine	Maine Revised Statutes (MRS), Title 17-A, Chapter 53, Section 1301(1)a	MRS, Title 17-A, chapter 53, Section 1301(4)	
Maryland	Annotated Code of Maryland (ACM), Title 7, Chapter 5, Sections 7-503 and 7-504	Maryland Courts, Article 7-202, Rule 4-353	
Massachu-setts	Massachusetts General Law (MAGL), Part IV, Title II, Chapter 280, Section 6B	MAGL, Part IV, Title II, Chapter 280, Section 6	
Michigan	Michigan Code of Criminal Procedure (MCCP), Act 175, Section 769.1J	MCCP, Act 175, Section 769.1J; Bannon et al. (2010), 10	Bannon et al. (2010), 10
Minnesota	Minnesota Revised Statutes (MNRS), Chapter 609, Section 0341	MNRS, Sections 631.48; 357.021(2), 357.021(6), and 480.15(10c)	State of Minnesota, "Application for a Public Defender"
Mississippi	Mississippi (MS) Code, Sections 99-19-20 and 32	MS Code, Section 99-19-73(6, 7)	
Missouri	Missouri Revised Statutes (MRS), Title XXXVIII, Chapter 560, Section .011	(MRS, Sections 595.045(8) and 488.0101.1	MRS, Section 600.090(1)
Montana	Montana Code (MC) (annotated), Section 46-18-231	MC (annotated), Section 46-18-232	
Nebraska	Nebraska Revised Statutes (NRS), chapter 28, sec-tion 105	NRS, sections 33-107.03, 33-106, and 24-703	NRS, section 29-3908

Penalty for Incomplete Payment or Nonpayment	Community Service Provision?	Incarceration for "Willful" Nonpayment?	Can Debtors Vote?
MRS, title 14, Chapter 502-A, Section 3142 (civil fine for contempt of court up to $500)	MRS, Title 17-A, Chapter 5, Section 1304(A) (2)	MRS, Title 17-A, Chapter 5, Section 1304(A) (1)	Bannon et al. (2010)
			Bannon et al. (2010)
	MAGL, Part IV, Title II, Chapter 279(1)	MAGL, Part IV, Title II, Chapter 279(7)	Bannon et al. (2010)
Bannon et al. (2010), 14	Bannon et al. (2010), 17	Bannon et al. (2010), 21–22	Bannon et al. (2010)
MNRS, Section 480.15			Bannon et al. (2010)
	MS Code, Section 99-19-20(2)a	MS Code, Section 480.15(10c)	Bannon et al. (2010)
	Bannon et al. (2010), 17	Bannon et al. (2010), 6	Bannon et al. (2010), 20
			Bannon et al. (2010)
	NRS, section 29-2278	NRS, sections 29-2206.01 and 29-2412	

(Table continues on p. 172.)

Table A2.2 *Continued*

State	Example of LFO (Fine or Fee) Statute	Example of Fees and Surcharges for Felony Convictions	Charge for Public Defense?
Nevada	Nevada Revised Statutes (NRS), Section 176.064	NRS, Section 176.0623 (2013)	
New Hampshire	New Hampshire Statutes (NHS), Title LXII, Chapter 651, Section 2(9)a	NHS, Title LXII, Chapter 618, Section 14	
New Jersey	New Jersey Revised Statutes (NJRS), Section 2C:43-3 (2013)	NJRS, Section 2C:43-3.3 (2013)	New Jersey Office of the Public Defender ($50 fee for a public defender)
New Mexico	New Mexico Statutes (NMS), Section 31-18-15(E)1	NMS, Sections 31-12-6 and 29-16-11	NMS, Section 31-16-7
New York	New York Penal Law (NYPL), Title E, Article 80.00	NYPL, Section 60.35(a)(i, ii)	Bannon et al. (2010), 12
North Carolina	North Carolina General Statutes (NCGS), Sections 15A-1340.17 and 15A-1362	NCGS, Article 28, Section 7A-304	Bannon et al. (2010), 6
North Dakota	North Dakota Century Code (NDCC), Chapter 12, Section 12.1-32-01	NDCC, Section 12.1-32-08(10)	NDCC, Section 12.1-32-08(1)(a)
Ohio	Ohio Revised Code (ORC), Title 29, Chapter 2929, Sections 18(B)3 and 2947.09	ORC, Section 2743.70 (2013)	Bannon et al. (2010), 12

Penalty for Incomplete Payment or Nonpayment	Community Service Provision?	Incarceration for "Willful" Nonpayment?	Can Debtors Vote?
NRS, Section 176.064 (2013)	NRS, Section 176.0623 (2013)	NRS, Sections 176.064(3)(d) and 176.065	Bannon et al. (2010)
Revised Statutes Annotated (RSA), Section 490:26-a(II-a) ($25 fee for payment plan)		NHS, Title LXII, Section 618:9	Bannon et al. (2010)
	NJRS, Section 2C:46-2(2)	NJRS, Section 2C:46-2(2)	State of New Jersey, Department of State, "Voter Registration and Voting"
	NMS, Section 31-12-3	NMS, Section 31-12-3(C)	Bannon et al. (2010)
	Bannon et al. (2010), 17	New York State Criminal Procedure Law (CPL), Section 420.10 (2012)	Bannon et al. (2010)
Bannon et al. (2010), 7	Bannon et al. (2010), 17	NCGS, Section 15A-1364(b)	Bannon et al. (2010), 29
NDCC, Section 12.1-32-05.	North Dakota Department of Corrections and Rehabilitation, "Parole and Probation . . . Community Service"	NDCC, Section 12.1-32-05	Bannon et al. (2010)
Bannon et al. (2010), 15	Bannon et al. (2010), 17	ORC, Section 2947.14	Bannon et al. (2010)

(Table continues on p. 174.)

Table A2.2   *Continued*

State	Example of LFO (Fine or Fee) Statute	Example of Fees and Surcharges for Felony Convictions	Charge for Public Defense?
Oklahoma	Oklahoma Statutes (OS), Section 2164	OS, Sections 21-142.18 and 20-1313.2(c)	OS, Sections 22-1355.14C and 22-1355A
Oregon	Oregon Revised Statutes (ORS), Section 161.625	ORS, Section 137.540(7, 11)	ORS, Section 161.665
Pennsylvania	Pennsylvania Consolidated Statutes (PCS), Title 18, Chapter 11, Section 1106; Pennsylvania Consolidated Statutes (PaCS), Title 42, Section 9728	Bannon et al. (2010), 9	
Rhode Island	Rhode Island General Laws (RIGL), Sections 12-19-23.2, 12-21-20, and 12-20-10	RIGL, Section 12-18.1-3	
South Carolina	South Carolina Code of Laws (SCCL), Section 17-25-350	SCCL, Section 16-23-50	SCCL, Section 17-3-30
South Dakota	South Dakota Codified Laws (SDCL), Title 22, Chapter 22-6-1, Section 23A-27-25.2	SDCL, Section 23A-27-27	
Tennessee	Tennessee Code Annotated (TCA), Sections 40-35-111 and 40-24	TCA, Sections 41-11-103 and 8-21-401(d)	TCA, Section 40-14-210

Penalty for Incomplete Payment or Nonpayment	Community Service Provision?	Incarceration for "Willful" Nonpayment?	Can Debtors Vote?
OS, Section 28-32.3	OS, Section 22-1514(4)	OS, Section 22-983	Bannon et al. (2010)
ORS, Sections 137.118 and 1.202(1); Chief Justice Order 11-027	ORS, Section 137.128	ORS, Section 161.685	ORS, Section 137.275
Bannon et al. (2010), 6	Bannon et al. (2010), 17	PCS, Title 42, Chapter 41, Section 4137(c)	Bannon et al. (2010)
	RIGL, Section 12-19-23.2	RIGL, Section 12-21-9	Bannon et al. (2010)
SCCL, Section 14-17-725		SCCL, Sections 17-25-340 and 17-25-350	Bannon et al. (2010)
	SDCL, Section 23A-27-25.1	SDCL, Section 23A-27-25.6	Bannon et al. (2010)
TCA, Section 40-24-101		TCA, Section 40-24-104	Bannon et al. (2010)

(Table continues on p. 176.)

Table A2.2   *Continued*

State	Example of LFO (Fine or Fee) Statute	Example of Fees and Surcharges for Felony Convictions	Charge for Public Defense?
Texas	Texas Statutes (TS), Chapters 42.15 and 43.03	Bannon et al. (2010), 10; Texas Code of Criminal Procedure (CCP), Sections 42.038 and 102.0215 (Government Code, (Harris County)	TS, Article 26.05
Utah	Utah Code (UC), Title 76-3-301	UC, Section 51-9-401	UC, Section 77-32-202
Vermont	Vermont Statutes Annotated (VSA), Title 13, Section 7252	VSA, Title 13, Sections 7252 and 7282	VSA, Title 13, Section 5240
Virginia	Code of Virginia (CV), Title 18, Section 18.2-10; Title 19.2, Section 19.2-340.1	Bannon et al. (2010), note 42	CV, Section 19.2-163.4:1
Washington	Revised Code of Washington (RCW), Sections 9.94A.760 and 9.94A.550	ACLU (2010), 65–69	RCW, Section 10.101.020
West Virginia	West Virginia (WV) Code, Section 62-5-7	WV Code, Sections 62-5-10, 62-11C-7, and 62-4-8	
Wisconsin	Wisconsin Statutes (WS), Section 973.05	WS, Sections 973.043, 973.044, 973.045, 973.046, 973.047, and 973.0438	WS, Section 977.075
Wyoming	Wyoming Statutes (WS), Section 6-10-102	WS, Sections 7-11-505, 6-10-102, 5-2-120, and 5-2-121	WS, Section 6-10-102
United States (federal)	Title 18, Sections 3571 and 3013(A)(2)(A)		

Source: Author review of online and University of Washington Law Library collection of state statutes.

Notes: State statute information is current as of June 2014. Each state is constantly amending laws and making new ones. In addition, the counties within states vary widely in how they interpret and operationalize state statutes, with resulting variations in practice.

Penalty for Incomplete Payment or Nonpayment	Community Service Provision?	Incarceration for "Willful" Nonpayment?	Can Debtors Vote?
TS, Sections 133.103(a) and 132.006 (Local Government Code, Harris County)	TS, Article 43.09(f)	TS, Article 43.03(a)	CCP (annotated), Article 42.12(22)(c)
	Utah Uniform Fine/Bail Forfeiture Schedule 2014:10		Bannon et al. (2010)
	VSA, Title 28, Section 808(7)	VSA, Title 13, Section 7180	Bannon et al. (2010)
Bannon et al. (2010), 14	Bannon et al. (2010), 17	CV, Section 19.2-354	Bannon et al. (2010), note 215
ACLU (2010), 65, 66	RCW, Section 9.94B.040	RCW, Sections 9.94A.634(3)(c) and 9.94A.631	Bannon et al. (2010)
WV Code, Section 62-4-17	WV Code, Section 62-4-16	WV Code, Sections 62-4-9 and 10	Bannon et al. (2010)
	WS, Section 973.05(3)(a)	WS, Section 973.07	Bannon et al. (2010)
		WS, Section 6-10-105	Bannon et al. (2010)

ments? If so, why? If they did not make regular payments, why not? What had been the consequences for them of making or not making regular payments? The open-ended portion of the interviews was digitally recorded, and the recordings were transcribed for analyses.

Case Studies

I used the first set of interviews and my observations of courtroom hearings to choose five more people who had experienced legal debt to interview as case studies. My aim was to expand the interview questions and incorporate initial findings from courtroom observations to get a better sense of how legal debt had affected these individuals' lives. Although five case studies can in no way be representative of the thousands of ex-felons riddled with legal debt in Washington, the analysis of their lives sheds light on how legal debt can accumulate, how debtors attempt to personally and institutionally manage their debt (via the criminal justice system, nonprofit organizations, or credit granting or collection organizations), and the individual, familial, and community consequences of paying or not paying debt. These case studies also allowed me to examine the effects of monetary sanctions on individuals' lives—how they perceived and experienced the LFO process and how legal debt affected them legally, financially, socially, and emotionally.

The case study interviews covered three subthemes. I recorded basic demographic information: respondent's age, race-ethnicity, education, housing and family situation, number of felonies, and times and duration of incarceration (if experienced). I explored interviewees' experiences and their perceptions about legal debt being imposed on them as a punishment. I also asked about each conviction and the associated LFO. I asked the case study interviewees about the amounts of their LFOs (and whether they knew what portions were fines, fees, or costs), how they were assessed the LFO (whether they could recall any discussion about indigence or ability to pay), and whether a payment plan had been established and, if so, by whom (such as a judge, probation officer, or clerk). I asked about any personal consequences for them of having legal debt. We discussed their attempts to make regular payments, their reasons for not making payments, and the consequences of either making regular payments or not making payments (such as warrants issued for nonpayment and violations of court orders, or incarceration). I analyzed the interview and case study transcripts in a way similar to my coding of the interviews with and observations of court personnel (see next section).

Amortization Tables

Table A3.1   Debt Accumulation over Five Years on an LFO Assessment of $1,347 (Average LFO Debt, Not Including Restitution, Among Interviewees), Including 12 Percent Simple Interest and $100 Annual Surcharge, by Payment Amount, 2004

	$0 Monthly Payment	$5 Monthly Payment	$31.25 Monthly Payment	$100 Monthly Payment
Sentencing day	$1,347	$1,347	$1,347	$1,347
At six months	$1,413	$1,388	$1,253	$899
At one year	$1,608	$1,545	$1,210	$330
At two years	$1,869	$1,735	$1,027	PAID
At five years	$2,653	$1,824	$256	
Difference between initial LFO and debt five years later	(+)$1,306	(+)$477	(−)$1,091	

Source: Author's calculations.
Notes: Interviewees who said that they were making a regular monthly payment paid $31.25 on average. Monthly simple interest is calculated only on the principal, not on any surcharges. In my initial examination of the growth of legal debt (Harris, Beckett, and Evans 2010), as explained to me by informants in Washington, I had calculated the interest on top of interest. Through subsequent research, I learned that "simple interest" is interest that accrues only on the principal owed, not on previous monthly interest charges or collection fees. I adjusted these amortization tables accordingly.

Table A3.2   Debt Accumulation over Five Years on an LFO Assessment of $9,204 (Average LFO Debt, Including Restitution, Among Interviewees), Including 12 Percent Simple Interest and $100 Annual Surcharge, by Payment Amount, 2007

	$0 Monthly Payment	$5 Monthly Payment	$31.25 Monthly Payment	$100 Monthly Payment
Sentencing day	$9,204	$9,204	$9,204	$9,204
At six months	$9,661	$9,635	$9,503	$9,146
At one year	$10,408	$10,345	$10,0120	$9,130
At two years	$11,613	$11,478	$10,772	$8,912
At five years	$15,226	$14,835	$10,667	$7,395
Difference between initial LFO and debt five years later	(+)$6,022	(+)$5,631	(+)$1,463	(−)$1,809

Source: Author's calculations.
Notes: Interviewees who said that they were making a regular monthly payment paid $31.25 on average. Monthly simple interest is calculated only on the principal, not on any surcharges. See note at table A3.1.

Chapter 4

Analysis of Online Washington Legislative Session Hearings About Legal Financial Obligations

My research assistant Jorge Martinez and I constructed a review of online legislative session hearings in Washington State regarding legal financial obligations. The bills included Senate Bill (SB) 6336 (2000), which extended the collection period for life among legal debtors (passed), SB 5168 (2004), which authorized the reduction of interest on LFOs (failed), and SB 5461 (2005), which changed limits on the costs of incarceration (passed). We located visual recordings of these three debates at the Washington State Legislature's tvw.org web page. Each of us watched the sessions three to five times and noted frequent themes that emerged, taking down illustrative quotes. The account I present in chapter 4 is representative of the dialogue in the three legislative hearings that Jorge and I observed.

Interviews with State Legislators

I supplemented our observations of the online legislative sessions with four interviews with Washington legislators. I initially sampled legislators who had been sponsors of LFO-related legislation. I used a set interview protocol with questions about why they supported the specific piece of legislation, what they understood its goals to be, and whether they had followed any of the outcomes of the legislation. I audiorecorded the interviews, transcribed them, transferred them to NVivo, and did open coding of the main themes.

My initial plan was to interview approximately fifteen policymakers—or at least enough of them to gather a sense of their orientation and discourse around monetary sanctions in Washington. I quickly learned that I would need to adjust my plan, for several reasons. The policymakers (or their staffs) would readily schedule meetings with me but then frequently cancel the interview the day before or even on the same day, citing new meetings that were more pressing; naturally, this made it difficult to interview policymakers at the state level. The legislators I did manage to interview had frequently cosponsored LFO-related bills, not out of a commitment to or particular stance on the issue but more as a result of their relationship with the bill's originator; essentially, they "were asked to sign on." As such, the four legislators I interviewed could not recall the point of the legislation, much less the details. My line of inquiry sheds light on the disconnect between the assumptions of those constructing monetary sanctions policy and the outcomes and consequences of the laws they create to enforce it.

Review of the Washington Association of County Officials Reports to the Washington Legislature

I obtained the financial data used in chapter 4 from a series of reports compiled by the Washington Association of County Officials (WACO). SB 5990 (2003 RCW, chapter 379, section 20) directed that "the Washington Association of County Officials shall report on the amounts of legal financial obligations collected by the county clerks to the appropriate committees of the legislature no later than December 1, 2004, and annually thereafter." The WACO reports contain limited amounts of legal financial data for each of the thirty-nine counties in Washington between 2004 and 2012: the total LFO collections recouped per year; the average dollars collected per open account receivable; the number of open accounts; the percentage change in the total collected between 2003 and the most current year of the report; and the distribution of total amounts recouped among victims, the state, and the county. Because no information is contained in the reports about the total outstanding uncollected LFOs, the number of related warrants issued, or staff size, I asked each county clerk's office for information to supplement the reports (table A4.1). The information was not consistently provided, however, and was often incomplete.

Cost Estimation of the Warren County Collection System

Warren County is an anomaly in some aspects: one of the smaller Washington counties in terms of population, it has a higher-than-average felony conviction rate (5.29 per 100,000 people versus 4.31 per 100,000 people for the state), the second-largest amount of LFO collections in the state, and the highest average dollar amount collected per open account. The county expends a lot of resources to monitor and collect from legal debtors, and it collects a large amount of LFO payments. I chose Warren County as an example for the cost-benefit analysis in order to detail the total possible resources used in the monitoring and sanctioning process (table A4.2).

The direct county expenses include the full-time staff of clerks who manage the public collection unit in Warren County (including six full-time positions and one hourly position). In fact, the collection unit had its own budget line in the Warren County 2011–2012 budget ($718,860). Indirect costs related to the county's monitoring and sanctioning of defendants are less clear. The costs associated with the weekly LFO court are unknown. I estimated total annual judicial time spent reviewing defendants' payment histories and sentencing additional jail days for

Table A4.1 LFO Characteristics of County Clerks in Five Washington Counties, 2011

	Warren[a]	Alexander	Langston	James	Santos
Number of outstanding cases with LFO debt	—	—	77,433	35,087	14,000
Total amount of outstanding debt from these cases	—	—	$329,022,596	$151,773,494	$79,549,471
Restitution debt outstanding	—	—	$210,633,067	$95,890,457	N/A
Fine or fee debt outstanding	—	—	$116,538,762	$52,728,224	—
Collection cost debt outstanding (interest, surcharges)	—	—	$1,850,767	$3,154,813	—
"Active payers"	—	Unknown[b]	—	N/A	—
Number of notices of delinquency	—	27,020	4,067	6,014	0
Number of summonses to appear for nonpayment issues	—	180	N/A[d]	N/A[e]	0[f]
Number of warrants for failure to appear (FTA)	—	N/A	N/A	N/A	0
Number of outstanding FTA warrants	—	N/A	N/A	N/A	0
Number of outstanding warrants for failure to pay (FTP)	—	N/A[c]	N/A	N/A	0
Number of people jailed for FTA	—	N/A	N/A	N/A	0

Number of people jailed for FTP	—	N/A	N/A	0
Average number of days spent in jail for FTP	—	N/A	N/A	0
Number of LFO cases sent to collections	—	0	4,176	"Less than 1,000"
Number of cases actively supervised by county clerk's office	—	0[g]	1,975	N/A[h]
Number of clerks working full-time on LFO collections	—	7[i]	2	5
Number of 100 percent full-time LFO clerks	—	0	1	0
Percentage of part-time clerks' time spent on LFO collections	—	0	25%	—

Source: Compiled by the author from information provided by county clerk's offices upon the author's request.

[a] After repeated contacts with the Warren County clerk's office, I was told that they would submit information, but I never received it.

[b] "Unable to report how many people make payments regularly; but we posted 70,388 payments toward adult[s] during 2011."

[c] "No specific data; can get number of warrants issued, but no way of distinguishing between warrants for nonpayment and other things."

[d] "In Langston defendants are not summoned to court for failure to pay."

[e] "(1) People get hearing notice for multiple violations, then get warrant issued. People usually will not be jailed simply because of nonpayment. (2) Did not keep a record of warrants issued."

[f] "We don't have the money in our budget to facilitate this."

[g] As told in interviews.

[h] "Define 'actively supervised.'"

[i] "We don't 'supervise' cases. We actively work a number of cases; this typically fluctuates between 35,000 and 40,000 cases at any given time."

Table A4.2 Estimated LFO-Related Costs and Revenue for Warren County, Fiscal Year 2011–2012

	Description	Amount
Costs		
LFO clerks' collection costs	Actual budgeted amount for 2011–2012	$718,860
Specialty courts: judicial time	Three three-hour hearings per month (12 months = 108 hours) × $81 per hour[a]	$8,748
Prosecutor	Approximate annual salary	$150,000
Warrant-related costs	Eight issued per week on average (416 per year) × $100[b]	$41,600
Jail days until first appearance	30 people per week on average[c] (1,560 per year) × $76.83 per day in jail	$119,855
Arraignment hearings	Clerks: $200[d] × 1,560 debtors per year = $312,000; judges: 10 hours per week (520 hours per year) × $81 per hour = $42,120	$354,120
Jail days as sanction for nonpayment	15 people sanctioned per week with 15 days in jail (225 jail days) × 52 weeks = 11,700 jail days × $76.83[e]	$898,911
Unknown costs	Sheriff warrant pickups; jail processing costs; court officials' health and retirement benefits; costs of court stenographer, bail clerk, and personal clerk	—
Conservative estimate of total yearly costs for LFO monitoring and sanctioning		$2,292,094

Revenue		
From Washington State AOC (for billing statements)	Offset costs not included in expenditures	−$60,000
Recouped to county		$1,829,889
Recouped to individual victims		$1,121,882
Recouped to crime victim fund		$133,441
Recouped to state		$277,690
Total amount recouped (state, county, and victims' restitution)		$3,362,903[f]

Source: Author's calculations from data in the Warren County 2011–2012 budget and Washington Association of County Officials (2012).

[a]Calculated from the average annual full-time salary for a superior court judge in Warren County in the 2011–2012 budget.

[b]According to interviews and observations of first appearance hearings, six to eight people are seen per day after being picked up on warrants for failure to pay.

[c]Conservative estimate based on interviews and observation (see note b).

[d]The cost charged to defendants for court costs as part of their LFO.

[e]The actual daily jail bed cost in Warren County in 2010 was $76.83, according to the website of the Washington Association of Sheriff and Police Chiefs (http://www.waspc.org/index.php?c=Jail%20Statistics, accessed April 8, 2016.).

[f]These revenue numbers, provided by the AOC report, do not total correctly.

not meeting the conditions of initial sentences by calculating one hour a week of the average judicial hourly wage (from the county 2011–2012 budget) multiplied by fifty-two weeks ($8,748). Warren County commonly issued warrants to monitor and sanction nonpayers and charged defendants $100 per warrant issued to them. Thus, I included a line in the budget for warrant-related expenses based on the average number of eight warrants issued per week, or 416 per year ($41,600). Because the one prosecutor assigned LFO cases was so involved on a daily basis with the monitoring (filling out paperwork for warrants, talking with legal debtors) and sanctioning (being present at first appearance hearings, managing the Thursday afternoon defendant meetings and court hearings) of LFOs, I included the average annual prosecutor salary as an LFO-related expense. Indirect costs also include the costs associated with defendants being arrested for a warrant. Warren County processed an average of six to eight debtors who had been picked up on LFO-related warrants and appeared before the court each day. I conservatively estimated the cost of jail days for six debtors per day (1,560 debtors per year).

I then calculated the expenses related to the arraignment hearings. It is extremely difficult to calculate the exact amount of court time (including judicial, prosecutor, defense attorney, bailiff, court transcriber, and clerk personnel hours) required to process people arrested on warrants for nonpayment or for not responding to a court summons regarding nonpayment. To calculate the expected costs of the LFO-related cases in arraignment hearings, I included the $200 in court costs that are charged to defendants upon conviction ($312,000) and calculated judicial time for 10 hours a week, or 560 a year ($42,120). When debtors were able to pay the minimum required for release, they were allowed to leave the jail; if they did not pay, they stayed in jail for their sanctioned number of days, which ranged, I observed, from ten to fifteen days, depending on how frequently they had been reprimanded or arrested for nonpayment. Thus, I calculated the costs related to sanctioned jail days for fifteen people per week (half of those arrested on warrants) sentenced to fifteen jail days. I arrived at an estimated 11,700 jail days imposed on legal debtors per year in Warren County ($898,911).

Chapter 5

Criminal Court Data, Observations, and Interviews with Court Officials

I analyzed data regarding the dollar value of the monetary sanctions imposed by Washington superior courts for all felony cases sentenced in the first two months of 2004 (N = 3,366). In 2007, when I began the study, the Washington State Sentencing Guidelines Commission (SGC) made individual-level data publicly available through a search program on its website. I selected a sample of cases sentenced in the first two months of 2004 to create the study's first database for statistical analysis. My graduate research assistant, Heather Evans, linked the data to financial sanction records from the Administrative Office of the Courts (AOC). The sample was drawn from the SGC database, which summarizes information entered from individual judgment and sentence forms submitted each month by every superior court in the state and provided by the AOC. I used convictions rather than individuals as the unit of analysis. The data include only the monetary sanctions assessed by Washington superior courts. Although Washington courts may now impose an impressive range of monetary sanctions, court data omit other potential sources of legal debt, including jail fees, DOC fees, and interest on unpaid legal obligations. In addition, the data capture the sanctions imposed for a single felony charge, yet many of those convicted of a felony offense are convicted of multiple charges; many also acquire multiple criminal convictions over time. The court conviction data thus shed light only on the magnitude of the monetary sanctions associated with a single felony charge.

The SGC database from which both the cross-sectional and longitudinal data were drawn includes information about defendants' race-ethnicity, gender, and age, as well as their case characteristics.[2] Although some Hispanic/Latino defendants were identified as such in the SGC database, some state courts identified defendants by race only, ignoring ethnicity or Hispanicity. As a result, some Hispanic defendants were not classified as Hispanic in the SGC database. I used Hispanic Surname Analysis (HSA) to estimate the proportion of white, black, and other defendants who were Hispanic. Using the U.S. census Spanish surname database, the HAS program assigns a numeric value between 0 and 1 to all surnames in the database. Numeric values are provided by the U.S. Census Bureau and represent the probability that a given surname corresponds to persons who identified themselves as Hispanic/Latino in the 1990 U.S. census.[3] The list used to identify defendants of Hispanic origin in the SGC data included only Spanish surnames classified by the Census Bureau as "heavily Hispanic." It is possible that applying the methodology led to the misidentification of some mainly white defendants as Hispanic. It is also possible that some Hispanics remain unidentified as such, as many Hispanics do not have surnames that are on the list generated by the Census Bureau.

Table A5.1   The Effects of Offense- and Offender-Related Factors on the Amount of
the Fines and Fees Assessed in Five Washington Counties, 2004

	Langston County	Santos County	James County	Warren County
Mean fines and fees[a]	$1,058	$1,823	$956	$2,530
SRA level (seriousness of offense)	0.3%	3.1%	3.5%	0.1%
Offender score (persistence)	0.5%		2.3%	
Male				
White	−5.5%	−6.7%		
Latino		17.5%		
Drug offense		128.9%	65.0%	67.5%
Violent offense				
Other offense		−51.1%	−29.0%	37.8%
Chose trial[b]	59.4%		73%	
Number of convictions	536	187	169	249

Source: Author's analysis of Washington State Sentencing Guidelines Commission (SGC) and Administrative Office of the Courts (AOC) (2004) data.
Notes: N = 1,649. Only statistically significant factors at the $p = 0.05$ level are shown. Reference county is Alexander.
[a]Restitution is not included.
[b]There were not enough cases to calculate the effect in this category for Santos County. See table A5.2 for coefficients and significance levels.

Analysis

My research assistant Heather Evans and I conducted the statistical analyses for this chapter together. We revised the analysis presented in table A5.1 from prior use of the data in two ways.[4] First, we replaced the variable measure, the percentage of a county population who voted Republican, with the 2004 proportions. (We had used data from 2000 in prior analyses.) And second, we replaced the percentage of a county budget spent on law and justice–related activities with a different indicator. The new variable includes the proportion of the county's general fund expenditures spent on law and justice. (The prior variable was the proportion of total expenditures spent on law and justice.) We reran the model we presented in the 2011 paper using the new variables. In terms of significance and direction, there were no differences in the results of the two models.

We constructed the analysis for table A5.1 in several layers. First, we pooled the data for all five counties and ran an ordinary least squares (OLS) regression (using logged fines/fees as the dependent variable). We included five dummy variables, using Alexander County as the reference category. The results show that Warren, Langston, James, and Santos Counties were significantly different from Alexander County: the fines and fees imposed on individuals sentenced in one of these counties were significantly higher, on average, than the fees imposed for the same offense in Alexander County. All of the coefficients were significantly different from Alexander County. That is, a person convicted in Warren could expect to be assessed almost 300 percent more in fines and fees than a person of the same race, gender, age, and offense type convicted in Alexander County.

Next, we ran regression models creating interaction terms between each county and one independent variable. To analyze the effect on the SRA score in each county, we ran the model:

$$\text{Fines/Fees(logged)} = \alpha + \beta_1 \text{(SRA)} + \beta_2 \text{(OffenderScore)} + \beta_3 \text{(Age)} \\ + \beta_4 \text{(Male)} + \beta_5 \text{(Latino)} + \beta_6 \text{(AfricanAmerican)} \\ + \beta_7 \text{(OtherRace)} + \beta_8 \text{(DrugOffense)} \\ + \beta_9 \text{(OtherOffense)} + \beta_{10}\text{(Trial)} + \beta_{11}\text{(Warren)} \\ + \beta_{12}\text{(Langston)} + \beta_{13}\text{(James)} + \beta_{14}\text{(Santos)} \\ + \beta_{15}\text{(Warren*SRA)} + \beta_{16}\text{(Langston*SRA)} \\ + \beta_{17}\text{(James*SRA)} + \beta_{18}\text{(Santos*SRA)}$$

To calculate the effect of being in a particular county (compared to Alexander), we developed tables for each independent variable. For example, the effect of SRA in Warren County is: −0.025239(SRA) + 0.0263994 (Warren: 0 or 1) = 0.00116. Note that outside of Warren County (Warren = 0) the effect of SRA is: −0.025239(SRA) + 0.0263994 (0) = −0.025239. Thus, the effect of SRA in Alexander County is −0.025239—or a 2.5 percent *decrease* in fines and fees assessed.

We used the conventional formula for calculating the effect of an independent variable on a logged dependent variable:

$$Y(\ln) = \alpha + \beta x$$

One-unit increase in β = an increase in Y of $[100(e\beta - 1)]\%$

Using this formula, we then calculated the interpretation of the effect—for example, of SRA (0.00116)—for each increase of one SRA point. A one-point increase in SRA was associated with a 0.1 percent increase in fines and fees assessed.

Separately, we ran each of the following models:

- SRA*Counties
- Score*Counties

- Male*Counties (model included gender as male/nonmale)
- White*Counties (model included race as white/nonwhite)
- Latino*Counties (model included race as Latino/non-Latino)
- Drug Offense*Counties (model included drug offense/nondrug offense)
- Violent Offense*Counties (model included violent offense/nonviolent offense)
- Other Offense*Counties (model included other offense/non-other offense)
- Trial*Counties

Selected results from each model are presented in tables A5.1 and A5.2.

Chapter 6

Interviews with Courtroom Officials

I draw on interview data to assess how LFOs affect legal debtors and analyze whether and how monetary sanctions contribute to the accumulation of disadvantage. The selection of the interviewees was purposive and accomplished through snowballing techniques.

Judges   Prior to conducting observational research in a courthouse, I sent an email request for an interview to the presiding judge, the presiding criminal judge, and two others within the courthouse. Judges often referred me to a colleague they knew had a special interest or calendar related to LFOs, and I would invite that judge for an interview. I interviewed a total of fifteen judges. The interviews lasted from one to two and a half hours, and I conducted them individually in each judge's office. The interviews consisted of a set of open-ended questions designed to begin a dialogue about the role of court officials in the sentencing of LFOs, how they interpreted the legal concepts of "willful" and "indigent," and what their overall perception was of monetary sanctions as a sentencing tool. One judge I interviewed, Judge Orth, knowing I was studying monetary sanctions, read excerpts from the court file of one of the defendants he had sentenced in his court. See figure A6.1 for excerpts from that file.

Attorneys   All but one of the attorneys I contacted and asked for an interview agreed to participate; one prosecutor refused. I interviewed

(Text continues on p. 195.)

Table A5.2 Selected Results from OLS Regression Models Pooling Conviction Data from Five Washington Counties, 2004

	County Coefficient	IV Coefficient	Interaction Coefficient	Interaction P Value[a]	Calculated Effect of IV	Interpretation of Effect	Adjusted R-squared
SRA (IV)							
Alexander	0.000	-0.025	N/A	0.000	-0.025	-2.47%	0.7319
Warren	1.286	-0.025	0.026*	0.016	0.001	0.10%	0.7319
Santos	0.837	-0.025	0.055***	0.000	0.030	3.05%	0.7319
James	0.140	-0.025	0.060***	0.000	0.034	3.46%	0.7319
Langston	0.421	-0.025	0.028**	0.001	0.003	0.30%	0.7319
Score (IV)							
Alexander	0.000	-0.014	N/A	0.001	-0.014	-1.39%	0.7304
Warren	1.335	-0.014	0.013	0.138	-0.001	-0.10%	0.7304
Santos	1.020	-0.014	-0.009	0.348	-0.023	-2.27%	0.7304
James	0.212	-0.014	0.038***	0.000	0.023	2.33%	0.7304
Langston	0.457	-0.014	0.019**	0.002	0.005	0.50%	0.7304
Men (IV)							
Alexander	0.000	0.047	N/A	0.276	0.047	4.81%	0.7262
Warren	1.402	0.047	-0.039	0.523	0.008	0.80%	0.7262
Santos	1.010	0.047	-0.013	0.868	0.034	3.46%	0.7262
James	0.295	0.047	0.054	0.455	0.100	10.52%	0.7262
Langston	0.498	0.047	0.020	0.711	0.067	6.93%	0.7262

(Table continues on p. 192.)

Table A5.2 *Continued*

	County Coefficient	IV Coefficient	Interaction Coefficient	Interaction P Value[a]	Calculated Effect of IV	Interpretation of Effect	Adjusted R-squared
Whites (IV)							
Alexander	0.000	0.041	N/A	0.141	0.041	4.19%	0.7275
Warren	1.384	0.041	−0.017	0.753	0.023	2.33%	0.7275
Santos	1.081	0.041	−0.110*	0.041	−0.069	−6.67%	0.7275
James	0.255	0.041	0.102	0.095	0.143	15.37%	0.7275
Langston	0.573	0.041	−0.098*	0.014	−0.057	−5.54%	0.7275
Latinos (IV)							
Alexander	0.000	−0.003	N/A	0.959	−0.003	−0.30%	0.7277
Warren	1.372	−0.003	0.114	0.211	0.111	11.74%	0.7277
Santos	0.975	−0.003	0.164*	0.032	0.161	17.47%	0.7277
James	0.348	−0.003	−0.216	0.126	−0.219	−19.67%	0.7277
Langston	0.512	−0.003	0.072	0.415	0.069	7.14%	0.7277
Drug offenders (IV)							
Alexander	0.000	0.041	N/A	0.163	0.041	4.19%	0.7738
Warren	1.220	0.041	0.474***	0.000	0.516	67.53%	0.7738
Santos	0.793	0.041	0.787***	0.000	0.828	128.87%	0.7738
James	0.233	0.041	0.460***	0.000	0.501	65.04%	0.7738
Langston	0.541	0.041	0.015	0.708	0.056	5.76%	0.7738

Violent offenders (IV)							
Alexander	0.000	-0.019	N/A	0.689	-0.019	-1.88%	0.6883
Warren	1.430	-0.019	-0.171	0.115	-0.189	-17.22%	0.6883
Santos	1.024	-0.019	-0.183	0.092	-0.202	-18.29%	0.6883
James	0.356	-0.019	-0.088	0.297	-0.106	-10.06%	0.6883
Langston	0.545	-0.019	0.057	0.402	0.039	3.98%	0.6883
Other offenders (IV)							
Alexander	0.000	-0.048	N/A	0.085	-0.048	-4.69%	0.7559
Warren	1.631	-0.048	-0.427***	0.000	-0.475	-37.81%	0.7559
Santos	1.442	-0.048	-0.667***	0.000	-0.715	-51.08%	0.7559
James	0.518	-0.048	-0.295***	0.000	-0.343	-29.04%	0.7559
Langston	0.554	-0.048	-0.026	0.492	-0.074	-7.13%	0.7559
Chose trial (IV)[b]							
Alexander	0.000	-0.122	N/A	0.337	-0.122	-11.49%	0.7293
Warren	1.372	-0.122	0.299	0.237	0.177	19.36%	0.7293
Santos	0.997	-0.122	(omitted)	(omitted)	(omitted)	(omitted)	0.7293
James	0.316	-0.122	0.670***	0.000	0.548	72.98%	0.7293
Langston	0.509	-0.122	0.588*	0.020	0.466	59.36%	0.7293
N = 1,649							

Source: Author's analysis of Washington State Sentencing Guidelines Commission (SGC) and Administrative Office of the Courts (AOC) (2004) data.
Note: Data shown are nonstandardized OLS regression coefficients. The reference county is Alexander.

[a]For Alexander County, this p-value is for the independent variable with no interaction.

[b]"Chose trial" was omitted because there were not enough cases in this category in Santos County.

*p < 0.05; **p < 0.01; ***p < 0.001 (two-tailed tests)

Figure A6.1   Excerpt from Judge Orth's File on the Defendant "Mr. Frank"

10/25/2007	Plea to possession of a stolen vehicle
12/14/2007	Sentenced $600 fines and fees
3/14/2008	Sentencing conditions violation hearing
5/6/2008	Clerks send notice mailed to appear for nonpayment
6/8/2008	Document: Order setting restitution—$1,410.13; total owed—$2,010.13
5/6/2009	Document: Court notice of violation

"Violations Specified: The above-named offender is in violation of his LFO payment schedule, and is delinquent in the amount of: $2,164.69. The total unpaid obligation is $2,164.69. Of which $1,410.13 is restitution; $600.00 court fines and fees; and $154.56 accrued interest."

"Supporting Evidence: To date Mr. Frank has made no payments in this matter. The defendant's scheduled monthly payment is $25.00. The LFO Section has sent the defendant numerous notifications along with phone calls regarding his delinquency with no response. Efforts by personnel with the Alexander Co. Court Clerk's Office to locate employment information or other assets has been futile and the crime victim has been very persistent."

5/18/2009	Notice of sentencing modification hearing—clerk's action required
6/09/2009	Failure to appear
6/19/2009	Bench warrant issued (bail $2,100 cash only)
9/24/2009	Arrested, hearing—Judge Weston pulled off SRA calendar—he appeared in front of her, and judge released him to DOC
10/1/2009	Document: Clerk's minutes: "Legal Financial Obligations are now totaling, including interest, $2,164.69" "The court imposes credit for time served. Order is signed. Order of Immediate Release is signed."
12/21/2010	Notice of violation: Failure to pay

"[Violations] Specified: The beginning balance as ordered by the court on 12/4/2007 . . . was $500 plus restitution TBD. The defendant has paid nothing since that time. The total unpaid obligation is now $2,547.02 of which $1,410.13 is restitution, $700 is court fines and fees, and $436.89 is interest."

"Supporting Evidence: In spite of payment due notices being sent out to the defendant's last known address since 2/7/2008, he has not paid anything and has not contacted this office to make other arrangements. Several attempts have been made to contact the defendant. Attempts have also failed to locate garnishment sources such as wages. The defendant's victim has contacted our office repeatedly for assistance but all administrative collection efforts have been exhausted."

Figure A6.1 *Continued*

	"Recommendation: It is respectfully recommended that the Court order the defendant to complete a comprehensive financial declaration for the purpose of determining the defendant's ability to pay. It is further recommended that a periodic review be scheduled by the court to insure his compliance with the appropriate payment and schedule."
1/03/2011	Clerks send notice mailed to [defendant to] appear for nonpayment
1/28/2011	Clerk's minutes—SRA out of custody calendar. Defendant appears with counsel—before SRA Judge. Hearing is continued to March 11, 2011. Defendant does not need to appear if he has made the first payment.
	Document: Order modifying probation and jail commitment "failure to comply with financial obligations . . . if defendant makes required payment he will not need to appear at next hearing . . . defendant shall return for a review hearing on March 1, 2011. Defendant shall pay at least $50 per month by the 1st day of each month, starting on March 1, 2011"—SRA Judge.
3/11/2011	On SRA calendar, FTA, BW $3,000 bail
3/14/2011	Document: Motion certification and order for bench warrant from SRA Judge
4/1/2011	Document: SRA in custody calendar clerk's minutes: "The court [SRA judge] modifies sentence. . . . Defendant to serve a term of 8 days in Alexander Co jail with credit for 8 days. Defendant to set a payment schedule with clerk's office to address his legal financial obligations."

Source: Author's notes from interview with Judge Orth.

fourteen attorneys, including at least one prosecutor and one defense attorney in each county. To better understand the role of monetary sanctions in the sentencing process, I asked both prosecuting and defense attorneys: What is the function of monetary sanctions as a sentencing option? Are they treated by court officials as a less punitive sentencing option? Or are monetary sanctions viewed, like incarceration, as an important tool to punish offenders and hold them accountable for their actions? Also, what roles do warrants and reincarceration play in the management of offenders with outstanding LFO accounts? Do you view LFOs as a helpful strategy that assists in monitoring offenders or as an impediment to the reentry process?

Community Corrections Officers   I called at least one CCO in each of the counties I studied to confirm the existence of the monitoring and sanctioning processes described by interviewees. I interviewed a total of six CCOs, all of them over the phone. My questions focused on how they monitored nonpaying individuals, what the consequences were for non-payment, and what types of hearings they held when they deemed legal debtors to be out of compliance with their community supervision.

Clerks   I attempted to interview the head clerk in each of the five counties. One clerk's office refused to participate, and another requested that I not audio-record the interview and that I not interview any other staff besides her. I asked the clerks: How many staff members do you have? What is your collection process? How do you communicate with judges about nonpaying debtors? And how do you determine that someone is a "willful" nonpayer?

Analysis of Interview Data

For each set of interviews, I used a set list of open-ended protocol questions, but I also allowed interviewees to veer off topic if they chose to do so. I audio-recorded all of the interviews, paid a research assistant to transcribe them, and then uploaded those documents into NVivo for analysis. In my first read-through of all the transcripts, I conducted open coding—I noted the key concepts, local terms, processes, events, and policies that emerged. In my second read-through, I grouped the codes into broader analytic themes—assessment of debtors, sanctions for nonpayment, representations of indigence, categorizations of debtors, interpretations of the law, and applications of the law. I then wrote short essays on the key themes, with excerpts from my interview notes that illustrated them.[5] The themes were informed and guided by the theoretical questions about criminal sentencing, court culture, and defendant-processing procedures. Throughout the book I have used representative excerpts from the interviews and observations to illustrate and discuss these key themes.

In attempting to make sense of the system of monetary sanctions, I frequently resorted to sketching out the relationships between themes, court officials, and legal concepts on large construction paper. What resulted was this book, which begins with a broad illustration of the monetary sanctions system and then provides in each chapter an increasingly tapered analysis of the layers of that system.

Ethnographic Observations of Courtroom Hearings

Much of my understanding of the LFO process is based on observations of sentencing and violation hearings. I observed eighty-five sentencing hearings and fifty violation hearings. Sentencing hearings occur either directly at the end of a plea hearing, where defendants plead guilty to an offense, or at a subsequent hearing post-conviction. I also conducted two hours of observations of pre-plea hearings in Warren County. I learned from interviewees that many defendants who appear at these hearings have been regularly arrested for nonpayment-related warrants.

I conducted fieldwork in five of the thirty-nine counties of Washington from 2008 to 2012. I selected these five counties on the basis of maximizing variation in LFO assessment and demographic composition. During my observations of sentencing hearings, I paid attention to the process of judicial assessment and court monitoring of monetary sanctions. In Washington, superior court adjudication and sentencing hearings are open to the public, so I would randomly attend county plea and sentencing hearings, using online court calendars to determine when these would occur. I sat in the audience section of the courtroom and hand-recorded my field notes about the dialogue between the court officials (judges, prosecutors, and defense attorneys) and the defendants. Using an observation sheet, I systematically recorded characteristics of the defendants and details of the case outcome, including the offense type, my estimation of the defendant's race, ethnicity, and age, whether the person was detained in jail, whether a public or private attorney was present, and the sentence outcome (including both physical and nonphysical punishments and all financial sentences).

I observed cases involving offenses ranging from assaults and assaults related to domestic violence to drug charges, driving under the influence, unlawful firearm possession, and forgery. The sentences imposed usually included a combination of conditions: drug and alcohol assessment and treatment, community service hours, a range in years of community supervision (probation), a certain number of days in jail or months in prison, and a monetary sanction (set at a minimum of $600). Besides my field notes about defendants' characteristics, I recorded details about each hearing in a handwritten journal during these observations. Using a method similar to the one I used for my analysis of the interview data, I typed my field notes and coded them using NVivo qualitative software for data analysis. NVivo was particularly helpful for organizing all of the codes I developed during the analysis of my interview and observational data.

To get an initial framing of the key codes, I began the analysis by printing hard copies of the field notes and then coding or identifying in the margins of the printouts the salient events, processes, and terms that emerged from my readings of the transcript. I mostly used an informal method I learned in my methodological training from Bob Emerson, who helped me see the importance of being close to my data, touching the words on the paper, and flipping back and forth through the pages to struggle with the observations I had recorded. After getting a sense of the key codes that were consistently developing from my rereading of the data, I formally coded the transcripts using NVivo on my computer. An inductive analytic approach allowed me to investigate the "meanings, intentions and actions of the research participants."[6]

To add further dimensions to the main themes, I examined my data for counterfactual examples. Noting contrary or diverging findings allowed me to highlight potential variation in respondents' experiences or understandings. The resulting book is an analysis of representative data taken from field notes and guided by current theoretical concepts and questions centered on the nature of criminal sentencing, court officials' interpretations of the people before them in court, and the subsequent processing decisions.

═ Notes ═

Chapter 1: The Criminal Justice System and Monetary Sanctions

1. I used pseudonyms to protect the identity of all subjects interviewed and observed.

2. Further, during clemency hearings, review members regular ask questions about defendants' ability to pay their LFOs upon release as an assessment of their readiness to be released from prison.

3. See 11 U.S. Code, section 523, subsections (a)(7) and (a)(13).

4. Nationally, monetary sanctions are assessed at every legal level from juvenile and adult criminal courts to civil and district courts. Here I briefly describe the other types of court financial sanctions, but my study is focused on monetary sanctions imposed at the felony level. See RCW 9.94A.760 and RCW 7.68.035. Clerk's fees and surcharges (RCW 36.18.020) are an example of a new fee added in 2012 (Harris, Evans, and Beckett 2010).

5. A person with, for instance, three felony convictions in three different Washington counties is charged $300 annually for unpaid LFOs (RCW 36.18.016[29]). Interest and collection charges are imposed on defendants who are incarcerated. Recent legislation allows felons, upon release from confinement, to apply for a waiver of accumulated interest and charges if they can provide an accounting of the amount of interest that accrued on nonrestitution LFOs during their incarceration and show that they have "personally made a good faith effort to pay and that the interest accrual is causing a significant hardship" (RCW 10.82.090). In King County, Washington, the clerk's office assesses a fee of $10 for all LFO payments that exceed $25 (KCC 4A.630.120). In North Carolina, a $25 late fee for failure to pay a fine or other court cost on time is imposed, as well as a $20 surcharge to set up an installment payment plan. See "[North Carolina] Court Costs and Fees Chart," effective October 1, 2014, http://www.nccourts.org/Courts /Trial/Documents/court_costs_chart-Oct2014.pdf (accessed January 19, 2016); see also "2011 Louisiana Laws, Revised Statutes, Title 13—Courts and Judicial Procedure, RS 13:996.55—Judicial Expense Fund . . .," http:// law.justia.com/codes/louisiana/2011/rs/title13/rs13-996-55/ (accessed

January 19, 2016); and North Carolina Legislature, "Article 28: Uniform Costs and Fees in the Trial Divisions: Costs in Criminal Actions," G.S. 7A-304 (§ 31.23[a] (Harris, Evans, and Beckett 2010).

6. The fifteen states were Alabama, Arizona, California, Florida, Georgia, Illinois, Louisiana, Michigan, Missouri, New York, North Carolina, Ohio, Pennsylvania, Texas, and Virginia (Bannon, Nagrecha, and Diller 2010). Washington State policy is consistent with these states' policies.

7. See, for example, Adamson 1983; Blackman 2008; Harris, Evans, and Beckett 2011; and Oshinsky 1996.

8. Others use the term "mass incarceration" (Garland 2001), but I prefer to use the term "mass conviction" when analyzing the contemporary relationship between social control and the criminal system. It is the stain of a felony conviction, above and beyond incarceration, that produces much of the related legal and societal stigma. Furthermore, the sentences imposed in addition to incarceration (such as monetary sanctions) generate other negative outcomes for defendants.

9. Bonczar 1997.

10. Guerino, Harrison, and Sabol 2011.

11. Glaze and Herberman 2013.

12. Uggen, Shannon, and Manza 2012.

13. Pettit and Western 2004, 160.

14. Uggen, Shannon, and Manza 2012.

15. Harlow 1998.

16. Ibid.

17. Bonczar 1997.

18. Harlow 1998.

19. Bonczar 1997.

20. Ibid.

21. New York State Division of Parole 2004.

22. Manza and Uggen 2006.

23. Saxonhouse 2004.

24. Clear 2007; Comfort 2007; Massoglia 2008.

25. Mauer and McCalmont 2013.

26. Travis 2005; see also the Federal Quality Housing and Work Responsibility Act of 1998 (QHWRA).

27. Pager 2007; Western 2006; Wildeman 2009.

28. Anderson 1990, 1999; Bobo and Thomson 2006; Pettit and Western 2004; Western 2006; Wheelock and Uggen 2008.

29. Alexander 2010; Garland 2001; Goffman 2014; Guerino, Harrison, and Sabol 2011; Manza and Uggen 2006; Pager 2007; Pettit 2012; Pettit and Western 2004; Ulmer and Kramer 2008; Wacquant 2000, 2001b; Western 2006; Wooldredge and Thistlethwaite 2004.

30. Rusche and Kirchheimer 1939/2009, 5.

31. Mitchell and Leachman 2014.

32. Henrichson and Delaney 2012; National Center for Education Statistics 2015.

33. See Weiss 1989; see also American Civil Liberties Union 2011 and Stillman 2014.

34. California Assembly Bills 109 and 117. See also Petersilia and Snyder 2013, 266; and Office of Governor Edmund G. Brown Jr., "Governor Brown Signs Legislation to Improve Public Safety and Empower Local Law Enforcement" (press release), April 5, 2011.

35. Provine 2007.

36. Bobo and Thompson 2006; Pettit and Western 2004; Manza and Uggen 2006; Pager 2007; Wakefield and Uggen 2010; Western 2006.

37. For exceptions, see Alice Goffman's (2009) work on the impact of felony warrants (many of which are imposed for nonpayment of monetary sanctions) or Alfred Blumstein and Kiminori Nakamura's (2009) research on the liminal legal status of released prisoners. See also Harris, Evans, and Beckett 2010, 2011; and Ruback, Shaffer, and Logue 2004.

38. RCW 9.94A.760.

39. A local public defense advocacy organization created a special "LFO attorney position"; in 2013 the ACLU of Washington conducted an investigation of monetary sanctions in a sample of counties across Washington; and between 2009 and 2013, several LFO-related bills were brought before the state legislature.

40. Forty-one of the interviews with felony defendants were collected by my colleagues Katherine Beckett and Heather Evans as part of a collaborative project in 2007.

Chapter 2: Criminal Monetary Sanctions in the United States

1. Rusche and Kirchheimer 1939/2009.

2. Oshinsky 1996, 42.

3. "For an offense committed on or after July 1, 2000, the court shall retain jurisdiction over the offender, for purposes of the offender's compliance with payment of the legal financial obligations, until the obligation is com-

pletely satisfied, regardless of the statutory maximum for the crime" (RCW 9.94A.760[4]).

4. Bishop 1923, section 940, 693; Darlington 1955; Holdsworth 1927, 43–44.

5. Stephen 1883, 57. See also Darlington 1955; and Westen 1969, 778.

6. Lepore 2009.

7. See Washington constitution, article 1, section 17: "There shall be no imprisonment for debt, except in cases of absconding debtors"; Oregon constitution, article 1, section 19: "There shall be no imprisonment for debt, except in case of fraud or absconding debtors"; Missouri constitution, article 1, section 11: "No person shall be imprisoned for debt, except for nonpayment of fines and penalties imposed by law"; Florida constitution, article 1, section 11: "No person shall be imprisoned for debt, except in cases of fraud." However, the Texas constitution (article 1, section 18) simply states that "no person shall ever be imprisoned for debt" and adds no qualifications.

8. *State v. Barklind,* 87 Wn.2d 814, 820 (1976).

9. *Williams v. Illinois,* 399 U.S. 235, 244 (1970).

10. See RCW 9.94A.760(10).

11. Harris, Evans, and Beckett 2010.

12. ACLU 2010; Harris, Evans, and Beckett 2010; Rosenthal and Weissman 2007. See also "Penalty Assessment and Surcharge Guide: Effective January 01, 2015," Phoenix: Arizona Administrative Office of the Courts, Court Services Division; and Arizona Revised Statutes (ARS), sections 12-116.01, 12.116.02, and 16-954.

13. RCW 7.68.035 and 36.18.016.

14. The names used for the five Washington counties that are the focus of this study (Alexander, Langston, Santos, James, and Warren) are pseudonymous.

15. Washington Association of County Officials (WACO) reports from 2006 to 2012. Additional information was obtained via personal correspondence with an Alexander County Council member.

16. McLean and Thompson 2007.

17. Cole et al. 1987; see also Hillsman Baker et al. 1987.

18. These courts can include district courts (misdemeanors and gross misdemeanors), municipal courts, and specialized courts such as traffic and domestic violence courts. See Feeley 1979; Gillespie 1980; Harris, Evans, and Beckett 2010; Ragona and Ryan 1983; Ryan 1983.

19. Gordon and Glaser 1991; see also Ruback, Shaffer, and Logue 2004.

20. Wheeler and Rudolph 1990.

21. Harris, Evans, and Beckett 2011.

22. Gordon and Glaser 1991; Harris, Evans, and Beckett 2011; Ruback and Clark 2010.

23. I provide a detailed state-by-state summary chart with citations in table A2.2.

24. Massachusetts General Law (MAGL), part IV, title II, chapter 280, section 6B; Arkansas (AR) Code, title 5, subtitle 1, chapter 4, subchapter 2, section 5-4-201; Alaska Code of Criminal Procedure (ACCP), title 12, section 12.55.035; Kansas Statutes (KS), chapter 21, article 4503a; Arizona Revised Statutes (ARS), section 13-808.

25. *Washington v. Curry*, 829 P.2d 166, 168 (Wash. 1992).

26. Ruback and Clark 2010.

27. 2011 Louisiana Revised Statutes (LRS), title 13, 996.55; North Carolina General Statutes (NCGS), 7A-304, section 31.23(a); California Penal Code (CPC), section 1465.8; Indiana Code (IC), title 33, article 37, chapter 4, section 1.

28. Texas Code of Criminal Procedure (CCP), title 2, article 102.020; RCW, section 43.43.7541. See also Tran-Leung (2009); and State of Texas, Office of Court Administration, "Justice Court Convictions: Court Cost Chart— 01/01/2014," http://www.txcourts.gov/media/683441/justicecourtconvictionscourtcostchart010114.pdf (accessed January 19, 2016).

29. See Administrative Office of the Courts 2015. See also ARS, sections 12-116.01, 12.116.02, and 16-954; and 730 Illinois Compiled Statutes (ILCS), section 5/5-9-1(c).

30. Florida Statutes (FS), section 55.03; Official Code of Georgia Annotated (OCGA), sections 17-14-14 and 7-4-12; RCW, sections 9.94A.760(1), 4.56.110(4), 10.82.090(1), and 19.52.020(1). In 2011 Washington passed legislation allowing defendants recently released from jail or prison to apply for a waiver of the interest (only on fines and fees, not on restitution) that accrued while they were incarcerated. If a defendant can detail the specific amount of interest that accumulated during his or her period of incarceration and show that the interest has created a "hardship," then the judge must waive the interest. The person must have made fifteen payments during an eighteen-month period to qualify for the waiver.

31. 725 ILCS, section 5/124A-10; 730 ILCS, section 5/5-9-3(e). For Arizona's delinquent fees, see ARS, sections 28-1630 through 28-1636. See also Arizona Citizens Clean Elections Commission, "Your Guide to Arizona's Political Process," http://www.azcleanelections.gov/about-us (accessed January 19, 2016).

32. See Anderson 2009; Tran-Leung 2009; Wright and Logan 2006. If the person cannot pay the fee up-front, then the amount is added to the judgment and sentence upon conviction.

33. Arkansas (AR) Code of 1987, section 16-827-213(2)(B)(i)(a).

34. RCW 2.70 and RCW 10.101. According to RCW, section 10.101.010(2), those determined to be "indigent but able to contribute" must establish a payment schedule and pay a monthly amount to the court during their adjudication; see Washington State Office of Public Defense 2007.

35. 725 ILCS, section 5/113-3.1; Ohio Revised Code (ORC), section 2947.23(A) (1)(a).

36. *Gideon v. Wainwright,* 372 U.S. 335, 40 (1963).

37. The *Miranda* warning reads: "[The individual] must be warned prior to any questioning that he [*sic*] has the right to remain silent, that anything he says can be used against him in a court of law, that he has the right to the presence of an attorney, and that, if he cannot afford an attorney one will be appointed for him prior to any questioning if he so desires"; *Miranda v. Arizona,* 384 U.S. 436, 480 (1966). Seattle police officers' reading of rights to suspects closely follows this wording; see Seattle Police Department (2015).

38. It is interesting to note that some jurisdictions indicate in their *Miranda* warning that suspects will not have to pay for their attorney. The Los Angeles County Police Department (LAPD) reads the following to juvenile arrestees: "You have the right to remain silent; anything you say may be used against you in court; you have the right to the presence of an attorney before and during any questioning; if you cannot afford an attorney, one will be appointed for you, *free of charge*, before any questioning, if you want" (emphasis added); see Chief of Police Charlie Beck to the Honorable Board of Commissioners, May 24, 2011, LAPD intradepartmental correspondence, BPC 11-0251. Another example comes from the Colorado Revised Statutes (CRS), section 16-18-101: "The sixth amendment of the constitution compels appointing counsel for indigent defendants but does not speak to whether convicted defendants of limited resources may be charged with the costs of their trial"; *People v. Fisher,* 189 Colo. 297, 539 P.2d 1258 (1975).

39. *James v. Strange,* 407 U.S. 136 (1972).

40. "The statute before us embodies elements of punitiveness and discrimination which violate the rights of citizens to equal treatment under the law"; *James v. Strange* 407 U.S. 142 (1972).

41. *Fuller v. Oregon,* 417 U.S. 40, 44 (1974). See Oregon Revised Statutes (ORS), section 161.665(3); *Oregon v. Fuller,* 12 Or. App., at 156, 504 P.2d, at 139 (1973).

42. Louisiana Code of Criminal Procedure (CCRP), 887(G); New Mexico Statutes (NMSA), section 66-8-102(E); Clerk of the Courts 2014.

43. For Marion County, Florida, see Lee 2009; see also Kentucky Revised Statutes (KRS), section 534.045.

44. Lee 2009. See also CPC, section 1203.1m; ARS, section 28-1444; and RCW, section 9.94.760.

45. City of Beverly Hills, Beverly Hills Police Department, "Jail Pay to Stay Program: Beverly Hills Police Jail," http://www.beverlyhills.org/citygov ernment/departments/policedepartment/jailpaytostayprogram/ (accessed September 25, 2013). Several California cities offer such programs. Huntington Beach has a similar program termed "Pay-n-Stay," which requires inmates to pay for two weeks prior to starting their sentence; the cost for the first day is $150 and each subsequent day is $110 per day. See City of Huntington Beach, California, "Pay-N-Stay Inmate Worker Program," http:// www.huntingtonbeachca.gov/Government/Departments/PD/divisions /investigation/PayandStayProgram.cfm?cross=true&department=police &sub=online_services&page=jail_pay&CFID=325598&CFTOKEN=76d69e 5e3ca0f589-7242351E-D9AA-6015-910B833166F511A1 (accessed January 19, 2016).

46. ARS, section 13-901; Alabama (ALA) Code, 1975, section 15-18-117. For Multnomah County, Oregon (ORS 423.570), see Multnomah County, "Supervision Fees FAQ," https://multco.us/dcj-adult/supervision-fees-faq (accessed January 19, 2016).

47. CPC, section 1463.13. See also *People v. Corrales*, 213 Cal. App. 4th 696, 700–702 (2013); and FS, section 948.034(1)(a). For a thorough discussion of "problem-solving" courts, see Paik 2011.

48. See ARS, section 16-954(D); and Arizona Citizens Clean Elections Commission, "Your Guide to Arizona's Political Process."

49. Transportation Trust Fund Task Force (2011); Delaware (DE) Code, title 11, section 4101(g)(1).

50. Nebraska Revised Statutes (NRS) 24-703: "(3) Except as otherwise provided in this subsection, a Nebraska Retirement Fund for Judges fee of six dollars shall be taxed as costs in each (a) civil cause of action, criminal cause of action, traffic misdemeanor or infraction, and city or village ordinance violation filed in the district courts, the county courts, and the separate juvenile courts."

51. RCW 13.40.192: "If a juvenile is ordered to pay legal financial obligations, including fines, penalty assessments, attorneys' fees, court costs, and restitution, the money judgment remains enforceable for a period of ten years. When the juvenile reaches the age of eighteen years or at the conclusion of juvenile court jurisdiction, whichever occurs later, the superior court clerk must docket the remaining balance of the juvenile's legal financial obligations in the same manner as other judgments for the payment of money."

52. RCW 13.40.056, 13.40.085, 13.40.198, 13.40.220, 13.40.640, 7.68.035, 43.43.690, and 7.21.030.

53. RCW 13.40.127.

54. Polk County, Iowa, Sheriff's Office, "Inmate Room & Board," https://www .polkcountyiowa.gov/sheriff/divisions/detention/inmate-room-board/

(accessed January 19, 2016); LRS 13:847E(1)(c): "A filing and processing fee of one hundred dollars for all felony expungement proceedings filed in the Twenty-Fourth Judicial District Court pursuant to the provisions of R.S. 44:9, regardless of whether the expungement is filed after a conviction is set aside and the prosecution is dismissed pursuant to the provisions of Code of Criminal Procedure Article 893."

55. See Pennsylvania Sentencing Alternatives (PACSA) 42, section 9721. See also Bannon, Nagrecha, and Diller 2010; Gordon and Glaser 1991; Harris, Evans, and Beckett 2010; Hillsman 1990; Morris and Tonry 1990; Tonry 1998.

56. Harris, Evans, and Beckett 2010.

57. Goffman 2014.

58. Braman 2007.

59. "For a felony conviction in a Washington court, the right to vote is provisionally restored as long as the person is not under the authority of the department of corrections. For a felony conviction in a federal court or any state court other than a Washington court, the right to vote is restored as long as the person is no longer incarcerated. (2)(a) Once the right to vote has been provisionally restored, the sentencing court may revoke the provisional restoration of voting rights if the sentencing court determines that a person has willfully failed to comply with the terms of his or her order to pay legal financial obligations. (b) If the person has failed to make three payments in a twelve-month period and the county clerk or restitution recipient requests, the prosecutor shall seek revocation of the provisional restoration of voting rights from the court"; RCW 29A.08.520.

60. See *Harvard Law Review* 2002.

61. ARS, title 13, chapter 8, section 13.810; KRS, 534.060(2)(a); ALA Code 1975, 15-18-62.

62. ORC, section 2947.23(i–ii).

Chapter 3: Defendant Experiences with Monetary Sanctions in Washington State

1. To manage prison populations and overcrowding, many states transport their prisoners to rented beds in other states' prison systems. As a result of this practice in Washington, Reuben had not seen his mother for seven years during his out-of-state incarceration. Legal debtors are constantly responsible for paying their legal debt (as discussed later in the chapter). Reuben regularly made payments on his LFOs while in prison from his monthly DOC stipend and from deductions taken from money that friends and family sent to him for his prisoner's account.

2. Bushway, Thornberry, and Krohn 2003; Laub and Sampson 2001, 2003.

3. Alexander 2010; Manza and Uggen 2006; Western 2006.

4. Abram and Teplin 1991; Swartz, Lurigio, and Goldstein 2000; Volkow 2001.

5. McLanahan 2009; see also Hirschi 1969.

6. The VPA is a mandatory LFO in Washington.

7. "Assisting Service" (pseudonym) is an Alexander County agency that connects with defendants who are not supervised by the DOC in completing their court-mandated community service hours. The term "dropping" refers to the DOC's decision to discontinue community service monitoring of a defendant. The defendant is supposed to seek assistance from Assisting Service, which then monitors the defendant's completion of community service hours and provides official reports to the Superior Court. While conducting research, I heard several judges and attorneys describe the impact of county fiscal constraints on the quality of Assisting Service's interactions with and monitoring of defendants. Defense attorneys and defendants often said that the organization had been unable to place them in a community service agency or had stopped communicating with and assisting them.

8. RCW 9.94A.760, notes, "Intent—Purpose—2003(c)379, sections 13–27."

9. Giordano, Cernkovich, and Rudolph 2002; Giordano, Schroeder, and Cernkovich 2007; Harris 2011.

10. See the work of Peggy Giordano and her colleagues (Giordano, Cernkovich, and Rudolph 2002; Giordano, Schroeder, and Cernkovich 2007). See also Maruna 2001; Maruna and Immarigeon 2004; Goffman 1963; and my own prior research on reentry after conviction and incarceration (Harris 2011).

Chapter 4: The Legal Intent of Monetary Sanctions Versus Real Outcomes

1. RCW 9.94A 1989(c)252, section 1 (emphasis added).

2. For information on state sentencing commissions, see National Association of Sentencing Commissions, "About Us," http://thenasc.org/aboutnasc .html (accessed February 1, 2013).

3. Bontrager, Bales, and Chiricos 2005; Frase 2005; Johnson 2006; Tonry 1995, 1998; Weber 1968, 657; Wooldredge and Thistlewaite 2004. For analysis, see Savelsberg 1992 and Steffensmeir and Demuth 2000.

4. The act created an advisory sentencing guideline commission, which was officially eliminated as an independent agency on July 1, 2011 (Engrossed Substitute Senate Bill 5891). On the same date, the Washington State Legislature created the Caseload Forecast Council (CFC), which assumed responsibility for the adult felony and juvenile disposition databases, the an-

nual sentencing statistical summaries, and the sentencing manuals. Furthermore, the CFC and the Sex Offender Policy Board (SOPB) were established within the Office of Financial Management (OFM) to serve in an advisory capacity to the governor and the legislature as necessary on issues relating to adult and juvenile sentencing.

5. Washington State Sentencing Guidelines Commission (2000).

6. The 2012 *Washington State Adult Sentencing Guidelines Manual* includes nine sentencing grids to be used depending on the type of offense (in particular drug offenses) and the date of conviction (Caseload Forecast Council 2012). Without detailing the ways in which policymakers' cultural orientations toward punishment are embedded in the guidelines (how they determined the offense seriousness levels) and in how they established alternative sentences (such as for special sex offenders, drug offenders, and first-time offenders) and set sentence enhancements (including criminal street gangs, sex offenses, and firearms and drug-related offenses), I would nevertheless note here the ongoing relationship between culture and punishment and the impact of individual and local-level ideology and emotions on the creation of law (Engen et al. 2003; Engen and Steen 2000).

7. RCW 9.94A.701.

8. RCW 9.94A.760; House Bill 1542 (1989, "Providing Retirement Benefits . . ."). The sentencing grid provides a presumptive range of sentences, but judges have the discretion to impose sentences below or above this range. If they do so, however, they must provide reasoning based on statute criteria and cite the defendant's eligibility for mitigating or aggravating circumstances; see RCW 9.94A.535, and *Blakely v. Washington* 542 U.S. 296, 124 S. Ct. 2531, 159 L. Ed.2d 403 (2004). These criteria include the victim assessment penalty (RCW 7.68.035); a domestic violence assessment (RCW 10.99.080); court costs (RCW 9.94A.760, 9.94A.505, 10.01.160, and 10.46.190); criminal filing fees; witness costs; sheriff service fees; a jury demand fee; extradition costs; fees for a court-appointed attorney (RCW 9.94.760), a court-appointed defense expert, and other defense costs (RCW 9.94A.760); DUI fines, fees, and assessments; a meth/amphetamine cleanup fine (RCW 69.50.440 and 69.50.401[a][1][ii]); a crime lab fee (RCW 43.43.690); a DNA collection fee (RCW 43.43.7541); and emergency response costs (RW 38.52.430). Courts may impose up to $10,000 for class C felonies, $20,000 for class B felonies, and $50,000 for class A felonies (RCW 9A.20.021).

9. RCW 10.01.160(1): "The court may require a defendant to pay costs. Costs may be imposed only upon a convicted defendant, except for costs imposed upon a defendant's entry into a deferred prosecution program, costs imposed upon a defendant for pretrial supervision, or costs imposed upon a defendant for preparing and serving a warrant for failure to appear."

10. See RCW 19.52.020.

11. RCW 9.94A.633(1)(a) and 10.82.030 (2010).

12. Currently, DOC officers monitor defendants only while they are under supervision. The DOC manages defendants' financial accounts when they are imprisoned and deduct monthly charges from any funds received from family or friends or for prison labor. These deductions can include payments for LFOs (20 percent), costs of incarceration (15 percent), crime victims' compensation (5 percent), savings accounts (10 percent), outstanding child support (15 percent), Prisoner Litigation Reform Act fees (20 percent), and any DOC postage debt owed (20 percent). Once inmates are released from what is called "community supervision" in Washington (effectively probation), the county clerks monitor their debt. The county clerks thus monitor the vast majority of legal debtors in Washington, and this is why my study focuses on them.

13. RCW 9.94A.760, notes, "Intent—Purpose—2003(c)379, sections 13–27."

14. RCW 9.94A.7602, 9.94A.7701, and 19.16.500 (1982, C65, section 1, "Public Bodies May Retain Private Collection Agencies to Retain Public Debts—Fees").

15. Washington SB 5454 (2000); RCW 3.62.020 and 3.62.04.

16. I use pseudonymous names for the counties in an attempt to protect the confidentiality of the people I interviewed and observed.

17. The Native American reservation takes up 39 percent of the territory within Santos County.

18. Caseload Forecast Council 2015.

19. Matthias and Klaversma 2009; Moon 2013.

20. Raaen et al. 2012; Texas SSP, section 103.0033. See also Texas Judicial Branch, "Collection Improvement Program," http://www.txcourts.gov /cip.aspx (accessed January 19, 2016).

21. The data presented and analyzed here were taken from a yearly report prepared for the Washington State Legislature by the Washington Association of County Officials. Every year since 2004, WACO has compiled a report for the legislature outlining the county clerks' recoupment results, analyzing the total amount of LFOs collected across the thirty-nine Washington counties, and comparing the amounts generated for restitution, the state crime victim fund, state revenue, and county cost recoupment.

22. The 2004 AOC data are the only information available for the average amount sentenced.

23. I obtained the outstanding LFO dollar amount from a personal communication with an Alexander County Council member.

24. There are several unknown costs associated with processing LFOs that I have not calculated. I do not know the number of hours that sheriffs spend locating debtors on their warrant pickups. Nor do I include jail processing costs (for example, booking fees, jail guards). Also, because many defen-

dants are poor, lack education, and have access to little to no health care, they tend to have several health concerns that must be addressed when they are brought into the jails. The counties bear this fiscal responsibility for jail-related health expenditures, which are not included in this analysis. And of course, besides the county expenditures on the LFO collection process not included here, the individual and social consequences of the legal debt system are costly and not easily calculable.

25. RCW 9.94A.760. The statute continues: "After restitution is satisfied, the county clerk shall distribute the payment proportionally among all other fines, costs, and assessments imposed, unless otherwise ordered by the court."

26. Once the restitution amount is paid in full, the interest that has accrued on the initial restitution amount is collected by the clerk and paid directly to the victim. After restitution and interest on restitution have been fully paid to victims, county clerks apply LFO payments first toward defendants' other court-imposed fines and fees, as noted earlier, and then toward the interest. A state-mandated formula for each fine and fee directs clerks' allocation of the funds (see table A4.1). For instance, the clerk redistributes 80 percent of the funds applied toward the $100 DNA fee to the state treasurer for deposit in the state DNA database account and 20 percent to the agency responsible for collection of the DNA sample.

27. LFO dollars retained as "county revenue" include all amounts going to the county, including the county current expense fund, the court current expense fund, local drug, cleanup, and lab funds, and local fines and penalties. Revenue items in the category "state revenue" include all revenues going to the state public safety and education accounts (State General Funds 40 and 54), the state Judicial Information System (JIS) account, crime lab funding, the state DNA account, various wildlife-related penalties, and the state Indigent Defense Fund (Washington Association of County Officials 2012, 11, note 16). In addition, a portion of the county revenue generated from LFOs is used to pay for staff and other collection-related expenses. Warren County also has a direct line item in its annual operating budget for county debt collections.

28. This information comes from my email exchange on August 18, 2014, with a Washington criminal defense attorney specializing in LFO process. RCW 9.94A.780(7) labels the collection surcharge an "annual assessment": "If a county clerk assumes responsibility for collection of unpaid legal financial obligations under RCW 9.94A.760 [which outlines monetary sanctions and the reallocation schema], or under any agreement with the department under that section, whether before or after the completion of any period of community custody, the clerk may impose a monthly or annual assessment for the cost of collections. The amount of the assessment shall not exceed the actual cost of collections. The county clerk may exempt or defer payment of all or part of the assessment based upon any of the factors listed in subsection (1) of this section. The offender shall pay the assessment under

this subsection to the county clerk who shall apply it to the cost of collecting legal financial obligations under RCW 9.94A.760."

Chapter 5: The Punishment Continuum

1. Stearns and Beggs 2010.

2. American Civil Liberties Union of Washington and Washington Association of Criminal Defense Lawyers 2010.

3. In Washington, all superior court judges are elected. If a vacancy occurs as a result of a death or resignation, the governor appoints a judicial officer to the bench, and he or she must run for election to the position during the next election cycle (RCW 10.101.010).

4. The Washington Supreme Court has held that, "to qualify for appointed counsel, it is not necessary that an accused person be utterly destitute or totally insolvent. Indigence is a relative term, and must be considered and measured in each case by reference to the need or service to be met or furnished. In connection with the constitutional right to counsel, it properly connotes a state of impoverishment or lack of resources which, when realistically viewed in the light of everyday practicalities, effectually impairs or prevents the employment and retention of competent counsel"; *Morgan v. Rhay*, 78 Wn.2d 116, 119–20, 470 P.2d 180 (1970). "All persons determined to be indigent and able to contribute, shall be required to execute a promissory note at the time counsel is appointed. The person shall be informed whether payment shall be made in the form of a lump sum payment or periodic payments. The payment and payment schedule must be set forth in writing" (RCW 10.101.020). Furthermore, three counties in Washington charge an indigent application fee of $10 or $25. For defendants who are unable to pay at the time of the screening, the amount is added to their judgment and sentence.

5. Offender scores and offense scores are explained in the next section.

6. "DNA" was the collection fee for the blood draw that would add the defendant's DNA to the national offender registry, and the DAC charge was the cost for the public defense provided by the Department of Assigned Council. The jail sentences were to be served concurrently, meaning that the defendant would spend a total of thirteen months in jail, less the seven days she had already served in jail awaiting her adjudication and sentencing.

7. Criminal defendants sentenced to electronic home monitoring are liable for the hook-up costs and for making monthly payments for their supervision and for rental of the monitoring device. They are also required to attend victim panel classes, which are educational sessions moderated by victims who discuss their experiences and the consequences of the criminal acts against them. Defendants enroll and serve as audience members. The cost of the classes ranges from $35 to $40, and the topics tend to focus on driving under the influence and domestic violence.

8. The financial declaration statement is a six-page documentation of income and household expenses, personal information (occupation, educational level, employment and employer's contact information), detailed income information, available assets and monthly expenses (housing, utilities, food and supplies, child-related expenses, transportation, health care), and debts. Clerks use this document to assess defendants' ability to pay their LFOs and establish the minimum payment (although most courthouses have a typical minimum amount that all defendants are expected to meet). A minimum payment amount is established for each of a defendant's convictions. After 2003, debtors received monthly statements and billings of their LFO debt, but as a result of budget cuts in 2010, they no longer receive those monthly statements. Thus, many debtors (in addition to those who are homeless and never receive the mailed statements) do not know that they have outstanding debt and do not know how to make the payments (Washington Association of County Officials, 2011 report; see also RCW 9.94A.760[10]). Although judges have the discretion to set the payment amounts, I never observed them doing so. Instead, they told defendants to see either their DOC-assigned officer after their release from prison or a clerk if they were not placed on DOC supervision.

9. These databases contain confidential information, including unemployment compensation and employment and wage data (RCW 50.13.020[2]).

10. Harris, Evans, and Beckett 2010.

11. To begin this analysis of how counties apply the state LFO statute, I investigated how case characteristics operate differently in the five counties. I pooled conviction data from the counties ($N = 1,649$ convictions) to first test whether there were differences between the five counties in the average amounts of the fines and fees imposed on defendants, trying to discern whether there were regular patterns in how judges in the five counties imposed fines and fees. Because Alexander County had the lowest average assessed fines and fees ($600), I compared Warren, Santos, James, and Langston Counties to Alexander County. I found large differences between counties in the LFO amounts that judges set, and I also found that each county had its own factors that affected the sentencing amounts.

12. If a defendant has already been assessed the $100 DNA fee on a prior felony, judges do not always impose the cost again. However, I observed judges imposing the fee on people with multiple prior felonies.

13. On what constitutes a "reasonable" fee, the state code reads: "A contingent fee of up to 50% of the first one hundred thousand dollars of the unpaid debt per account and up to 35% of the unpaid debt over one hundred thousand dollars per account is reasonable, and a minimum fee of the full amount of the debt up to one hundred dollars per account is reasonable" (RCW 19.16.500).

14. The contract mandates that "no debt may be assigned to a collection agency unless (a) there has been an attempt to advise the debtor (i) of the existence

of the debt and (ii) that the debt may be assigned to a collection agency for collection if the debt is not paid, and (b) at least thirty days have elapsed from the time the notice was sent and attempted" (RCW 19.16.500 1982 C65S1, "Public Bodies May Retain Private Collection Agencies . . .").

15. An enterprise fund is a government agency modeled as closely as possible on the private sector: as a "quasi" enterprise fund, the Santos County jail provides services and operates solely from revenue generated. The jail is a "quasi" enterprise fund because its budget is not 100 percent funded through revenue; technically classified as a "special revenue fund," the jail is subsidized by the government via sending agencies such as federal, state, and local law enforcement agencies, which are billed by the jail at varying and negotiated daily rates. In 2013 the negotiated daily rate with the Washington State DOC was $85 per body, the local city rate was $54.75, and the federal rate (for U.S. Immigration and Customs Enforcement [ICE] holds) was $84.51. The jail charges the county itself $81 per day per body for each Superior Court defendant sent there (paid out of the general county fund). The negotiated rate is meant to "entice" these agencies to send people to the county jail rather than other local county or city jails, since the rented bed spaces generate revenue that offsets the county's jail costs. If Santos County had an internal public collection unit that would heavily monitor and sanction nonpayers with jail, the clerk's office would be fiscally responsible not only for the employees in the collection unit but also for paying for each defendant sanctioned and housed in the local jail. Thus, for Santos County court officials, the surveillance and punishment of nonpayers is ineffective.

16. To illustrate a complete monitoring and sanctioning process within one Washington county, I selected Warren County for a couple of reasons: as mentioned, its processing schema to monitor legal debtors is meticulous and multilayered, and its practices and related ideology clearly map onto each collection and punishment stage. Each of Washington's thirty-nine counties has developed its own unique sentencing, monitoring, and sanctioning processes, though some may be similar. Without observations and interviews within every county to draw on, I do not know the extent to which Warren is similar to or different from all of the other counties. However, its informal practices and procedures are allowable under state statute, and thus it is possible that other counties operate in the same way, if not even more punitively.

17. In Alexander County, the original sentencing judge sometimes liked to have defendants' SRA hearing placed on his calendar in order either to adjust the payment schedule or to reprimand the defendant. Depending on the judge's calendar, these defendants would often have to wait (in jail) for several days until the hearing.

18. Some counties not analyzed here use a process termed "sitting out fines": legal debtors are incarcerated to "sit out" their LFO debt. They earn $50 a

day toward their LFO debt and are released from jail once the debt is fully "paid" in this way. For instance, in Gossett County, a fifty-six-year-old white woman was arrested and jailed on May 2, 2013, with a charge listed as "commit to jail to serve time" and her bond status listed as "sitting out fines." She was sitting out an LFO of $1,021; thus, at $50 a day, she would serve twenty days, and her legal debt on this specific offense account would be wiped clean when she was released.

19. Columbia Legal Services and ACLU of Washington 2014. This report's analysis of jail data in Benton County and found that approximately 20 percent of the people booked into the county jail each day were incarcerated for nonpayment of their court-imposed debts. The attorneys who wrote the report examined Benton County jail rosters, which identified people who were "sitting out fines" for lower court (not superior court) violations. They then estimated the number of superior court violators by identifying those who were incarcerated for sentencing violations and had been told by a judge that they had to pay a specific financial amount or go to jail. Thus, their estimate is an approximation, not an exact number.

20. Garland 1990, 283.

Chapter 6: Law in Action: Bureaucrats and Values

1. Laws of the Commonwealth of Pennsylvania, vol. 1, 2A, 185 (1929–1930).

2. Bannon, Nagrecha, and Diller 2010.

3. Watkins-Hayes 2009, 79. Watkins-Hayes's work centers on what she terms "catchall" bureaucrats (in comparison to Michael Lipsky's [1980] street-level bureaucrats). For Watkins-Hayes, the identity of workers is pivotal for how they view their clients and make processing decisions. Because my analytic strategy is to investigate the entire system of monetary sanctions, from the structuring of the law to its application to defendants, I do not focus on the individual identities of court workers. I do not believe, however, that had I taken this analytic route, the findings would be different. In particular, the organizing values that guide court actors in their decisions would still have been present even if I had used a different analytic lens through which to understand the provenance of those decisions. Furthermore, as Watkins-Hayes stresses, her actors (case workers) had much more all-encompassing decisions to make—on how to facilitate housing, education, and income payments and assess income, compliance, and intentions—whereas my actors (clerks) made a dichotomous decision: were payments made or not? Clerks deliberate on defendants' ability to pay and on whether or how to assist them during the monitoring of their debt, but their charge is not to help the defendants per se but rather to enforce the orders of the court.

4. Lipsky 1980.

5. Emerson 1969; Engen and Steen 2000; Frase 2005; Harris 2007; Hasenfeld 1972; Miethe 1987; Paik 2011; Tonry 1996, 1998.

6. Hasenfeld 1972.

7. Lipsky 1980, 13, 212.

8. "In a cognitive aspect, culture refers to all those conceptions and values, categories and distinctions, frameworks of ideas and systems of belief which human beings use to construe their world and render it orderly and meaningful. . . . When we talk of 'culture' we refer not just to intellectual systems and forms of consciousness but also to structures of affect and what might be called emotional configurations or 'sensibilities.'. . . These (socially constructed) sensibilities and mentalities have major implications for the ways in which we punish offenders. These cultural patterns structure the ways in which we think about criminals, providing the intellectual frameworks (whether scientific or religious or commonsensical) through which we see these individuals, understand their motivations, and dispose of them as cases. Cultural patterns also structure the ways in which we feel about offenders, not only through the evocative ritual processes . . . but also through the shaping of our sensibilities" (Garland 1990, 195). "Theoretically, these concepts make sense in terms of how our emotions and cognitive orientations surrounding crime, offenders and punishment, might impact the very laws we construct and how we apply them. However, in practice, ethnographic analyses of the relationship between local punishment practices and the cultural context are needed to better specify the theoretical linkage between culture and punishment and identify the 'particulars and matter of detail'" (200).

9. Garland 1990, 195.

10. See, for example, the public debate over Washington State Senate Bill E2SHB 1390 on March 30, 2015. If passed, this bill would have reduced the interest on nonrestitution LFOs from 12 percent to 2 percent and prioritized payment of LFOs on restitution obligations. Those testifying against the bill included a representative from the WSACC, a clerk from Alexander County, and a member of the Washington State Association of Counties. See "Senate Bill Report: E2SHB 1390" at: http://lawfilesext.leg.wa.gov/biennium/2015-16/Pdf/Bill%20Reports/Senate/1390-S2.E%20SBA%20LAW%202015.pdf (accessed January 19, 2016).

11. RCW 36.18.016(29) introduced clerk collection fees of up to $100 per case per year, and SB 6336 (2000) extended legal debt for the duration of debtors' lives. See the website of the National Association of County Recorders, Election Officials, and Clerks (NACRC), http://www.nacrc.org.

12. See Emerson 1969 and Harris 2007.

13. RCW 10.82.090 ("Interest on Judgments," notes, 2011, chapter 106, section 1).

14. VanDeVerr 1986.

15. In Warren County, a $2.95 clerk processing fee is charged per payment up to $50. Any payments above $50 are charged a 2.9 percent processing fee.

16. It was awkward for me to listen to these interactions that involved individuals' intimate financial situations. Many defendants assumed that I was an employee of the court. Some even asked me questions about where they should wait, or when the judge was coming out of his chambers. One man had been in line watching me write notes and watching others. He asked me a question about where payments should be made. I said, "I don't work here." He responded, smiling, "I know you just take names."

17. Paik 2011, 182.

Chapter 7: The Permanent Punishment

1. Rusche and Kirchheimer 1939/2002, 207.

2. Bronner 2012.

3. Bannon, Nagrecha, and Diller 2010; see also *Bernard Brown Sr. v. Walter A. McNeil et al.,* 591 F. Supp.2d, 1245 (M.D. Fla. 2008).

4. Urken 2012; see also *People of the State of Illinois v. Leonia Davis,* 216 Ill. App. 3d 884; 576 N.E.2d 510 (1991).

5. Rhode Island Family Life Center 2007.

6. Bannon, Nagrecha, and Diller 2010; see also chapter 1, note 6.

7. *People of the State of Illinois v. Leonia Davis,* 216 Ill. App. 3d 884; 576 N.E.2d 510 (1991).

8. *St. Louis American* 2014; Harvey et al. 2014. The number I provide for the recouped amount is different from the number in the report. I note the actual amount for the fiscal year ending 2012, while the ArchCity report notes the forecasted amount for 2013.

9. U.S. Department of Justice 2015, 42.

10. Emphasis added by the author.

11. See Bersani and Chapple 2007; Harris, Evans, and Beckett 2010; James 2004; Kalleberg 2013; Pager 2007; Peterson and Krivo 2010; Western 2006.

12. Pettit and Western 2010, 11. Today one out of every nine black men between the ages of twenty and thirty-four lives behind bars. See Pettit, Sykes, and Western 2009; Pettit and Western 2004; and Pew Charitable Trusts 2010.

13. Blackman 2008.

14. Ibid.

15. Du Bois 1903/1990; Muhammad 2010; Oshinsky 1996.

16. Oshinsky 1996, 21.

17. Ibid.

18. The Thirteenth Amendment states: "Neither slavery nor involuntary servi-

tude, except as punishment for crime whereof the party shall have been duly convicted, shall exist within the United States, nor any place subject to their jurisdiction."

19. Blackman 2008, 53; see also Mandle 1978.

20. DuBois 1903/1990.

21. See Louisiana State Penitentiary Museum Foundation, "Angola Museum," http://www.angolamuseum.org/.

22. (Louisiana) Prison Enterprises Board, meeting minutes, January 17, 2012, available at: http://wwwprd.doa.louisiana.gov/boardsandcommissions /MeetingMinutes/509_BOARD%20MEETING%20MINUTES%20JANU ARY%202012.doc (accessed January 19, 2016). See also Blackmon 2008; Daniels 1990; Oshinsky 1996; and Taylor 1993, 1999.

23. See Kafka 1925/1998, 1926/2009; and Dickens 1873/2008.

Appendix

1. Harris, Evans, and Beckett 2010.

2. Harris, Evans, and Beckett 2010, 2011.

3. Perkins 1993; Word and Perkins 1996.

4. Harris, Evans, and Beckett 2011.

5. Emerson, Fretz, and Shaw 1995.

6. Charmaz 2001, 337.

References

Abram, Karne, and Linda Teplin. 1991. "Co-occurring Disorders Among Mentally Ill Jail Detainees: Implications for Public Policy." *American Psychologist* 46(10): 1036–45.

Adamson, Christopher R. 1983. "Punishment After Slavery: Southern State Penal Systems, 1865–1890." *Social Problems* 30: 555–69.

Administrative Office of the Courts (AOC), Court Services Division. 2015. "Penalty Assessment and Surcharge Guide." Phoenix, Ariz.: AOC (effective January 1, 2015). Available at: http://www.azcourts.gov/Portals/27/SurchrgGuide012015.pdf (accessed January 19, 2016).

Alexander, Michelle. 2010. *The New Jim Crow: Mass Incarceration in the Age of Colorblindness*. New York: New Press.

American Civil Liberties Union (ACLU). 2010. "In for a Penny: The Rise of America's New Debtors' Prisons." New York: ACLU (October). Available at: https://www.aclu.org/files/assets/InForAPenny_web.pdf (accessed January 19, 2016).

———. 2011. "Banking on Bondage: Private Prisons and Mass Incarceration." New York: ACLU (November 2). Available at: https://www.aclu.org/sites/default/files/field_document/bankingonbondage_20111102.pdf (accessed January 19, 2016).

American Civil Liberties Union of Washington and Washington Association of Criminal Defense Lawyers (WACDL). 2010. "Brief of Amici Curiae, in *Washington v. Nason,* Supreme Court of the State of Washington." No. 82333-2. Seattle: ACLU of Washington and WACDL (February 4).

Anderson, Elijah. 1990. *Streetwise: Race, Class, and Change in an Urban Community*. Chicago: University of Chicago Press.

———. 1999. *Code of the Street: Decency, Violence, and the Moral Life of the Inner City*. New York: W. W. Norton.

Anderson, Helen A. 2009. "Penalizing Poverty: Making Criminal Defendants Pay for the Court-Appointed Counsel Through Recoupment and Contribution." *University of Michigan Journal of Law Reform* 42(2): 323–80.

Baldwin, James. 1961. *Nobody Knows My Name*. New York: Dial Press.

Bannon, Alicia, Mitali Nagrecha, and Rebekah Diller. 2010. "Criminal Justice Debt: A Barrier to Reentry." New York: New York University School of Law,

Brennan Center for Justice (October 4). Available at: http://www.brennan center.org/publication/criminal-justice-debt-barrier-reentry (accessed January 19, 2016).

Bersani, Bianca, and Constance Chapple. 2007. "School Failure as an Adolescent Turning Point." *Sociological Focus* 40(4): 370–91.

Bishop, Joel Prentiss, John Maxcy Zane, and Carl Zollmann. 1923. *Bishop on Criminal Law,* 9th ed. Chicago: T. H. Flood.

Blackman, Douglas A. 2008. *Slavery by Another Name: The Re-enslavement of Black People in America from the Civil War to World War II.* New York: Doubleday.

Blumstein, Alfred, and Kiminori Nakamura. 2009. "Redemption in the Presence of Widespread Criminal Background Checks." *Criminology* 47(2): 327–59.

Bobo, Lawrence D., and Victor Thompson. 2006. "Unfair by Design: The War on Drugs, Race, and the Legitimacy of the Criminal Justice System." *Social Research: An International Quarterly* 73(2): 445–72.

Bonczar, Thomas P. 1997. "Characteristics of Adults on Probation, 1995." NCJ-164267. Washington: U.S. Department of Justice, Bureau of Justice Statistics (December). Available at: http://bjs.gov/content/pub/pdf/cap95.pdf (accessed January 19, 2016).

Bontrager, Stephanie, William Bales, and Ted Chiricos. 2005. "Race, Ethnicity, Threat, and the Labeling of Convicted Felons." *Criminology* 43(3): 589–622.

Braman, Donald. 2007. *Doing Time on the Outside: Incarceration and Family Life in Urban America.* Ann Arbor: University of Michigan Press.

Brennan Center for Justice. N.d. *The State Survey on Enforcement Mechanisms for Collecting Fees.* New York: Brennan Center for Justice.

Bronner, Ethan. 2012. "Poor Land in Jail as Companies Add Huge Fees for Probation." *New York Times,* July 2, 2012.

Bushway, Shawn, Terence Thornberry, and Marvin Krohn. 2003. "Desistance as a Developmental Process: A Comparison of Static and Dynamic Approaches." *Journal of Quantitative Criminology* 19(2): 129–53.

Caseload Forecast Council. 2012. *2012 Washington State Adult Sentencing Guidelines Manual.* Olympia: State of Washington, Caseload Forecast Council. Available at: http://www.cfc.wa.gov/PublicationSentencing/Sentencing Manual/Adult_Sentencing_Manual_2012_20130815.pdf (accessed January 19, 2016).

———. 2015. "Statistical Summary of Adult Felony Sentencing, Fiscal Year 2014." Olympia: State of Washington, Caseload Forecast Council (March). Available at: http://www.cfc.wa.gov/PublicationSentencing/Statistical Summary/Adult_Stat_Sum_FY2014.pdf (accessed January 19, 2016).

Charmaz, Kathy. 2001. "Grounded Theory." In *Contemporary Field Research: Perspectives and Formulations,* 2nd ed., edited by Robert Emerson. Long Grove, Ill.: Waveland Press.

Clear, Todd R. 2007. *Imprisoning Communities: How Mass Incarceration Makes Disadvantaged Neighborhoods Worse.* New York: Oxford University Press.

Clerk of the Courts. 2014. "Fee Schedule." Miami-Dade County, Fla.: Clerk of the Courts, effective July 1). Available at: http://www.miami-dadeclerk.com /service_fee_schedule.asp (accessed January 19, 2016).

Cole, George F., Barry Mahony, Marlene Thornton, and Roger A. Hanson. 1987. "The Practices and Attitudes of Trial Court Judges Regarding Fines as a Criminal Sanction." Washington: U.S. Department of Justice, National Institute of Justice.

Columbia Legal Services and ACLU of Washington. 2014. "Modern-Day Debtors' Prisons: How Court-Imposed Debts Punish Poor People in Washington." Seattle: Columbia Legal Services and ACLU of Washington (January).

Comfort, Megan. 2007. "Punishment Beyond the Legal Offender." *Annual Review of Law in the Social Sciences* 3: 271–96.

Daniels, Pete. 1990. *The Shadow of Slavery: Peonage in the South, 1901–1969*. Chicago: University of Illinois Press.

Darlington, Ida, ed. 1955. "Southwark Prisons." In *Survey of London*, vol. 25, *St. George's Fields (the Parishes of St. George the Martyr Southwark and St. Mary Newington)*, 9–21. London: London County Council. Available at British History Online: http://www.british-history.ac.uk/survey-london/vol25/pp9-21 (accessed January 19, 2016).

Dickens, Charles. 2008. *Bleak House*. New York: Overlook Press. (Originally published in 1873.)

Du Bois, W.E.B. 1990. *The Souls of Black Folks*. New York: Vintage Books. (Originally published in 1903.)

Emerson, Robert. 1969. *Judging Delinquents: Context and Process in Juvenile Court*. Chicago: Aldine de Gruyter.

Emerson, Robert, Rachel Fretz, and Linda Shaw. 1995. *Writing Ethnographic Fieldnotes*. Chicago: University of Chicago Press.

Engen, Rodney, Randy Gainey, Robert Crutchfield, and Joseph Weis. 2003. "Discretion and Disparity Under Sentencing Guidelines: The Role of Departures and Structured Sentencing Alternatives." *Criminology* 41(1): 99–130.

Engen, Rodney, and Sara Steen. 2000. "The Power to Punish: Discretion and Sentencing Reform in the War on Drugs." *American Journal of Sociology* 105(5): 1357–95.

Feeley, Malcolm. 1979. *The Process Is the Punishment: Handling Cases in a Lower Criminal Court*. New York: Russell Sage Foundation.

Frase, Richard. 2005. "State Sentencing Guidelines: Diversity, Consensus, and Unresolved Policy Issues." *Columbia Law Review* 105: 1190–92.

Garland, David. 1990. *Punishment and Modern Society*. Chicago: University of Chicago Press.

———. 2001. *The Culture of Control: Crime and Social Order in Contemporary Society*. Chicago: University of Chicago Press.

Gillespie, Robert W. 1980. "Fines as an Alternative to Incarceration: The German Experience." *Federal Probation* 44(4): 20–26.

Giordano, Peggy, Stephen Cernkovich, and Jennifer Rudolph. 2002. "Gender Crime and Desistance: Toward a Theory of Cognitive Transformation." *American Journal of Sociology* 107(4): 990–1064.

Giordano, Peggy, Ryan Schroeder, and Stephen Cernkovich. 2007. "Emotions and Crime over the Life Course: A Neo-Meadian Perspective on Criminal Continuity and Change." *American Journal of Sociology* 112(6): 1603–61.

Glaze, Lauren E., and Erinn J. Herberman. 2013. "Correctional Populations in the United States, 2012." NCJ 243936. Washington: U.S. Department of Justice, Bureau of Justice Statistics. Available at: http://www.bjs.gov/content/pub/pdf/cpus12.pdf (accessed January 19, 2016).

Goffman, Alice. 2009. "On the Run: Wanted Black Men in a Philadelphia Ghetto." *American Sociological Review* 74: 339–57.

———. 2014. *On the Run: Fugitive Life in an American City*. Chicago: University of Chicago Press.

Goffman, Erving. 1963. *Stigma: Notes on the Management of Spoiled Identity*. New York: Simon & Schuster.

Gordon, Margaret A., and Daniel Glaser. 1991. "The Use and Effects of Financial Penalties in Municipal Courts." *Criminology* 29(4): 651–76.

Guerino, Paul, Paige M. Harrison, and William J. Sabol. 2011. "Prisoners in 2010." NCJ 236096. Washington: U.S. Department of Justice, Office of Justice Programs, Bureau of Justice Statistics (December). Available at: http://www.bjs.gov/index.cfm?ty=pbdetail&iid=2230 (revised February 9, 2012).

Harlow, Caroline Wolf. 1998. "Profile of Jail Inmates 1996." NCJ 164620. Washington: U.S. Department of Justice, Office of Justice Programs, Bureau of Justice Statistics (April). Available at: http://www.bjs.gov/content/pub/pdf/pji96.pdf (revised June 4, 1998).

Harris, Alexes. 2007. "Diverting and Abdicating Judicial Discretion: Cultural, Political, and Procedural Dynamics in California Juvenile Justice." *Law and Society Review* 41(2): 387–428.

———. 2011. "Constructing Clean Dreams: Accounts, Future Selves, and Social and Structural Support as Desistance Work." *Symbolic Interaction* 34(1): 63–85.

Harris, Alexes, Heather Evans, and Katherine Beckett. 2010. "Drawing Blood from Stones: Monetary Sanctions, Punishment, and Inequality in the Contemporary United States." *American Journal of Sociology* 115(6): 1753–99.

———. 2011. "Courtesy Stigma and Monetary Sanctions: Toward a Socio-Cultural Theory of Punishment." *American Sociological Review* 76(2): 234–64.

Harvard Law Review. 2002. "Criminal Law—Alabama Raises the Rates at Which Individuals in Jail for Nonpayment of Fines Earn Out Their Debts—HB 95, Reg. Sess. (Ala. 2002) (Codified at Ala. Code § 15-18-62 [1995 & Supp. 2002])." *Harvard Law Review* 116(2): 735–42.

Harvey, Thomas, John McAnnar, Michael-John Voss, Megan Conn, Sean Janda, and Sophia Keskey. 2014. "ArchCity Defenders: Municipal Courts White Paper." St. Louis: ArchCity Defenders. Available at: https://ia802303.us.archive.org/14/items/pdfy-iyuTY46j7R_fAvpK/ArchCity%20Defenders%20-%20Municipal%20Courts%20Whitepaper%20(2014).pdf (accessed January 19, 2016).

Hasenfeld, Yeheskel. 1972. "People Processing Organizations: An Exchange Approach." *American Sociological Review* 37: 256–63.

Henrichson, Christian, and Ruth Delaney. 2012. "The Price of Prisons: What Incarceration Costs Taxpayers." Los Angeles: VERA Institute of Justice, Center on Sentencing and Corrections (January).

Hillsman, Sally. 1990. "Fines and Day Fines." In *Crime and Justice: A Review of Research*, vol. 12, edited by Michael Tonry and Norval Morris. Chicago: University of Chicago Press.

Hillsman Baker, Sally, Barry Mahoney, George F. Cole, and Bernard Auchter. 1987. "Fines as Criminal Sanctions." Research in Brief Series. Washington: U.S. Department of Justice, National Institute of Justice.

Hirschi, Travis. 1969. *Causes of Delinquency*. Berkeley: University of California Press.

Holdsworth, William Searle. 1927. *A History of English Law*, 3rd ed. London: Methuen.

James, Doris J. 2004. "Profile of Jail Inmates 2002." NCJ 201932. Washington: U.S. Department of Justice, Bureau of Justice Statistics (July). Available at: http://www.bjs.gov/content/pub/pdf/pji02.pdf (revised October 12, 2004).

Johnson, Brian. 2006. "The Multilevel Context of Criminal Sentencing: Integrating Judge- and County-Level Influences." *Criminology* 44(2): 259–98.

Kafka, Franz. 1998. *The Trial*. New York: Schocken Books. (Originally published in 1925.)

————. 2009. *The Castle*. Oxford: Oxford University Press. (Originally published in 1926.)

Kalleberg, Arne. 2013. *Good Jobs, Bad Jobs: The Rise of Polarized and Precarious Employment Systems in the United States, 1970–2000s*. New York: Russell Sage Foundation.

Laub, John H., and Robert J. Sampson. 2001. "Understanding Desistance from Crime." *Crime and Justice* 28: 1–69.

————. 2003. "Life-Course Desisters? Trajectories of Crime Among Delinquent Boys Followed to Age 70." *Criminology* 41: 319–39.

Lee, Suevon. 2009. "Incarceration Fees Come Under Fire." *Ocala Star Banner*, December 20, 2009.

Lepore, Jill. 2009. "Annals of Finance: IOU." *The New Yorker*, April 13.

Lipsky, Michael. 1980. *Street-Level Bureaucracy: Dilemmas of the Individual in Public Service*. New York: Russell Sage Foundation.

Mandle, Jay R. 1978. *The Roots of Black Poverty: The Southern Plantation Economy After the Civil War*. Durham, N.C.: Duke University Press.

Manza, Jeff, and Christopher Uggen. 2006. *Locked Out: Felon Disenfranchisement and American Democracy*. New York: Oxford University Press.

Maruna, Shadd. 2001. *Making Good: How Ex-Convicts Reform and Rebuild Their Lives*. Washington, D.C.: American Psychological Association.

Maruna, Shadd, and Russ Immarigeon, eds. 2004. *After Crime and Punishment: Pathways to Offender Reintegration*. Cullompton, U.K.: Willan Publishing.

Massoglia, Michael. 2008. "Incarceration, Health, and Racial Disparities in Health." *Law and Society Review* 42(2): 275–306.

Matthias, John, and Laura Klaversma. 2009. *Current Practices in Collecting Fines and Fees in State Courts: A Handbook of Collection Issues and Solutions*, 2nd ed. Denver: National Center for State Courts.

Mauer, Marc, and Virginia McCalmont. 2013. "Lifetime of Punishment: The Impact of the Felony Drug Ban on Welfare Benefits." Washington, D.C.: The

Sentencing Project (November). Available at: https://www.ncjrs.gov/App/Publications/abstract.aspx?ID=269456 (accessed January 19, 2016).

McLanahan, Sara. 2009. "Fragile Families and the Reproduction of Poverty." *Annals of the American Academy of Political and Social Sciences* 621: 111–31.

McLean, Rachel L., and Michael D. Thompson. 2007. *Repaying Debts*. New York: Council of State Governments Justice Center.

Miethe, Terrance D. 1987. "Charging and Plea Bargaining Under Determinate Sentencing: An Investigation of the Hydraulic Displacement of Discretion." *Journal of Criminal Law and Criminology* 78(1): 155–76.

Mitchell, Michael, and Michael Leachman. 2014. "Changing Priorities: State Criminal Justice Reforms and Investments in Education." Washington, D.C.: Center on Budget and Policy Priorities (October 28).

Moon, David. 2013. "Trends in State Courts." Williamsburg, Va.: National Center for State Courts.

Morris, Norval, and Michael Tonry. 1990. *Between Prison and Probation: Intermediate Punishments in a Rational Sentencing System*. New York: Oxford University Press.

Muhammad, Khalil. 2010. *The Condemnation of Blackness: Race, Crime, and the Making of Modern Urban America*. Cambridge, Mass.: Harvard University Press.

Murphy, Don K. 2015. "Why Crime Doesn't Pay: Examining Felony Collections." Fort Myers, Fla.: Institute for Court Management, Lee County Clerk of the Court (May). Available at: http://www.ncsc.org/~/media/files/pdf/education%20and%20careers/cedp%20papers/2015/why%20crime%20doesnt%20pay-examining%20felony%20collectionsmurphy.ashx (accessed January 19, 2016).

National Center for Education Statistics (NCES). 2015. "Fast Facts: Expenditures." Washington, D.C.: NCES, Institute of Education Sciences (IES). Available at: http://nces.ed.gov/fastfacts/display.asp?id=66 (accessed January 19, 2016).

New York State Division of Parole. 2004. "Parolee Facts." Albany: New York State Division of Parole (March).

Nieto, Marcus. 2006. "Who Pays for Penalty Assessment Programs in California?" CRB 06-003. Sacramento: California Research Bureau (February). Available at: https://www.library.ca.gov/crb/06/03/06-003.pdf (accessed January 19, 2016).

Oshinsky, David M. 1996. *Worse Than Slavery: Parchman Farm and the Ordeal of Jim Crow Justice*. New York: Simon & Schuster.

Pager, Devah. 2007. *Marked: Race, Crime, and Finding Work in an Era of Mass Incarceration*. Chicago: University of Chicago Press.

Paik, Leslie. 2011. *Discretionary Justice: Looking Inside a Juvenile Drug Court*. New Brunswick, N.J.: Rutgers University Press.

Perkins, Colby R. 1993. "Evaluating the Passel-Word Spanish Surname List: 1990 Decennial Census Post Enumeration Survey Results." Working Paper 4. Washington: U.S. Census Bureau, Population Division.

Petersilia, Joan, and Jessica Greenlick Snyder. 2013. "Looking Past the Hype: 10

Questions Everyone Should Ask About California's Prison Realignment." *California Journal Politics and Policy* 5(2): 266–306.

Peterson, Ruth, and Lauren Krivo. 2010. *Divergent Social Worlds: Neighborhood Crime and the Racial-Spatial Divide.* New York: Russell Sage Foundation.

Pettit, Becky. 2012. *Invisible Men: Mass Incarceration and the Myth of Black Progress.* New York: Russell Sage Foundation.

Pettit, Becky, Bryan Sykes, and Bruce Western. 2009. "Technical Report on Revised Population Estimates and NLSY 79 Analysis Tables for the Pew Public Safety and Mobility Project." Cambridge, Mass.: Harvard University.

Pettit, Becky, and Bruce Western. 2004. "Mass Imprisonment and the Life Course: Race and Class Inequality in U.S. Incarceration." *American Sociological Review* 69(2): 151–69.

———. 2010. "Incarceration and Social Inequality." *Daedalus* 11(Summer).

Pew Charitable Trusts. 2010. "Collateral Costs: Incarceration's Effect on Economic Mobility." Washington, D.C.: Pew Charitable Trusts. Available at: http://www.pewtrusts.org/~/media/legacy/uploadedfiles/pcs_assets/2010/collateralcosts1pdf.pdf (accessed January 19, 2016).

One in 100: Behind Bars in America 2008. Philadelphia: Pew Charitable Trusts (February 28). Available at: http://www.pewtrusts.org/en/research-and-analysis/reports/2008/02/28/one-in-100-behind-bars-in-america-2008 (accessed January 19, 2016).

Provine, Doris Marie. 2007. *Unequal Under Law: Race in the War on Drugs.* Chicago: University of Chicago Press.

Raaen, Niel, John Matthias, Alisa Kim, and Daniel Hall. 2012. "Study of the Effectiveness of Collections in the Florida Courts: A Report to the Florida Clerks of Court Operations Corporation." Williamsburg, Va.: National Center for State Courts (November 26). Available at: http://www.flccoc.org/collections/ncsc/ccoc%20report%20final%20submitted.pdf (accessed January 19, 2016).

Ragona, Anthony J., and John Paul Ryan. 1983. "Misdemeanor Courts and the Choice of Sanctions: A Comparative View." *Justice System Journal* 8(2): 199–221.

Rhode Island Family Life Center. 2007. "Court Debt and Related Incarceration in Rhode Island." Providence: Rhode Island Family Life Center (May).

Rosenthal, Alan, and Marsha Weissman. 2007. *Sentencing for Dollars: The Financial Consequences of a Criminal Conviction.* Syracuse, N.Y.: Center for Community Alternatives, Justice Strategies.

Ruback, Barry, and Valerie Clark. 2010. "Reduce Disparity in Economic Sanctions." In *Contemporary Issues in Criminal Justice Policy,* edited by Natasha Frost, Joshua Freilich, and Todd Clear. New Brunswick, N.J.: Rutgers University Press.

Ruback, R. Barry, Jennifer N. Shaffer, and Melissa A. Logue. 2004. "The Imposition and Effects of Restitution in Four Pennsylvania Counties: Effects of Size of County and Specialized Collection Units." *Crime and Delinquency* 50: 168–88.

Rusche, Georg, and Otto Kirchheimer. 2009. *Punishment and Social Struc-*

ture. New Brunswick, N.J.: Transaction Publishers. (Originally published in 1939.)

Ryan, Dennis M. 1983. "Criminal Fines: A Sentencing Alternative to Short-Term Incarceration." *Iowa Law Review* 68: 1285.

Savelsberg, Joachim. 1992. "Law That Does Not Fit Society: Sentencing Guidelines as a Neoclassical Reaction to the Dilemmas of Substantivized Law." *American Journal of Sociology* 97(5): 1346–81.

Saxonhouse, Elena. 2004. "Note: Unequal Protection: Comparing Former Felons' Challenges to Disenfranchisement and Employment Discrimination." *Stanford Law Review* 56: 1597.

Seattle Police Department. 2015. "Advising Persons of Right to Counsel and Miranda" (title 6, policy 6.150). In *Seattle Police Manual* (Seattle, Wash.: Seattle Police Department, effective January 1). Available at: http://www.seattle .gov/police-manual/title-6---arrests-search-and-seizure/6150---advising -persons-of-right-to-counsel-and-miranda (accessed January 19, 2016).

Stearns, Travis, and Breean Beggs. 2010. "Brief of Amicus Curiae, in *State of Washington v. Nason,* 168 Wn.2d 936; 233 P.3d 848 (2010)." Seattle: Washington Defender Association and the Center for Justice (February 8).

Steffensmeier, Darrell, and Stephen Demuth. 2001. "Ethnicity and Judges' Sentencing Decisions in Pennsylvania: Hispanic-Black-White Comparisons." *Criminology* 39(1): 145–78.

Stephen, James Fitzjames. 1883. *A History of the Criminal Law of England.* London: Macmillan.

Stillman, Sarah. 2014. "Get Out of Jail, Inc.: Does the Alternatives-to-Incarceration Industry Profit from Injustice?" *New Yorker,* June 23.

St. Louis American. 2014. "Update: Unarmed Teen Michael Brown Killed by Ferguson Police." *St. Louis American,* August 10, 2014.

Swartz, James, Arthur Lurigio, and Paul Goldstein. 2000. "Severe Mental Illness and Substance Use Disorder Among Former Supplemental Security Income Beneficiaries for Drug Addiction and Alcoholism." *Archives of General Psychiatry* 57(7): 701–7.

Taylor, William Banks. 1993. *Brokered Justice: Race Politics and Mississippi Prisons, 1798–1992.* Columbus: Ohio State University Press.

———. 1999. *Down on Parchman Farm: The Great Prison in the Mississippi Delta.* Columbus: Ohio State University Press.

Tonry, Michael. 1995. *Malign Neglect: Race, Crime, and Punishment in America.* New York: Oxford University Press.

———. 1996. *Sentencing Matters.* New York: Oxford University Press.

———. 1998. "Intermediate Sanctions." In *The Handbook of Crime and Punishment,* edited by Michel Tonry. New York: Oxford University Press.

Tran-Leung, Marie. 2009. "Debt Arising from Illinois' Criminal Justice System: Making Sense of the Ad Hoc Accumulation of Financial Obligations." Washington, D.C.: Shriver National Center on Poverty Law (November).

Transportation Trust Fund Task Force. 2011. "Report on Conditions, Planning, and Revenue Options for Support of the Transportation Trust Fund." Wilmington: Delaware Department of Transportation (March 31). Available at:

http://www.deldot.gov/information/community_programs_and_services
/ttf_task_force/pdf/Final_Transportation_Trust_Fund_Task_Force_Report
_033111.pdf (accessed January 19, 2016).

Travis, Jeremy. 2005. *But They All Come Back: Facing the Challenges of Prisoner Reentry*. New York: Urban Institute Press.

Uggen, Christopher, Sarah Shannon, and Jeff Manza. 2012. "State-Level Estimates of Felon Disenfranchisement in the United States, 2010." Washington, D.C.: The Sentencing Project (July). Available at: http://sentencingproject.org/doc/publications/fd_State_Level_Estimates_of_Felon_Disen_2010.pdf (accessed January 19, 2016).

Ulmer, Jeffery, and John Kramer. 1996. "Court Communities Under Sentencing Guidelines: Dilemmas of Formal Rationality and Sentencing Disparity." *Criminology* 34(3): 383–407.

Urken, Ross Kenneth. 2012. "Debtors' Prison Is Back and Just as Cruel as Ever." *Daily Finance*, August 30. Available at: http://www.dailyfinance.com/2012/08/30/debtors-prison-is-back-and-just-as-cruel-as-ever/ (accessed January 19, 2016).

U.S. Department of Justice. 2015. *Investigation of the Ferguson Police Department*. Washington: U.S. Department of Justice, Civil Rights Division (March 4). Available at: http://www.justice.gov/sites/default/files/opa/press-releases/attachments/2015/03/04/ferguson_police_department_report.pdf (accessed January 19, 2016).

U.S. Department of Justice. Bureau of Justice Statistics. 1991, 1997, and 2004. "Survey of Inmates of State and Federal Correctional Facilities." ICPSR 6068, 2598, and 4572. Ann Arbor, Mich.: Inter-university Consortium for Political and Social Research (ICPSR) (producer and distributor), 2007-02-28. Available at National Archive of Criminal Justice Data (NACJD), http://dx.doi.org/10.3886/ICPSR06068 (1991); http://dx.doi.org/10.3886/ICPSR02598 (1997); and http://dx.doi.org/10.3886/ICPSR04572 (2004) (accessed January 19, 2016).

VanDeVeer, Donald. 1986. *Paternalistic Intervention: The Moral Bounds of Benevolence*. Princeton, N.J.: Princeton University Press.

Volkow, Nora. 2001. "Drug Abuse and Mental Illness: Progress in Understanding Comorbidity." *American Journal of Psychiatry* 158: 1181–83.

Wacquant, Loïc. 2000. "The New 'Peculiar Institution': On the Prison as Surrogate Ghetto." *Theoretical Criminology* 4: 377–89.

———. 2001b. "The Advent of the Penal State Is Not a Destiny." *Social Justice* 28(3): 81–88.

Wakefield, Sara, and Christopher Uggen. 2010. "Incarceration and Stratification." *Annual Review of Sociology* 36: 387–406.

Washington Association of County Officials (WACO). 2003–2012. "Report to the Washington Legislature on the Fiscal Impact of ESSB 5990, or Chapter 379, Laws of 2003 and SSB 5256, or Chapter 362, Laws of 2005." Reports for the Washington State Association of County Clerks (WSACC). Olympia: WACO.

Washington State Office of Public Defense. 2007. "Update on Criteria and Standards for Determining and Verifying Indigency." Olympia: Washington State Office of Public Defense (October).

Washington State Sentencing Guidelines Commission (SGC). 2000. "The Sentencing Reform Act at Century's End: An Assessment of Adult Felony Sentencing Practices in the State of Washington." Report to the Governor and the Legislature. Olympia: Sentencing Guidelines Commission (January). Available at: http://www.cfc.wa.gov/PublicationSentencing/Research/Sentenc ingReformActReportCenturyEnd.pdf (accessed January 19, 2016).

Watkins-Hayes, Celeste. 2009. *The New Welfare Bureaucrats: Entanglements of Race, Class, and Policy Reform*. Chicago: University of Chicago Press.

Weber, Max. 1968. *Economy and Society*. Berkeley: University of California Press.

Weiss, Robert P. 1989. "Private Prisons and the State." In *Practicing Criminal Justice*, edited by Roger Matthews. London: Sage Publications.

Westen, Derek A. 1969. "Fines, Imprisonment, and the Poor: 'Thirty Dollars or Thirty Days.'" *California Law Review* 57(3): 780–87.

Western, Bruce. 2006. *Punishment and Inequality in America*. New York: Russell Sage Foundation.

Wheeler, Gerald R., and Amy S. Rudolph. 1990. "New Strategies to Improve Probation Officers' Fee Collection Rates: A Field Study in Performance Feedback." *Justice System Journal* 14(1): 78–94.

Wheelock, Darren, and Christopher Uggen. 2008. "Punishment, Crime, and Poverty." In *The Colors of Poverty: Why Racial and Ethnic Disparities Persist*, edited by Ann Chih Lin and David R. Harris. New York: Russell Sage Foundation.

Wildeman, Christopher. 2009. "Parental Imprisonment, the Prison Boom, and the Concentration of Childhood Disadvantage." *Demography* 46: 265–80.

Wooldredge, John, and Amy Thistlethwaite. 2004. "Bilevel Disparities in Court Dispositions for Intimate Assault." *Criminology* 42(2): 417–56.

Word, David L., and R. Colby Perkins Jr. 1996. "Building a Spanish Surname List for the 1990s (A New Approach to an Old Problem)." Technical Working Paper 3. Washington: U.S. Census Bureau, Population Division (March).

Wright, Ronald, and Wayne Logan. 2006. "The Political Economy of Up-Front Fees for Indigent Criminal Defense." *William and Mary Law Review* 47: 2045–87.

Cases Cited

Bernard Brown Sr. v. Walter A. McNeil et al., 591 F. Supp.2d 1245 (M.D. Fla. 2008)

Bearden v. Georgia, 461 U.S. 660, 103 S. Ct. 2064, 76 L. Ed.2d 221 (1983)

Blakely v. Washington, 542 U.S. 296, 124 S. Ct. 2531, 159 L. Ed.2d 403 (2004)

Brown v. Plata, 131 S. Ct. 1910 (2011)

Fuller v. Oregon, 417 U.S. 40 (1974)

Gideon v. Wainwright, 372 U.S. 335 (1963)

James v. Strange, 407 U.S. 128 (1972)

Madison v. State of Washington, 78598-8 (Wash. Sup. Ct. 2007)

Miranda v. Arizona, 384 U.S. 436 (1966)

Morgan v. Rhay, 78 Wn.2d 116, 119–20, 470 P.2d 180 (1970)

NST v. Washington, 232 P.3d584, 586 (Wash. Ct. App. 2010)

Oregon v. Fuller, 12 Or. App., 504 P.2d (1973)

People v. Corrales, 213 Cal. App. 4th 696 (2013)

People v. Fisher, 189 Colo. 297, 539 P.2d 1258 (1975)

People of the State of Illinois v. Leonia Davis, 216 Ill. App. 3d 884; 576 N.E.2d 510 (1991)

Tate v. Short, 401 U.S. 395, 91 S. Ct. 668, 28 L. Ed.2d 130 (1971)

(State of) Washington v. Barklind, 87 Wn.2d 814 (1976)

(State of) Washington v. Blazina, 89028-5 (Wash. 2015)

(State of) Washington v. Bower, 823 P.2d 1171, 1173 (Wash. Ct. App. 1992)

(State of) Washington v. Curry, 118 Wn.2d 911, 829 P.2d 166 (Wash. 1992)

(State of) Washington v. Nason, 233 P.3d 848, 853 (Wash. 2010)

(State of) Washington v. Stone, 268 P.3d 226 (Wash. Ct. App. 2012)

Williams v. Illinois, 399 U.S. 235 (1970)

═ Index ═

Boldface numbers refer to figures and tables.

accountability: culture of, court officials' reliance on, 15; offender and system, distinction between, 150; in policy rhetoric, 82–84; varying meanings of, 149–50

African Americans: incarceration and monetary sanctions experienced by male, 6–7, 156, 216n12; social control through incarceration, 157–58

Angola Prison, 158

attorneys: appointed, qualification for, 211n4; "auto-jail" issue, prosecutors' differing opinions on, 133–34; defense, emotional impact of defendants' monetary sanctions on, 70–72; defense attorneys' role in monetary sanction process, 101; discretion exercised by prosecutors, 129–31; interviews with, 190, 195; prosecutors' role in monetary sanction process, 101; public defenders, charging indigent defendants for, 42–45, 59–60

"auto-jail" policy, 22, 99–100, 115–16, 133–34

Baldwin, James, 52, 140
Baltimore, Maryland, 153
Bearden, Danny, 21
Bearden v. Georgia, 21–22, 120
beliefs. *See* values and beliefs
Blackmon, Douglass, 158
Bower, Robert Wayne, 22
Brown, Jerry, 11
Brown, Michael, 152
Brown v. Plata, 10–11

Center for Justice, 100

civil unrest: monetary sanctions and, 152–53

collections: collection improvement programs, 89–90; monitoring processes (*see* monitoring); paternalism in, 144–49; payment review of Warren County's "Unit," 145–49; personal responsibility as guiding value in, 140–41; private agencies, 25–26, 81–82, 89–90, 104–5, 111, 113, 122, 212–13n14; "sitting out fines," 213–14n18; "The Unit" in Warren County, 114–15

community corrections officers, 195–96

community service, 50–51, 207n7

convict leasing, 157

county clerks: ability to pay, assessment of, 104–5, 212n8; discretion exercised by, 104, 113, 119–20, 131–33, 140–41, 143–44; interviews with, 196; monetary sanction process, role in, 101, 116, 154; restitution payments, disbursement of, 104; types of, 131–32

criminal justice system: costs of, 9–11; culture of punishment and (*see* culture); deferred prosecution, 66–68; discretion and autonomy of court officials, 125–26 (*see also* discretion); felony convictions, 6–8, 11; incarceration (*see* incarceration); monetary sanctions as fiscal support for, 85, 87–93, 151–52; private for-profit entities involved in, 10 (*see also* collections, private agencies); processes and procedures for monetary sanctions (*see*